O'Neill on Film

O'Neill on Film

John Orlandello

Rutherford • Madison • Teaneck
Fairleigh Dickinson University Press
London and Toronto: Associated University Presses

© 1982 by Associated University Presses, Inc.

Associated University Presses, Inc.
4 Cornwall Drive
East Brunswick, N.J. 08816

Associated University Presses Ltd
69 Fleet Street
London EC4Y 1EU, England

Associated University Presses
Toronto M5E 1A7, Canada

Library of Congress Cataloging in Publication Data

Orlandello, John, 1943–
   O'Neill on film.

  Bibliography: p.
  Includes index.
  1. O'Neill, Eugene, 1888–1953—Film adaptations.
I. Title.
PS3529.N5Z763   1982   812'.52   80-70627
ISBN 0-8386-2291-7   AACR2

```
812.52 O58o

Orlandello, John, 1943-

O'Neill on film
```

Printed in the United States of America

To my mother
and to the memory of my father

Contents

Acknowledgments	9
Introduction	11
1 *Anna Christie* (1923 and 1930)	21
2 *Strange Interlude* (1932)	38
3 *The Emperor Jones* (1933)	51
4 *Ah, Wilderness!* (1935) and *Summer Holiday* (1948)	66
5 *The Long Voyage Home* (1940)	89
6 *Mourning Becomes Electra* (1947)	103
7 *Desire under the Elms* (1958)	116
8 *Long Day's Journey into Night* (1962)	131
9 *The Iceman Cometh* (1973)	146
Conclusion	162
Filmography	168
Bibliography	174
Index	179

Acknowledgments

I am deeply indebted to the late Professor Marvin Felheim for his invaluable encouragement and guidance during the early stages of this project. I would also like to thank the many other friends and colleagues who gave me support and assistance, especially Professor George Kurman for his perceptive comments and keen editorial help, and Connie Bassil for her constant support and multifarious assistance throughout this project. I am indebted to several sources for the photographic material used, including Cinemabilia, Jerry Ohlinger's Movie Materials, and the Museum of Modern Art, and I also wish to thank Robert Grillo for his help in searching out many of the stills for me. Finally, I would like to thank the film departments of the Museum of Modern Art and the Library of Congress for providing me with screenings of many of the films discussed in this book.

Introduction

The plays of Eugene O'Neill have been a continuing source for film adaptation, spanning fifty years of Hollywood history from the era of silent film with the 1923 adaptation of *Anna Christie* to 1973 with the American Film Theatre version of *The Iceman Cometh*. O'Neill, unlike Shaw or Tennessee Williams, was not intimately connected with the film versions of his work, which he sold outright, retaining no control over the final product. His association with the medium of film began and essentially remained merely a financial one. As a young man, O'Neill tried to earn money by writing film scripts, which were apparently comedies and romances, and in 1915 it was reported that one had been sold and was to be produced. Nothing ever came of these youthful ventures in screenwriting—no scripts were ever produced, nor has any survived.[1] At about the same time, O'Neill wrote a one-act play called *The Movie Man* that reflected his idea of the film industry as exploitative. This slight comedy deals with an American movie producer who goes to Mexico to stage a revolution in order to film it, with battles and executions occurring only when there are advantageous filming conditions.

During the early 1920s O'Neill's interest in film was revived when he saw Wiene's *Cabinet of Dr. Caligari,* which, as he said, made him "aware of wonderful possibilities . . . never dreamed of before."[2] O'Neill was fascinated by the stylized theatricality of the filmic expressionism, a style that would influence his dramatic work but would seldom be used in the film adaptations of his plays. It is known that O'Neill, partly influenced by expressionist films, reworked *The Emperor Jones* for film treatment. Nothing came of this experiment and little is known of the specifics of his ideas. The silent-film adaptation of *Anna Christie* in 1923 was the first of O'Neill's actual connections to the film industry and it was an auspicious beginning. O'Neill was impressed with the film version as a successful translation from one medium to another of the themes and spirit of his work. Encouraged by this happy union of stage and screen, O'Neill worked on scenarios of *The Hairy Ape* and *Desire under the Elms,* which he gave to Richard Watts, Jr., of the *New York Herald Tribune* for his appraisal. Watts's comments remain the only source of information on these scenarios, which were never produced and have since been destroyed.[3] The alterations made on *Desire under the Elms* are treated in the specific analysis of the much later film adaptation of that work. While there was a subsequent film version of *The Hairy Ape*, with no connection to O'Neill's scenario, it will not be discussed in this book since the film is currently unavailable through either film archives or film rental. By the end of the 1920s O'Neill would no longer make any attempts at writing for the film, nor, indeed, give it very much artistic consideration. Nonetheless, many of his works were still to be adapted, and while O'Neill would not be actively involved in the process, the adaptations brought O'Neill wider popular renown, and his name in association with a film assured it serious critical attention.

The 1930s saw four more O'Neill works put on film. In 1930 a sound version of *Anna Christie* was released to considerable attention and acclaim both as a work of O'Neill's and as the sound-film debut of Greta Garbo. Soon after, in 1932, O'Neill's massive Pulitzer Prize–winning play *Strange Interlude* was released. This adaptation, perhaps more than any other, soured O'Neill's attitude to the film industry. In 1933 a film called *The Constant Woman*, very loosely based on a one-act play by O'Neill called *Reckless*, was released. The film apparently had little to do with O'Neill's original and has not been preserved; hence it will not be discussed in this study. *The Emperor Jones* was adapted to film in 1933 and became a powerful vehicle for Paul Robeson. The first film version of *Ah, Wilderness!*—the only work other than *Anna Christie* that was twice adapted to film—was released in 1935. There is no indication that O'Neill ever saw any of the films made from his works during the 1930s—reports from friends and reviews of the films dissuaded him from seeing them.

During the 1940s O'Neill would have four more encounters with Hollywood. *The Long Voyage Home* (1940) brought to the screen four of O'Neill's early one-act plays about life at sea. O'Neill saw the film and was impressed by it, especially liking, as he said, "the talkless parts of the picture."[4] *The Hairy Ape* was adapted to film in 1943 and, as mentioned earlier, the film is currently unavailable and cannot be discussed in this study. In 1947 O'Neill's massive trilogy *Mourning Becomes Electra* was reverentially brought to the screen by Dudley Nichols, who had earlier worked on the screenplay for *The Long Voyage Home*. O'Neill was consulted about the film but had no actual part in its production. The last work of O'Neill adapted to film during his lifetime was *Summer Holiday*, released in 1948, which was a musical remake of MGM's earlier version of *Ah, Wilderness!*

Three other works of O'Neill were adapted to film after his death, the first of these being *Desire under the Elms*, wich was released in 1957. Curiously, this play, which O'Neill himself had reworked for film in the mid-1920s, would be among the last of his works put on film. In defiance of the terms of O'Neill's will,[5] *Long Day's Journey into Night* was sold to the films by his third wife, Carlotta, and released in 1961. The film was produced by Ely Landau, who would later produce *The Iceman Cometh*, which is currently the last adaptation of O'Neill's work on film. Released in 1973, *The Iceman Cometh* was produced in association with the American Film Theatre organization, which, for two years, adapted major works of the modern theater to film. Oddly enough, O'Neill had envisioned such a use for film in 1929, saying that "the day may come when there will develop a kind of Theatre Guild 'talkie' organization that will be able to rely on big cities for its audiences."[6] The American Film Theatre was precisely this sort of organization, and O'Neill's work was fittingly the premier presentation of its short-lived two seasons of operation.

The union of O'Neill works and Hollywood would seem a difficult and problematic one. The austerity of O'Neill's tragic vision, the often titanic scale of the plays, and the frequently incendiary nature of the themes of the works would seem to make them unlikely choices for film adaptation. Nonetheless, the fifty-year history of O'Neill screen adaptation (longer than that of any other modern playwright) and the thirteen screen treatments of his work evidence an enduring cinematic fascination with America's foremost dramatist. The reasons for this are several: the adapted plays of O'Neill had generally been popular and often controversial stage successes; the name of O'Neill, with his several Pulitzer Prizes and the Nobel Prize for literature, assured the films heedful reception; and finally, the tragic strain in O'Neill's works, not ideally suited to the cinema, was attenuated by an underpinning of melodramatic flair quite suitable to the medium.

Just as the adaptations themselves represent a long and varied period in Hollywood's history, so do many other variables come into play in the quality of the screen versions of O'Neill. Producers, directors, actors, cameramen, and scenarists involved in the films have been widely varied. The quality of the plays themselves and their suitability to film adaptation are diverse. The many variant elements that account for the success or failure of the individual film renderings of O'Neill lead to interesting and problematic questions about adaptive process in general. Before going on to examine specifically the results of the translation of O'Neill from one medium into another, it would be useful to survey some of the essential theoretical considerations that have informed the study of film adaptations generally.

The arts of stage and screen are similar in many respects: both are mimetic forms of entertainment—physical recreations of reality using actors, settings, props, and lighting; both generally tell stories dealing with social, emotional, and psychological aspects of human experience, and are performed or displayed for an audience. There has been little argument concerning the features that the stage and screen share, but there has been and still is a good deal of controversy over the way in which stage and screen can and, indeed, should use these shared features differently.

Allardyce Nicoll, for example, in his book *Film and Theatre* (1936), seeking to explain the failure of many film adaptations of plays, said: "The basic reason seems to be simply this—that practically all effectively drawn stage characters are types and that in the cinema we demand individualization."[7] The point is partially true, but it cannot be insisted upon as absolute. Nicoll's idea is founded on his argument that the theater is the realm of artifice and the cinema is the medium of truth—or realism. But the cinema is equally comfortable in both of these provinces. Expressionism, for example, is a viable filmic form. In examining an expressionist film such as *Caligari, Metropolis, The Crowd,* or many other films that have aspects of expressionism (in the sense of stylized nonrealism), we could scarcely find the characters less effective simply because they have elements of stylization. Typical of the controversy concerning stage-to-screen adaptations, Eric Bentley responded in a 1947 essay to Nicoll's oversimplifications, saying: "One cannot say, with Mr. Nicoll, that undecorated reality suits the screen, and fine words the stage. Such a belief is a hangover from the days of silent films."[8] Bentley's view allows greater latitude of subject matter in both film and theater, finding both fantasy and realism appropriate to either. He questions the idea that theatricality is inherently uncinematic, saying finally that "dramatic art is possible on both stage and screen. On both it could fulfill its function of presenting an account of human experience deeply and truly."[9]

Similar critical controversies have emerged with Susan Sontag's essay "Film and Theatre" and Pauline Kael's essay on Kracauer's *Theory of Film: The Redemption of Reality*. Sontag argues against Erwin Panofsky's idea that the job of the cinema is one of "manipulating and shooting unstylized reality in such a way that it has style."[10] Sontag suggests that Panofsky is insisting on the dynamics of the silent screen and, as did Bentley's remarks on Nicoll, decries the notion that realism is the only viable film form.[11] Likewise, Kael takes to task Kracauer's idea that film necessarily "gravitates toward unstaged reality" and the idea that "the artificiality of stagey setting of compositions runs counter to the medium's preference for nature in the raw."[12] This idea leads to Kracauer's assertion that an "obscure railroad station" is more cinematic than "the painted splendour of an enchanted woods." Kael simply answers this assertion as follows: "An obscure railroad station may be enchanting, so may painted woods."[13]

Such controversies lead to an important central idea of Sontag's essay—"that there is no reason to insist on a single model for film."[14] This point would seem indisputable. In a medium—and industry as well—such as cinema, which is so complex, so conglomerate, fed by so many sources and informed by a multiplicity of people in varying capacities, it seems impossible to insist on a single model for effectiveness in adapting stage works to the screen. A related point is well made by James Hurt in his introduction to *Focus on Film and Theatre*:

Historically each stage in the development of the film has raised new questions and has brought about fresh resolutions in the relationship of film to theatre. . . . The theoretical interrelationships are as complex as their historical ones, and indeed the historical development of each art and their reciprocal influence have made theoretical comparisons difficult and short-lived.[15]

The relationship between theater and film is complex both theoretically and practically. No single theory, as suggested above, seems to satisfy the particular problems and mechanics of all stage-to-screen adaptations. Successful adaptations of a dramatic work can range as widely as from Kurosawa's *Throne of Blood* (which has totally transmuted Shakespeare's *Macbeth* into the terms of cinema and Japanese culture), to Cukor's *Dinner at Eight*, which more or less just takes a witty and successful stage play and brings it to the screen unaltered. These perhaps very disparate examples represent the widest polarity in adaptation. Both of these film adaptations, however, have several common features: they both were made by fine directors, they both had superb actors for the style of the work, both remain quite faithful to the spirit of the work on which they are based, and they both remain stylistically consistent throughout.

Adaptations from stage to screen, then, it would seem, can be either very similar or very different in form to the plays on which they are based and still be successful. The effectiveness of adapted works certainly does not lie in mere fidelity to the original. Neither does it stand in any direct proportion to the worth of the stage work on which it is based. Not all of Shakespeare's adapted plays have resulted in superior films, whereas many rather slight plays have, such as *Camille, Way Down East,* or *Twentieth Century*. And certainly in the case of adapted plays of O'Neill, the intrinsic worth of the play itself has not determined the success of the film adaptation.

Criticism of stage-to-screen adaptations has tended to seek the answer to the question of effectiveness by assuming rules that should be followed in adapting a stage work to the screen. It is commonly held that a certain amount of dialogue must be cut in bringing a play to the screen, that stage dialogue, in the words of screenwriter Dudley Nichols, "must be condensed, synopsized."[16] The point is generally well taken, yet it need not be axiomatic. It would seem more important to look at the need for, and the quality of, the synopsis rather than to assume it as an absolute. Many plays have been successfully adapted without radical cutting of the original texts, among them Nichols's *Who's Afraid of Virginia Woolf?*, Wyler's *The Little Foxes*, and Kazan's *A Streetcar Named Desire*. "Talkiness" is no longer automatically considered uncinematic. It is, likewise, generally felt that film versions of plays must "open up" the stage work, that is, break it out of the confines of the spatially enclosed stage structure. The cinema, of course, has distinct advantages over the stage in the ability to make rapid spatial changes and to treat space fluidly, yet this kind of treatment may not be apt for all film adaptations. Certain works thematically and psychologically require that a sense of confinement be maintained even on film. *A Streetcar Named Desire, The Caretaker,* and *The Little Foxes,* mentioned in a different context above, are equally good examples of this point. Two widely different films—Kurosawa's version of *The Lower Depths,* and Hawks's *Twentieth Century*—are also examples of films that are effective while necessarily maintaining the sense of confined space of the original stage works. Merely to open up some scenes physically by bringing them outdoors, out of the confines of the studio setting, often results in simply underlining the hybrid film/theater nature of the adapted work. It is not enough merely to employ the convention of opening up; the crucial question of space must be more completely rethought and reworked for film. Properly understood, filmic space is the entire compositional area on the screen and this space can be manipulated or, to use Panofsky's phrase, "dynamized" by film techniques, such as depth of focus, camera angle and movement, light and shadow, and other compositional elements. Moreover, the treatment of space should be consistent throughout and should support, or cinematically augment, the themes of the work.

No "single model" in Sontag's phrase, nor any single a priori assumption can satisfactorily form the basis for evaluation of all or even most stage to screen adaptations. Rather, a multiplicity of considerations ought to be taken into account, such as the time of the film's release and relevant social and ethical mores; the variously determinant roles of producer, director, cameraman, and scenarist as these intervene between the original work and the adaptation; the actors and their suitability to the roles they play, both in terms of craft and the cinematically important factor of physical appropriateness; finally and importantly, the faithfulness of the adaptation to the original work. André Bazin defined a good adaptation as one that "results in a restoration of the essence of the letter and the spirit"[17] of the original work. Bazin's use of the term "restoration" is apt. An adaptation should revivify, reestablish, indeed, recreate the atmosphere, mood, characters, and themes of the original work within the aesthetic dynamics of the adapting medium.

This study of the adapted works of O'Neill will examine both the effectiveness of the films themselves, as films, and the equally important consideration of their validity as adaptations of the original works. The analyses will often closely compare the original text, situations, dialogue, stage directions, to the handling of similar elements in the film versions to discover the aptness of the transformation from one medium to another. Since the adaptation of the stage drama to screen has many creators—the scenarist, the director, the actors, and the technicians who contribute some share of the total work—it is necessary to consider a wide range of influences on the finished product. Finally, the films will be treated in chronological order according to release dates; criticism contemporary with the release of the films will frequently be used as a significant reflection of both changing critical currents and general ideas about the nature of the adaptive process from stage to screen.

NOTES

1. Louis Sheaffer, *O'Neill: Son and Playwright* (Boston: Little, Brown and Company, 1968), p. 312.
2. Louis Sheaffer, *O'Neill: Son and Artist* (Boston: Little, Brown and Company, 1973), p. 351.
3. Richard Watts, Jr., *New York Herald Tribune*, November 7, 1927.
4. Sheaffer, *O'Neill: Son and Artist*, p. 546.
5. Ibid., p. 560.
6. Barbara and Arthur Gelb, *O'Neill* (New York: Harper's, 1960), p. 719.
7. Allardyce Nicoll, *Film and Theatre* (New York: Crowell, 1936), p. 165.
8. Eric Bentley, "Realism and the Cinema," in *The Playwright as Thinker* (New York: Harcourt, 1946), reprinted in James Hurt, ed., *Focus on Film and Theatre* (Englewood Cliffs, N.J.: Prentice-Hall, 1974), p. 57.
9. Ibid.
10. Susan Sontag, "Film and Theatre," reprinted in *Film Theory and Criticism* (New York: Oxford University Press, 1974), p. 251.
11. Ibid.
12. Siegfried Kracauer, *Theory of Film: The Redemption of Physical Reality* (New York: Oxford University Press, 1960), p. 175.
13. Pauline Kael, *I Lost It at the Movies* (Boston: Little, Brown and Company, 1965), p. 259.
14. Sontag, p. 251.
15. James Hurt, *Focus on Film and Theatre* (Englewood Cliffs, N.J.: Prentice-Hall, 1974), p. 2.
16. John Gassner and Dudley Nichols, *Twenty Best Film Plays* (New York: Crown Publications, 1943), "The Writer and the Film" by Nichols, p. xxxiii.
17. André Bazin, *What Is Cinema?*, vol. 1, Hugh Gray, trans. (Berkeley: University of California Press, 1967), p. 67.

O'Neill on Film

1
Anna Christie

(1923 and 1930)

The first of O'Neill's works to reach the screen was *Anna Christie*, directed by John Griffith Wray under the personal supervision of Thomas Ince as producer. Riding the crest of the popularity of the play, which had seen a very successful New York run and an equally successful national tour, O'Neill sold the rights to the play for the sum of $25,000 to be divided equally between himself and the play's producer.[1] The film adaptation starred Blanche Sweet and was released in 1923. O'Neill's first encounter with the film industry was a happy one and, as pointed out in George Mitchell's article on Ince in *Films in Review*, "It received laudatory reviews from virtually all critics." Robert Sherwood called it "a credit to Mr. Ince and to movies." And it was chosen for special screening before the National Board of Review.[2] Mordaunt Hall said of it: "Here is a picture with wonderful characterization that tells a moving and compelling story—a film which is intensely dramatic, and one that will win new audiences for the screen."[3] The film had long been unavailable in this country until the Museum of Modern Art, in 1975, acquired a print of it from the Soviet Union with Serbo-Croatian titles; the titles have since been translated and the film is now, fortunately, available again.[4] The silent version of *Anna Christie* probably suffered neglect because it was so vastly overshadowed by the enormously successful later sound version starring Greta Garbo in her talking debut—a work to be discussed later.

While the film was nominally directed by Wray, it clearly retains the stamp of Ince, who, as producer, always insisted on complete supervision of the entire production of everything that came from his studio. Ince required elaborate shooting scripts, or production blueprints, which he would have to approve and stamp "shoot as is" before the director could begin work on the film, and Ince would generally edit the film himself on completion of the shooting. Ince's style generally included a penchant for dramatic titles (i.e., those bearing dialogue, rather than narrative titles) and this was indeed suitable to the first stage-to-screen adaptation of an O'Neill play. The work of Ince is also characterized by a great concern for the narrative flow of the story, and the cutting of his films is generally dynamic and fast-paced. Ince was also a pioneer in the use of location shooting. All these worked well in the adaptation of *Anna Christie* and resulted in a work that is both cinematically effective and faithful to the spirit of the original.

A central consideration in most stage-to-screen adaptations is the opening up of the play (or spatially breaking it out of the confines of the limited stage set). While opening up is not always necessary or even advisable for all screen adaptations, it can often be cinematically effective in supporting and augmenting the themes of the original work. The silent adaptation of *Anna Christie* is an interesting example of the viability of spatially expanding the limited setting of the play. Whereas O'Neill's play takes place in only two locations—a decrepit wharf saloon known as Johnny-the-Priest's, and the deck and cabin of Chris Christopherson's barge—the film version adds other locations suggested in the play and in so doing expands the play both spatially and temporally. The structure of the play is tight, covering the span of only nineteen days. It begins when Anna is twenty years old and newly arrived in New York from Saint Paul to visit her father, Chris. She moves to the barge that Chris operates and, soon after, meets the rough sailor Mat Burke, with whom she falls in love. Mat shares her love and wants them to marry, but is disgusted by Anna's confession of her past life as a prostitute. Mat rejects her but later that evening returns and agrees to marry her if she vows that he is the only man she has ever loved. The play ends with Chris and Mat about to sail the next day for South Africa, while Anna remains on the barge to await their return. During the course of the play we learn that Anna, at the age of five, had been sent from Sweden to live with relatives on a farm in Minnesota; that she was badly treated by them and sexually abused by her fifteen-year-old cousin; as a result she was forced to leave and drifted into a life of prostitution. The film version visualizes these past events and takes us to the locations only mentioned in the play.

The beginning of the film is set in Sweden fifteen years before the central action of the play. We see Anna as a child of five on the day that her mother receives a letter from her relatives in America suggesting that she send Anna to live a better life with them in Minnesota. The film then crosscuts to Chris, who is in Shanghai without enough money to get home to his family in Sweden. At this point a title card appears announcing that it is fifteen years later; we are now at the point of the central action of the play. The structure of the film now faithfully follows that of the play, with one other important divergence. During the speech in which Anna tells of the hardships of her past and eventual selling of her body, the film again visualizes the events through a flashback to the farm and a train station in Saint Paul. The opening up and time manipulation in the film version work well since they are adroitly paced and directed and visually support essential themes of the original work, as a closer analysis of details and images from these portions added to the play in its film treatment will suggest.

The film opens with shots of the sea, which will become the dominant image and central theme of the work. Anna's fated connection to the sea is foreshadowed in two significant details from the brief prologue set in Sweden. The young Anna first appears on screen holding a seashell to her ear, and later is seen playing in a boat at the water's edge. It is at this point that she is to be sent to America to live with her mother's relatives. The details of the seashell and boat establish Anna's inexorable link to the sea—or "Ol' davil," as Chris so often calls it. The following brief scene with Chris in Shanghai foreshadows Anna's fate in a somewhat different way. We see Chris holding a doll that he has bought to take home to his daughter. He counts his money and discovers that once again he does not have enough cash to book passage home. (Chris, like the seafarers in *The Long Voyage Home,* seems to be mysteriously and helplessly bound to the sea and a life of wandering.) Chris, angry at being unable to get home, throws the doll down on the deck of the ship, breaking it. There is now a dissolve from the doll to the child Anna back home, followed by another dissolve from Anna to the smashed doll, which Chris picks up from the deck and throws into the sea. A visual analogy is set up between Anna and the broken doll that foreshadows the unpleasant fate in store for her in Minnesota, a fate that she will blame on her father's neglect. The final shot in this sequence, of the doll thrown into the ocean, also suggests Anna's fated affinity with the sea.

The second major sequence added to the play occurs late in the film during Anna's long speech telling the whole truth of her past. As Anna narrates the events of her past there is a flashback to visualize the actions. We see her on the farm, carrying a large pail of water to the farmhouse, which is ugly and unkempt. We then see her unpleasant young cousin grab her in a sexually aggressive way (in the play she clearly implies that she is raped by the cousin). She tells her uncle of the event and both decide that she must leave the farm. We now see Anna at a train station. A man eyes her with obvious designs. Later the same night she is still at the station. There is a closeup as she counts her money, knowing that she does not have the funds to get away (paralleling the earlier shot of Chris counting his money to get home, suggesting their similar entrapment by circumstances). The same man still watches and follows her—"So, the job in St. Paul," she says, as the film cuts back to the present time of the action.

As Anna, Blanche Sweet creates a convincingly realistic portrait of the hardened and cynical character. Sweet, famous for several earlier films with Griffith, including *The Lonedale Operator* and *Judith of Bethulia,* was physically well suited to the role of Anna. She was quite different from the type of gently winsome heroines, such as Lillian and Dorothy Gish or Mary Pickford, popular in silent film. Blanche Sweet was a robustly handsome

ANNA CHRISTIE (1923) Ince Studios. Directed by John Griffith Wray. With Blanche Sweet. (Blanche Sweet as Anna soon after her entrance, a robustly handsome rather than typically pretty actress.)

rather than typically pretty actress and she played Anna with a suitable tough kind of determination. She is altogether rougher and more slatternly than Garbo's Anna was to be in the later film version, which romanticizes and softens the character.

Several details and situations added to the play work as reminders of Anna's recent past: her costume upon entering is tawdry; she roughly lights a match on the saloon table to light her cigarette; she is about to leave the saloon with a man (a situation not in the play) when Marthy lies about Chris being away; and finally, the flashback discussed earlier visualizes events of the recent past. Whereas the fact of Anna's prostitution is attenuated in the later film, here it is emphasized.

One scene that was not in the original play was, perhaps, added as a concession to morality. Toward the end of the film, when Anna has been rejected by Burke and is about to leave New York, we see her standing by the edge of the pier about to commit suicide by throwing herself into the river. This would, of course, suggest her sense of guilt and shame and satisfy both potential censors and moralists watching the film. That the film was not a great financial success was, as suggested by several critics, probably owing to its realistic portrayal of a controversial subject. It is also likely that audiences accustomed to action and adventure films from the studio of Ince were not prepared for a film such as *Anna Christie*.

While the film had only limited commercial success, it was indeed a critical success and still holds up well after more than fifty years since its release. Much of the success of the film is owing to the fine performance of Blanche Sweet in the title role and also the performances of George Marion as Chris and, to a lesser degree, William Russell as Mat Burke. George Marion had played Chris in the original New York production of the play and would play the role again seven years later in the sound version. He seems more suited to the role in the silent film than he does in the later sound film. He captures more of the weathered roughness of the character and what O'Neill called his "obstinate kindliness" than he would in the later film. William Russell as Mat Burke is aptly crude, overbearing, and yet childlike. Eugenie Besserer, appearing only in the first scene as Marthy, is suitably bedraggled in her small role. She certainly is not as memorable as Marie Dressler in the later film version—in a role that was expanded specifically for Dressler's talents. Of course, scope for all of the above merits could only exist within the competent directional framework provided by the Wray-Ince collaboration.

The film clearly reflects the narrative flow as well as attention to details and atmosphere that are characteristic of the Ince style. Kenneth Macgowan, in *Behind the Screen*, argued that Ince's style, in which "action is pared down to the bone and then fleshed with exact and appropriate details,"[5] was perfectly suited to O'Neill's *Anna Christie*. The precise use of images to characterize visually the dramatis personae of *Anna Christie* are abundant in the work, especially in connection to the title character as analyzed above. Lewis

ANNA CHRISTIE (1923) Ince Studios. Directed by John Griffith Wray. With Blanche Sweet, and Eugenie Besserer as Marthy. ("You're me, forty years from now.")

ANNA CHRISTIE (1923) Ince Studios. Directed by John Griffith Wray. With Blanche Sweet, George Marion, and William Russell. (Anna confesses the sins of her past to the appalled Chris and Mat.)

Jacobs, in *The Rise of the American Film*, attributed the general success of Ince's films to both the direct method of storytelling in his films and fine use of atmosphere. He said:

> Ince's narrative flair was enhanced by his feeling for human relationships, space, and nature. Sweeping landscapes, imposing mountain ranges, desert wastes—all these he brought into play to give his films color, to heighten dramatic moods.[6]

In *Anna Christie* the use of the atmosphere of the sea is indeed effective in intensifying the moods and characterizations of the work. From the very beginning of the film, with its shots of the ocean, mountains, and clouds, to the very end of the film, with the shot of Chris looking out into the foggy and mysterious sea, we are in a convincingly realistic world of natural forces that seem to dominate the lives and fates of the characters of the film. One small but very revealing use of imagery from nature occurs near the end of the film when Anna decides that she must tell Burke the truth of her past, thereby risking his rejection. As she talks to her old father, Chris, with the title "I just can't go on fooling him," we see rain running down the windowpanes of the barge cabin. This image supports the sense of melancholy that Anna feels in the scene, as elsewhere the film has taken full advantage of the expressive use of natural elements. For example, the storm sequence, in which Anna and Mat's fates coincidentally collide, is aptly intense and dramatic. This sequence contains quick and frenetic cutting, and its rhythms and images heighten the dramatic importance of this first of several turbulent encounters between Anna and Mat Burke.

The film version of *Anna Christie*, released one year prior to Ince's death, is a praiseworthy culmination of the career of an important and often historically neglected producer-director-editor. Ince himself was pleased with the film and its critical reception. He is supposed to have said of it, " made it for the highbrow critics who say that Thomas Ince can't make anything but box-office pictures."[7] O'Neill's first encounter with the film industry was much more felicitous than many later ones. He was impressed and pleased with the film, calling it "a delightful surprise . . . remarkably well acted and directed and in spirit an absolutely faithful transcript of the play."[8]

"GARBO TALKS!" announced marquees all over the country on the opening of the 1930 adaptation of O'Neill's *Anna Christie*. Only at the University Theatre, near Harvard, where O'Neill had briefly studied playwriting, was he not adumbrated by Miss Garbo's superstardom; here the marquees read "O'NEILL'S *ANNA CHRISTIE* WITH GRETA GARBO."[9] It had been only seven years since Blanche Sweet had played Anna on the silent screen, and now O'Neill's play would become a landmark in film history as the vehicle for the "talkie" debut of Greta Garbo. O'Neill had sold the visual rights to his play in 1922 and was now paid only $7,500 more for the dialogue rights.

ANNA CHRISTIE (1930) MGM. Directed by Clarence Brown. (Publicity still for *Anna Christie*.)

Although *Anna Christie* turned out to be one of the biggest financial successes of the film versions of O'Neill's plays, it was, ironically, the one for which he was paid the least. Much of his future disenchantment with the film industry stemmed from this and other examples of what O'Neill considered to be exploitation. O'Neill never saw the sound-film version of his play. Knowing and respecting the screen power of Garbo, he feared that the sound version of *Anna Christie* would be, as he said, "all to the Garbo and very little of the O'Neill."[10]

Indeed, Garbo's presence in the film was the thing most paramount when the film was released in March of 1930. Both popular and critical interest in the film centered on the presence of Greta Garbo in her first sound film. Curiously enough, according to Samuel Marx in his recent book *Mayer and Thalberg: The Make-Believe Saints*, Irving Thalberg of MGM had wanted Shaw's *Saint Joan* for Garbo's sound debut; but when Shaw refused to sell the rights, Thalberg settled on *Anna Christie* as a second choice. Marx points out also that Garbo originally refused to play the role, considering it "degrading to Swedes," and only agreed after Thalberg threatened to cut off her salary if she did not do it. The fact that Garbo had lost most of her savings in the crash of 1929 made Thalberg's threat quite convincing.[11] Nonetheless, the role of Anna seemed ready-made for Garbo. she was then twenty-five, close in age to the character, and naturally had the Swedish accent that O'Neill had written into the dialogue. Garbo's rich, mellifluous voice and, more importantly, her ability to make the transition from silent to talking pictures as so many other actors had not were the things on which audiences and critics alike focused their attention.

Creighton Peet's review in *Outlook* magazine is a typical example of critical attention to Garbo's voice in the film. He begins his review saying:

> Greta Garbo's voice, not to keep you in suspense any longer, is the deepest I have ever heard in a woman . . . so deep and mannish that when she says "I love you, I love you!" it is necessary to look twice at the screen to know whether it is she or Charles Bickford who is talking.[12]

His preoccupation with Garbo's voice does not end here; he goes on to say later in his review that "there is some question, however, about her voice. I am afraid it is going to startle a lot of people out of seven year's growth."[13] The exaggerated and somewhat obsessive nature of these comments—the review is very brief and discusses little else—stands as evidence not only of the power of Garbo's voice, but also of the importance and novelty of all the sound elements in early talkies. Mordaunt Hall's review displays a similar preoccupation with Garbo's voice: "The low enunciation of her utterance came somewhat as a surprise . . . for her delivery is almost masculine."[14] Given all the ballyhoo concerning Garbo's first words on the screen, it seems almost comical that they should have been O'Neill's colorfully prosaic line—"Gimme a whiskey—ginger ale on the side. And don't be stingy, baby."

Clarence Brown, the director of the sound version of *Anna Christie*, was familiar with Miss Garbo's particular talents and her enormous interest for audiences, having already directed her in *Flesh and the Devil* in 1927. (He would also direct her later in *Anna Karenina* [1935] and *Marie Walewska* [*Conquest*] in 1937, and is reputed to be Garbo's favorite director.)[15] He was well aware of the dramatic impact of the first entrance of Garbo as Anna. O'Neill had made Anna's entrance of consequence to the first act of the play, by placing center stage the door marked "Ladies' Entrance," through which Anna would inevitably enter. Brown, in the film version, borrows the stage convention and keeps this door centered in the background of every shot in the scene. Here the "held shot" and static camera tend to direct our attention to the door, and its central placing, along with a very slight upward tilt of the camera, further emphasize it. Anna's entrance in the film is delayed for thirty-four minutes, well into the second reel, and audiences are reputed to have applauded lavishly the patently prosaic first line.[16]

This adaptation of *Anna Christie* does not begin at a point in time previous to the central action of the play as did the earlier sound version, yet the screenplay also alters the opening of the play to make the exposition more graceful and natural. Employing the filmic capability of fluid treatment of space, the film opens on the barge rather than in the bar as O'Neill wrote it.

ANNA CHRISTIE (1930) MGM. Directed by Clarence Brown. With George Marion and Marie Dressler. (Chris forces the reluctant Marthy to leave in preparation for Anna's arrival.)

ANNA CHRISTIE (1930) MGM. Directed by Clarence Brown. With Greta Garbo. (Garbo as the world-weary prostitute.)

With this first scene on the barge we are introduced to Chris and Marthy in their own world. Visual details of the barge, the general atmosphere of clutter, disorder, and sordidness are presented so as to contrast later with the order imposed on this world by Anna. Sound plays a major role in this opening scene as well; the repeated and foreboding sound of the foghorn is heard in vivid contrast to the song "In the Good Old Summer Time" being played on an old scratchy Victrola. We first see only Marthy on the barge, and see it as her home, which prepares us for the scene later in which Chris falteringly suggests, and she knows, that she must leave it now that Anna is coming. She is drunk; Chris soon joins her in that condition, and they decide to go ashore to get more to drink. The film then introduces us to the sordid environment of the waterfront and to the fog, which will visually and symbolically play so great a part in the film.

Several changes from, and similarities to, O'Neill's play are worth noting. The name of the bar to which Chris and Marthy go is not the same as in the play. O'Neill's Johnny-the-Priest's may have been too controversial and offensive to the Catholic moviegoing audience, so its name is changed to just "Bar." Johnny-the-Priest himself becomes Johnny-the-Harp. (The silent version of *Anna Christie* does not change these names, owing to the less stringent censorship in 1923.) When Chris and Marthy arrive at the bar, Johnny gives Chris the letter from Anna that has just arrived. In the play we have already met Johnny before the entrance of Chris and Marthy and have heard that he had not seen Chris "in a dog's eye." This makes the immediate entrance of Chris, to receive the letter and news of Anna's arrival, seem contrived. The film's treatment of this scene puts less strain on our credulity as we are lead to believe that Chris goes there every day. The almost immediate arrival of Anna, another convenient coincidence, is the same in the film as in the play. Brown has maintained the conventionally stagey sequence of events: exit Chris to get something to eat and sober up, followed immediately by the ringing of the bell at the "Ladies' Entrance"; enter Anna, who finds Marthy also in the back room, which makes possible another convenient method of exposition.

O'Neill described Anna in the stage directions as "a tall, blond, fully developed girl of twenty, handsome after a large Viking-daughter fashion, but now run down in health and plainly showing all the outward signs of belonging to the world's oldest profession."[17] Garbo's face and figure fit this physical description almost perfectly. The outward signs of her being a prostitute are primarily the low cut of her blouse, the velvet bow tied at her neck, and the tough swagger of her walk. The following scene between Anna and Marthy follows the text of the play faithfully, except for a few minor changes in dialogue to make it sound more natural, and even Garbo changes some of O'Neill's "yusts" to "justs."

The shooting of the scene between Anna and Marthy is essentially static and stock early studio work. The camera almost always shoots the speaker rather than the listener, taking little advantage of the cinematic potential of characterizing through response and reaction. Anna and Marthy instantly recognize each other for what they are, and Anna clearly reflects her cynical self-image in saying to Marthy, "You're me, forty years from now." As Marthy, Marie Dressler perfectly embodies what O'Neill wanted in this character—"her jowly, mottled face, with its thick red nose . . . her figure is fat and flabby . . . but there still twinkles in her blood-shot eyes a youthful lust for life which hard usage has failed to stifle; a sense of mocking humor, but good tempered"[18]—almost as much a description of Marie Dressler as of Marthy. Frances Marion, scenarist for the film, suggested Dressler for the role to Clarence Brown, who was skeptical, thinking Dressler too "slapstick" for the role, but she was tested and Brown found her to be the perfect Marthy.[19] Because of Dressler's comic talents and audience appeal, the part of Marthy is expanded in the film. She is given two scenes that are not in the play—the opening scene of the film mentioned earlier, and a later scene added to the film. When Anna and her new love, Mat Burke, are at an amusement park, we meet Marthy again. Now her comedy takes on a different edge. Anna is embarrassed and feels shame in Mat's presence for knowing such a woman, or "wharf rat," as he calls her.

Marthy's role in this added scene suggests a somewhat moralistic approach to the character that is absent in the play. She realizes that she is interrupting and endangering Anna's reputation and relationship with Mat and feels guilty. But Marthy knows when to "beat it," as she has so often said earlier; and in this scene she backs off without letting Mat know that she knows more about Anna than she seems to, or more than Anna wants Mat to know. Comedy resurfaces at the end of this essentially melodramatic scene as Marthy shuffles drunkenly off, after having asked for a quarter to buy a drink, since she "hasn't had a drink in a month." Mordaunt Hall comments on this duel aspect of Dressler's performance, saying: "She, with all of Marthy's bibulous nature, elicits sympathy from the dissolute woman and often she relieves the sordid atmosphere with effective comedy."[20]

The roughness of O'Neill's characters is generally softened in this film version. As Marthy has been somewhat softened and sentimentalized in this film version, so have the characters of Anna, Chris, and Mat Burke. In the film Anna is more obviously and sentimentally romantic. Soon after meeting Burke, she is knitting a sweater for him. The scene in the amusement park, added for filmic interest, also underlines Anna's girlishly romantic nature through her responses to Burke, and his childlike pride in feats of strength in the amusement-part games. Burke's character is also modified in the film version. A notable deletion from the film version is Mat's threat to kill Anna after she has revealed the details of her dissolute past. He is still O'Neill's bossing and bullying Burke, but the film reduces the element of potential violence in his nature.

Anna's father, Chris Christopherson, seems also to be presented more

ANNA CHRISTIE (1930) MGM. Directed by Clarence Brown. With Greta Garbo and George Marion. (Anna with her father Chris on his newly "domesticated" barge.)

ANNA CHRISTIE (1930) MGM. Directed by Clarence Brown. With Greta Garbo and Charles Bickford. (Anna is infatuated with Mat during the amusement park scene.)

sympathetically in the film than in the play. Through the cinematic tricks of soft focus, gauzy filters, and haloing back lighting—especially in the scene in which he first encounters Anna—he is shown as kindly and paternal, less clumsy and weatherbeaten than O'Neill describes him in the stage directions. George Marion, who had played Chris in the original stage production and in the earlier silent-film version, plays Chris again, but he is nearly ten years older than he had been in the original production of the play. He is less the rough, broad-shouldered, thick-necked, he-manly old seafarer that O'Neill describes in the stage directions, and more the gentle, old, kind, and forgiving father.

The film's structure, as mentioned earlier, closely follows the play's structure. Even the act divisions are signaled by titles explaining the change of locale and time. The only scene other than the first (set on the barge) that is added to the fim is the one in the amusement park. This comes shortly after the initial meeting of Anna and Mat. There is a quick cut to Anna and Mat soaring down the slope of a rollercoaster. The cutting from the previous shot on the barge to this one on the rollercoaster is the quickest and most radical spatial transition in the film. The editing of the following sequence is much faster in tempo than other scenes in the film. We follow Anna and Mat on the rollercoaster ride by means of rear projection. Mat rings the bell on the strength-testing maching five times, visually interesting because of the unusual camera angle—filmed from atop the machine. This is followed by a series of quick cuts as Mat demonstrates his lung strength and his skill at throwing a baseball. All of this sequence is aimed at further characterizing Mat Burke; his childlike naiveté and his need to display his masculinity are well captured cinematically; and Anna responds with "appropriate" pleasure. This sequence also reintroduces Marthy and, through the confrontation between Anna and Marthy, acts as a prelude to Anna's subsequent confession to Mat of her past life. Mat's rejection of Marthy and her type ironically sets up the following scene, in which he finds out that Anna is, in a manner of speaking, Marthy forty years ago.

This scene set at the carnival is the most traditional example of opening up in the film. It was generally assumed that a screenplay should move the adapted play out of the confines of the studio for effective film treatment. Frances Marion, adapter and screenplay writer for the film, suggests this idea in talking about her work on *Anna Christie:*

> In writing the scenario of *Anna Christie,* I had adhered as closely as possible to the text of the O'Neill play, except for the necessary changes which had to be made to give the picture movement away from the confines of a dilapidated old tub tied up at the pier.[21]

Whether or not such changes are in fact "necessary" is an idea that is theoretically questionable, as often mentioned in this study. The more important consideration is the way in which the film is opened up and the relevance of such changes and their consistency within the whole work. The carnival sequence seems rather obtrusive stylistically. While it works well enough in capturing qualities of the character of Mat, it makes Anna too traditionally girlish and romantic.

There are several other kinds of opening up in the film that are more appropriate to the general atmosphere and themes of the film. Several shots of the sea punctuate the film, as in the silent version, to suggest the importance of the sea as a force in the lives of all the characters. Somewhat less effective are the several atmospheric shots in the film, which have a bogus studio quality. A number of shots on the deck of Chris's barge aim at creating atmosphere through a densely foggy effect. The storm at sea combines studio action and rear projection with modest effectiveness. Many of the exterior shots are very dimly lighted, which helps to make them more convincing, yet the exterior shots in this film are less effective than in the earlier silent version of the film. Nonetheless, since the mood of *Anna Christie* depends so heavily on O'Neill's metaphorical sense of the sea—its threatening, mysterious, and fateful power—it is necessary that this be suggested by the film.

The fact that this film is a product of the early sound studio and the speaking debut of the already legendary Garbo would tend to make the interior scenes and verbal dynamics of the work of preponderant concern. The studio sequences are handled in a generally static way, most often employing a fixed camera and relatively long takes. As suggested by the contemporary reviewers of the film, it was the presence of Garbo acting with words that was of most concern to the listeners and watchers of the film. The power of Garbo's screen presence, much clearer now than it was at the time of the release of *Anna Christie*, was captured in Richard Dana Skinner's insightful review of the film:

> She can arrest and hold attention with a single gesture. Behind the almost mask-like quality of her face one feels a burning intensity, not alone of feeling and emotion, but also of will and intellect—a sort of sullen superiority to her surroundings.[22]

Skinner also praises Garbo's mastery of acting through dialogue that "enables her to time gesture more accurately, to give them added distinctness and purpose, and to increase the impact of her occasional and rare moments of explosive action."[23]

There is indeed intensity and intelligence in Garbo's performance throughout the film, but especially in the long climactic speech in which she confesses the truth of her past life as a prostitute. During the speech she completely dominates both her father and Mat Burke and the viewer as well. At this point Anna must again become tough, hard, and determined. She is, in a sense, fighting for her life, for respect, and for the love of Mat Burke. Garbo is very convincing in the speech, with pacing and shadings of inflection that make the speech spellbinding, as it must be to be effective. The conflict between her love for Mat and her hatred of men generally for the way they have used her becomes palpably alive. The speech is shot with Anna standing between the two men, visually as well as dramatically dominating them, and a slight upward tilt to the camera magnifies her power. (Indeed, Garbo is scrupulously filmed throughout by William Daniels, who was her favorite cameraman at MGM.)

The power and presence of Garbo in the leading role seems to be chiefly responsible for both the critical and the commerical success of *Anna Christie*. Clarence Brown's direction of the film is competent if unexciting, and the overall effect of the film is weakened for several reasons. There is a static quality to the shooting of interior scenes partly owing to the lack of sophistication of sound-recording devices at the time. Characters do not often move when they speak and there is generally very little camera movement in the film. Usually the camera assumes a fixed position during scenes with dialogue and most scenes are shot from only one side of a room or setting. The more spatially fluid scene in the amusement park, while visually interesting and dramatically effective in its reintroduction of Marthy, is essentially inconsistent with the style of the rest of the film. And several of the atmospheric shots, while necessary to the theme and mood of the work, remain realistically unconvincing.

As an adaptation of O'Neill's play, the film follows the original in outline more than in essence. Anna is less the hardened and cynical former prostitute that Blanche Sweet had been in the silent version, or that O'Neill envisioned in writing the character. Garbo in costume and general manner is somewhat glamorized and romanticized. There is less of a kind of fatalism in Anna's connections to the sea and her seafaring father, Chris, and seafaring lover, Mat. An important line in the play that relates to all of their fates is cut from the film. After Anna's confession of her past, Chris is deeply hurt and feels responsible. In consolation Anna says, "Don't bawl about it. There ain't nothing to forgive anyway. It ain't your fault and it ain't mine, and it ain't his either. We're all poor nuts, and things happen, and we just get mixed in wrong, that's all." This important theme of resigned fatalism, which is repeated so often in most of O'Neill's later works, is not fully realized in the characterizations, moods, and atmosphere of Brown's adaptation of *Anna Christie*.

NOTES

1. Louis Sheaffer, *O'Neill: Son and Artist* (Boston: Little, Brown & Co., 1973), p. 104.
2. George Mitchell, *Films in Review* 2 (October 1960): 481.
3. Mordaunt Hall, *New York Times*, December 10, 1923, p. 20.
4. Notes supplied by the Museum of Modern Art give the following information on the titles used in their print of the film: "This version of Anna Christie was re-edited in the Soviet Union when the film was

released there in 1930, and new Russian titles were written. Therefore, the titles in this print are not the original ones, but translations from the Russian, with some assistance from the play of Eugene O'Neill, prepared by the Department of Film of the Museum of Modern Art."

5. Anonymous, *Exceptional Photoplays* (December–January 1925), reprinted in *American Film Criticism* (New York: Liveright, 1972), p. 153.

6. Lewis Jacobs, *The Rise of the American Film* (New York: Harcourt Brace, 1939), p. 205.

7. Mitchell, p. 481.

8. Sheaffer, p. 104.

9. Ibid., p. 353.

10. Ibid., p. 104.

11. Samuel Marx, *Mayer and Thalberg: The Make-Believe Saints* (New York: Random House, 1976), p. 123.

12. Creighton Peet, *Outlook* 29 (February 26, 1930): 350.

13. Ibid., p. 356.

14. Mordaunt Hall, *New York Times*, March 15, 1930, p. 5.

15. Andrew Sarris, *The American Cinema* (New York: E. P. Dutton and Company, 1968), p. 228.

16. Norman Zierold, *Garbo* (New York: Stein and Day, 1969), p. 12.

17. Eugene O'Neill, *Anna Christie* (New York: Liveright, 1922), p. 111.

18. Ibid., p. 103.

19. Frances Marion, *Off with Their Heads* (New York: Macmillan Company, 1972), p. 196.

20. Hall, p. 22.

21. Frances Marion, p. 198.

22. Richard Dana Skinner, *Commonweal* 2 (March 26, 1930): 591.

23. O'Neill, p. 87.

2
Strange Interlude

(1932)

O'Neill's *Strange Interlude* was brought to the screen in 1932, produced by the legendary "boy wonder of Hollywood," Irving B. Thalberg, and the results were nothing short of disastrous. Thalberg, the intellectual and literary-minded producer at MGM, thought he had the formula for good box office. When asked by a friend what good box office meant, he answered with assurance: "A combination of a star and the title that the public wants to see."[1] *Strange Interlude* had both of these qualities—it starred Norma Shearer and Clark Gable, and the "strangeness" of the play had attracted a great deal of attention since its premier in early 1928—and yet the film was still a failure both financially (it cost $654,000 to make and made only $90,000 during its first five years of commercial release) and, more importantly, artistically. As Samuel Marx puts it in his book *Mayer and Thalberg: The Make-Believe Saints:* "It was not even a *succès d'estime*."[2]

Thalberg as a producer was extremely well intentioned and very favorably inclined to films based on literature and the theater. He had earlier (1930) produced O'Neill's *Anna Christie* with Garbo, and he later produced several adaptations of other works from literature—including *The Barretts of Wimpole Street* (1934), *Mutiny on the Bounty* (1935) *Romeo and Juliet* (1936), and Garbo's *Camille* (1936). Thalberg assigned the direction of *Strange Interlude* to Robert Z. Leonard, who would later become associated with such glamorous MGM star vehicles and musicals as *Dancing Lady* (1932), *The Great Ziegfeld* (1936), and *Ziegfeld Girls* (1941), but his work with *Strange Interlude* remains uninspired. The scenarists, or those who cut O'Neill's play from over five hours to an hour and fifty minutes, were Bess Meredith, C. Gardner Sullivan, and Leonard himself. The most important problems with the film seem to lie in its scenario. O'Neill's vast "novelistic" play, with its own perhaps overworked intensity on stage, becomes merely a skeletal plot outline in the film version.

Although O'Neill himself refused to see it, he knew enough about the adaptation for it to raise his sternest damnation of Hollywood and its "dreadful hash of attempted condensation and idiotic censorship."[3]

On stage *Strange Interlude* was a great success; Sheaffer summarizes the early history of the play as

> the greatest success of O'Neill's career, the most talked about play of the decade . . . and one of the most profitable presentations in the Theatre Guild's history. The O'Neill drama gave four hundred and forty-one performances on Broadway, played three seasons on the road (most of the time there were two touring companies), and brought the author the third Pulitzer Prize, and eventually netted him about two hundred and seventy-five thousand dollars, a sum that included half his share of the seventy-five thousand dollar movie rights.[4]

A great part of the success of the play was doubtless due to its novelty—the extraordinary length and the use of the asides. But there was certainly more to its success than mere novelty. The play, despite its flaws—redundancy, a certain pretentiousness, and overreaching—has great theatrical power, both in its patently melodramatic actions laced with philosophy and psychology, and its often moving and poetic language. The play met with almost unanimous critical praise. George Jean Nathan called it "the finest, profoundest drama of O'Neill's career."[5] Joseph Wood Krutch, writing in *The Nation*, argued that the play managed to "give something—some depth, some solidity—which no play has ever had, and its strange method does make possible a kind of virtue new to dramatic art."[6] He went on to say even more eulogistically that O'Neill had

> taken a story which is not only longer than the ordinary story of a play, but one which invites, or rather demands, that brooding subtlety of treatment impossible in the ordinary dramatic form, and made out of it something which not only holds every one of our faculties employed but remains, like one of the greatest modern novels, to tease the mind with new discoveries to be made in its labyrinthine passages.[7]

Such criticism may be unduly biased in O'Neill's favor—Nathan and Krutch were highly sympathetic O'Neillophiles. The O'Neillophobe, Robert Benchley, called it "just another nine-act play."[8] But the kind of criticism that Nathan and Krutch could write about the play would be utterly impossible with the film version, which strips the play of most of its complexity, its reverberation of themes, and most of its poetry.

In a remarkably insightful article written by Robert Littell (one that Sheaffer in his biography quotes at length because of its obvious biographical significance), Littell makes an astute point about the play *Strange Interlude* in particular and O'Neill's writing in general. He said that O'Neill was an exception among writers in that his strength and his weaknesses are inseparable and the several faults, while they remain faults, serve also as allies of his strength. What distinguishes all his plays here and there, and *Strange Interlude* most of the way through, is a groping, smoldering, passionate sincerity many times more intense, relentless and mysterious than that of any other American playwright—and nearly all foreign ones also. O'Neill seems to be burrowing in the depths of human nature, not so much because he finds interesting dramatic material in these psychological catacombs, but because the search profoundly concerns him personally. The endless burrowing is a mole's progress toward salvation—his own salvation far more than that of his own characters.

If O'Neill could cease to identify his own search with that of the characters, if he could stand further away from them, they would be clearer, realer, but they would lose much of the mystery and the integrity which their author's fumblings, quite as much as his passions, help to give them. And if O'Neill had three grains more of humor which causes an author to laugh mistrustfully at his own solemnities, he could not indulge himself so freely in just those inarticulate cries of cosmic pain which make his characters, a great deal of the time, singularly strange and moving creatures.[9]

Littell's words, written in 1929, remain among the most elucidating and important commentaries on O'Neill. It is indeed the "groping, smoldering, and passionate sincerity," the descent into "psychological catacombs," and the power and pathos of the "inarticulate cries" (this last phrase seeming to predict what Edmund says in *Long Day's Journey* about his poetic "stammerings" as the "native eloquence of . . . fog people")[10] that give O'Neill's best plays, *Strange Interlude* among them, their energy and theatrical importance. *Strange Interlude* is a flawed but fascinating and powerful work; the film version strips it of its groping and passionate energy, its poetic language, and puts very little else into it to replace these qualities.

The film, like the play before it, was keenly anticipated because of O'Neill's fame and, in the case of the film, the stars who acted in it. Stark Young said that the film was "regarded in advance as the highest attempt of the moving picture so far as serious art."[11] But he goes on to say that, after seeing only a scene or two, it was apparent that it was nothing more than "a photographed stage play." Young's review is almost entirely negative, attacking the absurd cutting of the play, the actors, and the scenes added to the film. Young's account is fairly typical of most of the critical response to the film. Richard Dana Skinner placed most of the blame on censorship, which left the story hollow.[12] Alexander Bakshy called it "an uninspiring cross-breed of the stage and screen,"[13] and considered the two principal roles miscast. Mordaunt Hall took quite a different view in a puzzling review that called the film "engrossing and compact." Hall oddly asserts that "the script has been arranged in an able fashion, so that one is not conscious of any deletions" (which would be impossible for anyone who is even casually acquainted with the script). She

STRANGE INTERLUDE (1932) MGM. Directed by Robert Z. Leonard. With Norma Shearer and Clark Gable. (Nina and Ned in the garden of the Evans's Long Island estate.)

goes on to make the even more problematic point that "the ending is different from the play, but it is done with a deft hand."[14] The ending is one of the few parts of the film which does not substantially alter the play.

While the main fault with the film lies in the bowdlerization of its screenplay, which takes only enough from the play to exaggerate its soap-opera quality, its casting is also a serious problem. Norma Shearer and Clark Gable were cast in the leading roles mainly because of their presumed box-office appeal (and in the case of Shearer, because she was the wife of the producer, Irving Thalberg). They were not particularly successful in terms of box office or artistry. Each lacked the weight and power necessary to the characters of Nina and Ned Darrell. Shearer lacked the passion required for Nina who emotionally controls the lives of nearly all the men in the play. Richard Watts, Jr., put it nicely:

> Miss Shearer, apparently filled with reverence at the thought of the classic lines she is reciting, but at the same time understanding little about them, makes Nina Leeds, the neurotic heroine, a good healthy normal young woman, who ages prettily and isn't much bothered about her tragedies.[15]

STRANGE INTERLUDE (1932) MGM. Directed by Robert Z. Leonard. With Norma Shearer, Clark Gable, and Alexander Kirkland. (Nina, Ned, and Sam—living out their love triangle.)

Watts also summed up the nature of Gable's performance, saying succinctly: "Mr. Gable is always a dashing juvenile, particularly when he powders his hair and pretends to be an old man."[16] Shearer's beauty is too cold for the role of Nina, and Gable's winning manner has very little to do with the petulant, coldly scientific character of Ned Darrell. The role of Sam Evans, Nina's weak and passive husband, whom she marries only for practical reasons, is adequately played by Alexander Kirkland. The role of Sam suffers less than the others because he is less important in the play to begin with. Ralph Morgan plays Charlie Marsden, the "Oedipus-wrecked" (to use Watts's phrase), old, neurotic mother's boy with fine style, even though his is one of the most severely cut roles in the film, becoming caricature rather than character. All of the characters in the film are, in fact, oversimplified or broadened into caricature, or as Richard Dana Skinner said of Norma Shearer: "She lacks all sense of greatness—as does the altered play itself."[17]

Even a cursory look at the extent and quality of the cutting in *Strange Interlude* makes clear the impossibility of "greatness" or completeness or thematic reverberation in the screenplay for *Strange Interlude*. Because of the length and complexity of the play, I will outline only the most important changes, chronologically, act by act. All page references in parentheses are from *Nine Plays by Eugene O'Neill* (Random House, 1932). Most of the major specific changes made in the screenplay—ideas, suggestions, implications, or particular lines or images deleted in the film—are as follows:

Act 1: Marsden's important and psychologically revealing speech on sexuality and his fear of it (487–88). Discussion between Marsden and Professor Leeds of Nina's psychic condition since the death of Gordon (490–96). Professor Leeds's asides on loneliness and feelings of guilt over his intervention in Nina's affair with Gordon (504–5).

Act 2: Marsden's asides showing fear in the presence of Ned Darrell, who could scientifically analyze his problem (516–17). Nina's speeches contrasting the image of God the Father to "God the Mother"; the idea of female-image diety central to Nina's personality and self-concept (524–26). Details of Nina's recent past—the prostituting of herself as the self-inflicted punishment for betrayal of Gordon Shaw (526–29).

Act 3: Nina's asides on her pregnancy and her keeping it a secret from her husband in order to keep the child as her own (531–33). All references by Nina and Mrs. Evans to her pregnancy by her husband, Sam, which must lead to abortion because of cogenital insanity in his family (531–37).

Act 4: All references to Nina's abortion (549–57). Nina's asides which reflect on the idea that the dead Gordon Shaw had been the "real father" of the child she has aborted (565). Most of Nina's appeals to Ned Darrell for "scientific" and purely objective advice on her plan to have a child by another man (566–67).

Act 5: Nina's cosmic imagery of birth, the womb, and maternity (573–74). Repeated references to "God the Mother" imagery (590–91).

Act 6: Nina's asides of her affair with Darrell (593–94). Marsden's asides on his fear and loathing of women (598). Nina and Darrell's reminiscence about their affair of a year ago (610–11).

Act 7: Darrell's jealousy of and bitterness toward Sam (620–22/3). Nina's imagery of "rotting" as reflecting her fear of menopause (619). Nina's thoughts on the end of her roles of wife and mistress, replaced only by the role of mother (620).

Act 8: Nina's attempts to get Darrell to tell the child that he is the true father. Darrell's hostility to Nina; his realization that Gordon II is "really the son of Gordon Shaw" (654–55).

Act 9: Gordon and Madeline's discussion of the death of Sam, and Gordon's feelings of hostility toward his mother (666–68). All references to Nina's "change of life." Marsden's asides on being able to possess Nina after "the long interlude of war with life" is concluded (669). Nina's reference to her prime of life as "this tangled mass of love and hate and birth" (673). Nina's spoken idea that "sons pass through their mother to become their father again." Marsden's view of the years of sexual potency as "interludes" of "trial and preparation." Nina's important line which supplies the title of the play:

"Our lives are merely strange, dark interludes in the electrical display of God the Father." (681).

The summary of deletions, which does not pretend to be exhaustive, suggests the nature and extent of the changes in the film version of *Strange Interlude*. The play is essentially a sexual biography of the character Nina, and the psychologically connecting roles of daughter, wife, mistress, and mother. O'Neill, though he frequently denied it, shows a greal deal of the influence of Freud here, as he does in many other works.[18] The play is a parade of Freudian complexes—psychologically convoluted relationships between Daughter/Father (Nina and Professor Leeds), Son/Mother (Marsden and his mother, and Gordon II and Nina), Son/Father (Gordon II and his nominal father, Sam, and his biological father, Ned Darrell). In the film the Freudian aspects of these relationships are greatly diminished, weakening the psychological core of the work.

Likewise, Nina's psychology, central to which is her concept of deity imagined in both male and female form, is drastically reduced in the film. In the play she imagines "God the Father" as "the modern science God" who is cold and indifferent: "How could that God care about our trifling misery of death-born-of-birth?"[19] She thinks of the male deity in association with pain, cruelty, and images of lightning, as in the important line amazingly cut from the film: "Our lives are merely strange, dark interludes in the electrical display of God the Father."[20] To imagine deity in female form, for Nina, is to make greater sense of life, suffering, and death. She says:

> We should have imagined life as created in the birth pain of God the Mother. Then we would understand why we, Her children, have inherited pain, for we would know that our life's rhythms beat from Her great heart, torn with the agony of love and birth. And we would feel that death meant reunion with Her, a passing back into Her substance, blood of Her blood again, peace of Her peace. Now wouldn't that be more logical and satisfying than having God a male whose chest thunders with egotism and is too hard for tired heads and thoroughly comfortless.[21]

Nina's concept of the Mother God is crucial to her characterization and to the structure and movement of the whole play, since all the other (male) characters in the play are important primarily in relation to her. These ideas on deity are, of course, weighty matters for a Hollywood film, and would also create problems of censorship because of their seeming irreverence; but completely to eliminate this important aspect of the play, as has been done in Leonard's film, is essentially to alter the thematic content of the story and to devitalize the relationships that exist in it. The Motion Picture Production Code, penned in 1930 by Martin Quigley and the aptly named Reverend Lord, insisted upon the cinema's upholding of the sanctity of marriage and the home, disallowed the depiction or explicit suggestion of illicit sex, and forbade the use of the word *God* except in a clearly reverential way. But the Production Code was not so rigidly enforced until after 1934 and many other films of the early 1930s were more mature in their treatment of adult themes.

The play also involves frank discussions of sexual frustration, abortion, extramarital affairs, and promiscuity as a kind of "martyrdom to a lost love." These were subjects that simply could not be treated frankly in a Hollywood film of 1932. The film version retains very vague traces of all these subjects, except abortion, which is totally cut, making the most radical change in the play's story; but the mere traces of sexual frankness that remain are devoid of all development, complexity, or thematic importance. The censoring of these subjects necessarily leads to a change in the relationships which form the core of the play. Alexander Bakshy made this point clearly in his review of the film:

> Nina's sexual make-up as it is seen by O'Neill is the core of the play, which alone gives it unity and meaning. In the screen version . . . this inner significance of Nina's relationships with her four men is largely lost. The pentagon has been reduced to a triangle, with Nina's husband and her doctor-lover contending for her favors, instead of Nina herself trying to hold all the strings in a balanced relationship that is completely satisfying to herself.[22]

In other words, apart from the innovation of the asides, the film is a fairly conventionalized soap opera. Censorship accounts for other minor, and somewhat ludicrous, cuts in the play. Even though the film, in its sketchy resemblance to the play, is a story of love and passion, most of O'Neill's words having to do with the subject of passion must be cut. Among the words excised from the play are *promiscuity*, *kissing* and *petting*, *carnal*, *sex*, *sexual*, *slut*, and the word *passion* itself.

Much is taken away in this film version, but very little else is done cinematically to replace the losses. There are some routine and fairly conventional attempts to open up the play for filmic treatment; for instance, there is an exterior scene at the beginning of the film showing Marsden coming to the Leeds's apartment (he passes a crippled soldier on crutches, which serves as a visual analogue to the war death of Nina's fiancé, Gordon); there is a brief shot of Nina arriving home in a car after the death of her father; there are also brief exterior scenes at the various locations of the film—Sam and Nina's suburban cottage, the Evans's home in upstate New York, and the Evans's Long Island estate; there is also the location shooting for the yacht race (which is the setting for act 8 of the play). None of these exterior shots is treated with any particular filmic effectiveness. Most of the city exteriors are unconvincing studio sets, and the yacht race merely intercuts location shooting with studio shooting for the dialogue.

Not only are the attempts to open up the play visually pedestrian, but they tend to be thematically irrelevant. There are three scenes in the film that were

STRANGE INTERLUDE (1932) MGM. Directed by Robert Z. Leonard. With Norma Shearer and Alexander Kirkland. (Nina and Sam after their wedding ceremony.)

not part of the original play, and these suggest the conventionalizing nature of the adaptation. The first is a visualization of the wedding of Sam and Nina, which happens between acts 2 and 3 of the play. The wedding scene is traditionally romantic and is out of keeping with the nature of the union of Nina and Sam. For Nina this is merely a marriage of convenience—a way to occupy her time and feel useful. Following the wedding scene another brief scene is added that shows Nina and Sam running through the picturesquely pretty woods; Nina carries flowers—the scene is again conventionally romantic. Nina says, "It was a divine honeymoon," and continues with a brief speech, added to the screenplay, which is inappropriate to both O'Neill's Nina and the Nina of most of the film version. In a line from the end of act 2 which is cut from the film, Nina says:

> Sam is a nice boy. Yes, it would be a career for me to bring a career to his surface. I would be busy—surface life—no more depths, please God. But I don't love him, Father.[23]

The feeling of these lines is anything but romantic, and the fact that the film version romanticizes the marriage is typical of its overall bowdlerization of the play, and changes in the ethos of the relationships of the characters. The film, moreover, retains enough of O'Neills dialogue to make such changes essentially inconsistent.

Another brief scene, generally incongruous with the style of the whole, is added to the film. It is roughly based on act 3 of the play, in which Mrs. Evans pleads with Nina to abort the child she is carrying, because of congenital insanity in the Evans family. She tells Nina about Sam's aunt, who is insane and lives in the attic of the house. In the film, Mrs. Evans takes Nina up to the attic to show her the insane relative. The Gothic quality of the scene, reminiscent of *Jane Eyre*, seems strangely out of place in this film. There is also less logical need for Mrs. Evans to resort to this method of proof in the film, because Nina is not pregnant, whereas in the play Mrs. Evans is trying to convince Nina to have an abortion. The sequence in the film is handled in a traditional mystery-thriller way. Nina and Mrs. Evans, in the dark and dusty attic, approach a locked door. The sound of manic laughter is heard. Mrs. Evans unlocks the door and opens it. The film quickly cuts to within the room, and Nina's face is seen in terror, hand covering her mouth, and a muffled scream is heard. The laughter of the madwoman grows louder. This sequence, like other added sequences, does little for the momentum of the story and contributes nothing to the meaning of the film. And, perhaps more importantly, it is out of keeping with the style of the rest of the film.

Not only is the visual treatment of the film uninspired, but also the treatment of the audio quality in the handling of the asides. O'Neill's unprecedented and unorthodox—to the modern realistic theater—use of asides was the single most important factor in the enormous interest centered on his play. The stream-of-consciousness device was well known to both the sophisticated and the nonsophisticated. (Curiously enough, Groucho Marx in *Animal Crackers* [1930] does a parody of O'Neill's technique—he walks away from a group of people, talks to himself, and then turns to the camera and says, "I am having a strange interlude," which suggests the popular renown of O'Neill's technique.) While the asides are, owing to postsynchronization dubbing, technically more workable and graceful in the film version, they lose much of their impact because of the drastic nature of their cutting in the screenplay. (From the summary above of the cuts made in the play, it is obvious that most cuts were in the asides.) The unusual length of the play and preponderance of asides makes it necessary to cut many of them entirely and many in part, for film adaptation. (Helen Hayes, according to Sheaffer's biography of O'Neill, claims to have cut many of the asides during the original production of the play without O'Neill's even realizing it.) There are indeed too many asides in the play and they tend to overburden it with ideology and philosophical speculation. But the film version can be faulted for the way in which it cuts the asides. It would be possible to do the play (and film) without any of the asides, but once the film adaptation has chosen to retain the device, it should work thematically and cinematically, but it does not. Nearly all of the interesting, poetic, and provocative asides were excised, and the ones retained lack both the self-examining and self-revealing qualities which is their only raison d'être in the work. The scenario for *Strange Interlude* does not really allow the characters enough depth for either self-revelation or self-examination, the qualities which elevate O'Neill's play above the level of mere soap opera or melodrama, to which it is closely akin.

Since the film version of *Strange Interlude* was done only five years after the advent of the talkies, experimentation with sound would have been of great interest and importance. Mordaunt Hall, in the *New York Times,* and Regina Crewe, in the *New York American,* found the asides admirable and exciting both because of their novelty and because of their suitability to sound film. Hall makes the questionable assertion that "in view of the fact that the players do not have to move their lips . . . these utterances are all the more interesting."[24] Crewe waxed poetical about the asides: "Whispers that come from nowhere like thoughts. Thoughts that spring unbidden from the darkest depths of the consciousness. Thoughts that come unwanted to the mind. Lips are silent, still. Souls speak."[25] Crewe's comments seem more rhapsodic than astute. Most of the other critics found the asides problematical; foremost among them was Richard Watts, whose evaluation of the asides is much more convincing:

> the theory was shrewd enough, but in practice there are difficulties. The acting seemed to conceal the emotions expressed in the "asides," instead of dramatizing them. The result is that the secret thoughts are sometimes strange and even comical, but seldom poignant.[26]

Watts seems to be right in faulting the actors' speaking of the asides and the director's manner of presenting them (Leonard apparently experimented unsuccessfully with "double-takes" for the asides),[27] rather than the device itself. The device of audible thought, while historically more at home in the theater, is not necessarily alien to film. Rouben Mamoulian first used the voice-over to express inner thought in *City Street* (1931). The soliloquies in Olivier's film of *Hamlet,* for example, are used to extraordinary filmic effect, because of the varied method of shooting them—using several different angles to shoot the face of the "speaker" and intercutting this with supporting visual imagery. Another example of filmically effective use of thought made audible would be in Fellini's *8½;* during much of the film we share the confused thought processes of the director within the film. Here again, because of a wide variety of camera angles and the tempo of the voice-overs, they advance rather than retard the action of the film. Robert Leonard's direction of the asides in *Strange Interlude* remains as unimaginative as the handling of other elements in the film.

The film adaptation of *Strange Interlude* shares several common features

Strange Interlude (1932)

with the films made of *Mourning Becomes Electra* and *Desire under the Elms*. All three are based on plays of O'Neill's that delve deeply into psychological (or perhaps more accurately in the overused word *Freudian*) problems, relationships, and complexes. All three of the film versions share, with quantitative differences, obvious problems reflecting their hybrid film/theater natures. And all three, although made in three different decades, had to undergo a certain amount of censorship before being made acceptable to the mass medium of film. Edward Murray, in his book *The Cinematic Imagination*, considered each of these plays "too theatrical" (again, an overworked term) for successful screen adaptation. But whereas *Strange Interlude* and *Desire under the Elms* are not successful either as motion pictures or as film records of important stage plays, *Mourning Becomes Electra*, despite its flaws as a film, has integrity in being a faithful and true-to-spirit adaptation, with some cinematic value as well. The film of *Strange Interlude* has neither its own integrity as film, nor the lesser integrity of a faithful film record of an important and interesting work of theatrical art. O'Neill never saw the film, but reports of it only confirmed his dislike for Hollywood. Shortly after the film was released, he wrote in a letter to Robert Sisk that he

> really didn't give a damn what they've done to it. . . . Outside the money the films simply don't exist for me, and nothing they do or don't do seems of the slightest importance to my work as a playwright.[28]

O'Neill here, as elsewhere, was being perfectly honest in calling his relationship to Hollywood a purely financial one.

The film version of *Strange Interlude* begins with a title card explaining the nature of the work we are about to see: "In order to fully understand his characters, Eugene O'Neill allows them to express their thoughts aloud. As in life, these thoughts are quite different from the words that pass their lips." This title expresses the tension between levels of psychological awareness, and different aspects of personality in the characters of O'Neill's dramas. José Quintero, the foremost interpreter of O'Neill's works on the contemporary stage, has made a similar point about O'Neill's work which seems relevant to the failure of *Strange Interlude:*

> Every time I have done any of his plays I have had a sense of existing in two entirely separate kinds of realities: the commonplace, photographic reality and the interior reality of fantasy. I think the struggle of these two realities—where the impossible can happen among the commonplace, where the figures become regal, monumental and totally equipped for tragedy—gives that unbelievable tension to his works.[29]

It is just this kind of tension that is lacking in the film version of *Strange Interlude*. The drastic cutting of ideas, complexities of character, and thematic possibilities from the original work for the film version also strips the drama and its characters of this tension between interior and exterior life. While the opening title of the film invites the audience to perceive this tension, the nature of the film makes it impossible for us to do so. The thoughts that we hear in the film are not really so different from the words that the characters speak—since the asides revealing this psychic tension were largely cut from the film's script. This adaptation lacks, perhaps understandably, the philosophic level of the play; but, less understandably, it lacks the passion in the play's melodramatic events, certainly at home in the film medium.

NOTES

1. Samuel Marx, *Mayer and Thalberg: The Make-Believe Saints* (New York: Random House, 1975), p. 217.
2. Ibid.
3. Louis Sheaffer, *O'Neill: Son and Artist* (Boston: Little, Brown and Co., 1973), p. 547.
4. Ibid., pp. 288–89.
5. Ibid., p. 255.
6. Ibid., p. 276.
7. Ibid.
8. Ibid., p. 288.
9. Ibid., pp. 245–46.
10. Eugene O'Neill, *Long Day's Journey into Night* (New Haven, Conn.: Yale University Press, 1956), p. 154.
11. Stark Young, *New Republic* 72 (September 14, 1932): 124.
12. Richard Dana Skinner, *Commonweal* 16 (October 5, 1932): 539.
13. Alexander Bakshy, *Nation* 135 (September 28, 1932): 292.
14. Mordaunt Hall, *New York Times*, September 1, 1932, p. 24.
15. Richard Watts, Jr., "Review," *New York Herald Tribune*, quoted in *Literary Digest* 114 (September 24, 1932): 18.
16. Ibid.
17. Skinner, p. 539.
18. Sheaffer, p. 224. O'Neill, in response to Joseph Wood Krutch's comment that *Strange Interlude* seemed influenced by Freudian psychology, wrote: "I feel that although *Strange Interlude* is undoubtedly full of psychoanalytic ideas . . . any artist who was a good psychologist . . . could have written it without ever having heard of Freud, Jung, Adler and Co." Several years later, in response to a professor who was writing a dissertation on the psychological implications of his writings, O'Neill wrote that there was "no conscious use of psychoanalytical material in any of my plays."
19. Eugene O'Neill, *Strange Interlude*, in *Nine Plays by Eugene O'Neill* (New York: Random House, 1932), p. 524.
20. Ibid., p. 525.
21. Ibid., p. 524.
22. Bakshy, p. 292.
23. *Strange Interlude*, p. 528.
24. Watts, *Literary Digest*, p. 18.
25. Ibid.
26. Ibid.
27. Robert C. Roman, "O'Neill on the Screen," *Films in Review* 9 (June–July, 1958): 298.
28. Sheaffer, p. 407.
29. José Quintero, *If You Don't Dance They Beat You* (Boston-Toronto: Little, Brown, and Company, 1974), p. 223.

3
The Emperor Jones

(1933)

O'Neill's experimental and expressionist play *The Emperor Jones* was the third of his works to reach the screen. He sold the rights to the film to two young filmmakers named John Krimsky and Clifford Cochran for the sum of $30,000. Financial troubles probably prompted O'Neill to give Hollywood the rights to this play, even after the disappointing job it had done with *Strange Interlude* the year before. Dudley Murphy, a somewhat undistinguished director whose past career included *Confessions of a Co-ed* and *The Sport Parade*, was chosen to direct the film for United Artists. DuBose Heyward, the author of *Porgy*, seemed a likely choice as scenarist. O'Neill met Heyward and approved of his ideas for the screenplay. Paul Robeson was chosen to play the leading role, and O'Neill was naturally pleased with this choice, since he himself had discovered Robeson to play the part on stage after many difficulties had arisen with the original Emperor, Charles S. Gilpin.[1] (And Robeson had been very successful in the controversial first production of *All God's Chillun Got Wings* in 1924.) The film was shot in Paramount's old Astoria, Long Island, studio, and was released in September of 1933.

The translation of *The Emperor Jones* from stage to screen introduces several important questions about the nature of such adaptations in general. First, being primarily an expressionist play (apart from the realistic and expository first scene) and written very much in outline or scenario form, it would seem to lend itself very well to screen treatment. (Edward Murray, in his book *The Cinematic Imagination*,[2] discusses this aspect of the play quite fully.) But this film adaptation chooses rather to reduce the expressionist aspects of the play in favor of a very long and graphic treatment of past events in Brutus Jones's life, only some of which O'Neill had suggested in the play.

Scene 1 of O'Neill's play, a long and primarily expository dialogue between

THE EMPEROR JONES (1933) United Artists. Directed by Dudley Murphy. With Paul Robeson and Dudley Digges. (Smithers warns Jones of the dangers that face him in escaping from the island.)

Jones and his corrupt partner, Smithers, becomes the source of the action of nearly the first two-thirds of the film. There is some argument for the viability of this restructuring, or refocusing, of *The Emperor Jones* for filmic treatment, since the first scene of the play is its longest and is essentially in a realistic mode. But, in modifying the narrative to emphasize the linear development of Jones's progress to the point of becoming Emperor, the film version clearly shifts focus away from the compelling expressionism of all but scene 1 of O'Neill's play, in favor of a chronological progression of events in essentially realistic style.

Not only do scenarist Heyward and director Murphy take the play's facts concerning the earlier life of Brutus Jones, but they also invent many other situations to connect events that the play merely suggests. This refocusing of the play for film treatment is a source of both many of its strengths and its ultimate weakness—a weakness stemming from the film's inadequacy in blending the styles of the earlier realistic portions of the film with the fantastical and expressionistic scenes of its conclusion. Whereas the play opens with Jones's frightening moment of truth that his cardboard dictatorship has fallen apart, the film opens with young and ambitious Brutus Jones at a Baptist revival meeting and traces chronologically the following twelve years of his life from this point to the denouement on the island—the point at which the play had begun.

While it is not uncommon in the adaptive process from stage to screen to use this method of attack from an earlier point in time, the film version of *The Emperor Jones* pushes this process too far, introducing scenes and characters that are extraneous to both the central action and the essential themes of the adapted work. In the first scene of the play we learn several facts about Jones's earlier life—that he had worked for ten years on a Pullman train; that he had killed two men, a black friend and a white prison guard, that he had broken out of jail and escaped by sea; that he had stowed away on a ship and reached the island on which he is now "Emperor"; and that he had tricked the natives of his island into believing that he was invincible—except from a silver bullet. From this rather sketchy outline the film manages, with obviously necessary additions, to dramatize forty-five of the total of seventy-two-minutes' running time of the film.

Here is an outline of the film's structure:

Part One, or the events leading up to Jones's arrival on the island, including the Baptist revival meeting, Brutus Jones's work as a Pullman porter, several scenes set in nightclubs and romantic rivalry between Jones and Jeff, his fight with and murder of Jeff, his term in prison, murder of the guard and escape from prison, and finally his landing on the island. These events take up thirty minutes of the film's total running time of seventy-two minutes.

Part Two, or the action on the island, can be divided into two parts. The first shows us Brutus Jones's situation when he first arrives on the island: his capture by the king's guards, his being brought before the king, his deals with Smithers, the attempt of the king's guard to kill Jones with blank cartridges in the revolver which sets up the myth of Jones's invulnerability, and finally Jones's assuming total rule. These actions take up another fifteen minutes of the film's total running time. It is not until the last twenty-seven minutes of the film that the adaptation is actually based on specific scenes from the play. Only one-third of the film's total running time is devoted to the Emperor's flight in the jungle, which makes up the emotional and psychological core of the original work.

The adaptation is indeed strongest, as suggested by several of its original reviewers, in presenting the "added portions." Those facts that are implicit in the play are carefully made explicit in the film. Whereas O'Neill had developed Jones's character primarily along psychological lines, the film version develops his character more concretely in a linear progression of situations. An idea from Stanley Kauffmann's "Notes on Theater and Film" seems relevant here; he contrasts the "vertical" form of the theater to the "horizontal" form of the film: "The theater works predominantly by building higher and higher in one place. The film, despite the literally vertical progress of frames, works predominantly in a lateral series of places."[3] In the film version of *The Emperor Jones* we do see the progression of Jones's life in terms of a "lateral series of places." The character is personalized and individualized to a greater extent by the various contexts in which we see him operate. O'Neill began the play at the end of Jones's career; we don't see all of the facets of his personality that account for the possibility of his becoming Emperor, or the characteristics that make it impossible for him to maintain this role. The film, in a sense, simplifies things for the audience. We are well prepared for the situation on the island, and for the fantasies that haunt him as he tries to escape through the jungle. But. as will be discussed later, it is at this point that the film becomes least effective.

The play's lengthy exposition in scene 1 contains all the facts necessary to understand the fantasy sequences that follow. We learn that Jones is overweeningly proud—proud of his physical person, his strength, his position, his cunning, his foresight, and, most important to his tragic downfall, proud of his intelligence. In his pride he considers himself utterly invincible. He rests secure in the knowledge that he has had the foresight to put his money in a foreign bank, and that he has been able to twist circumstances to his own advantage (as in his several deceptions of the natives), and that he has had the intelligence to learn the natives' language so as better to swindle them. We also learn that he has killed two men, the first a black man, for whose murder he was imprisoned, and the second, a white prison guard. Finally, when Smithers, his white partner, sets the seeds of fear in him about the jungle at night, we learn that he is "a member in good standin' o' de Baptist Church."[4] (His Baptist upbringing, a mere mention in the play, becomes very important in the film.) The picture of Jones that we get in the first scene of O'Neill's play is of a man who is aggressive, condescending to his native subjects, overly self-confident, superstitious, and obviously ripe for a fall.

The film version realistically roots all of these characteristics in concrete details and actual situations. The film opens with a Baptist church meeting, a hierophantic minister invoking the Lord, and the congregation singing and clapping hands. We learn that this is a meeting gathered especially in preparation for Brutus Jones's departure to seek his fame and fortune outside his own community. Murphy foreshadows the island sequence in the opening montage. The film's titles are superimposed over a tribal jungle dance accompanied by the rhythmic beating of a tom-tom. A slow lap dissolve follows which momentarily superimposes the tribal dance and the church meeting. Jones's present and future are analogized in this opening sequence. This filmic device implies a connection between both of these situations as Jones will see and use them. He later invokes his Christian past as a means of using one religious "superstition" to combat another, the primitive tribal superstition that threatens him in his attempted escape from the jungle (i.e., his orthodox Baptist upbringing will, by the time of the end of the film, be powerless to combat the atavistic forces that haunt him). Jones is caught between these two worlds, believing in neither, but attempting to use whichever one might work to his advantage.

In order to visualize Jones's overweening pride and vanity, Murphy cleverly intersperses a series of mirror images throughout the film. Indeed, it is in a reflection that we see Brutus Jones for the first time in the film. He is proudly gazing at himself in his new Pullman porter's uniform. After Jones has successfully invested money in a business deal, we again see him proudly looking into a mirror (in a low-angle shot, which generally gives greater height to the character being photographed, and adds to the sense of power and importance). Mirror images will become very important later in the film in the sequence in Jones's palace. We see only his reflection as he decides on the name "Emperor Jones," and in the following shot we see him in a new mirror, which now has a carved crown at the top of its frame—again, a low-angle shot magnifies his stature and importance. This mirror with the crown seems to become an image of the ephemeral nature of Jones's position as Emperor, suggesting that this is merely an "image" or role without solidity. This idea is continued when we later see Jones's reflection in this same crowned mirror while he sleeps, as news is being brought to him that his "Empire" has collapsed and that all his servants, guards, and court have deserted him.

The metaphorical visual imagery discussed above is but one way in which Murphy has filmically concretized the aspects of Jones's character suggested by O'Neill in the first scene of the play. The overall refocusing of the narrative works along the same lines (i.e., toward the concretization and individuation of Jones's character). A key point made by Allardyce Nicoll in his pioneering if now somewhat outdated study of stage and screen seems relevant here:

> Practically all effectively drawn stage characters are types [whereas] in the cinema we demand individualisation, or else we recognize stage figures as types and impute greater power of independent life to the figures we see on the screen.[5]

O'Neill's Brutus Jones on stage is indeed an Everyman (both black and white, as O'Neill is quite consciously translating the themes and structure of Greek tragedy into contemporary American terms, as he does more obviously in *Mourning Becomes Electra* and *Desire under the Elms*). Jones's rise to and fall from power because of pride (hubris) and a series of miscalulations (hamartia) are essentially classical and in this sense transcend racial boundaries. In O'Neill's play Brutus Jones is a type in Nicoll's sense, a type of tragic hero whom we meet at the critical turning point in his life, at the moment when his fall begins, and it is this fall that makes up the action of the play. The film version is, as suggested before, quite a different story. It is the story of an extremely enterprising and aggressive young black man who rises from his humble Southern small-town background to become the Emperor Jones, with a series of romances, mishaps, and murders along the way. His fall from fortune (and the job of Emperor) becomes, at worst, an addendum, and, at best, a logical conclusion to all the action that has preceded his jungle flight. In very substantially expanding the actions which precede his actual situation on the island, the film version lays greater emphasis on his rise to power than his fall, and stresses the particularity rather than universality of the character.

Whereas the action of the play occurs entirely in the span of one day, the action of the film covers a much longer, though indeterminate, time span—at least ten years of Jones's life. The film is substantially opened up, bringing in many more locations than did the play. We first meet Jones with his girlfriend, Dolly, in church. She sees him off on the train, where he will begin his new job as Pullman porter. On the train we meet his friend, Jeff, who teaches him the ropes of the job. Soon after, he and Jeff are in Saint Louis, where Jones meets Jeff's girlfriend, Ondine, and begins a relationship with her. Back on the train Jones becomes involved in an investment deal (which seems to be fraudulent but profitable) with the president of a large corporation. At a nightclub in New York, Jones and his new girlfriend, Belle LeDuc, sit with Jeff and Ondine. A fight ensues between the two women competing for Jones's attention. Some time later, Jeff and Jones are seen shooting craps in another bar, with a blues singer performing in the background. The dice are found to be loaded and a fight breaks out. Jeff is fatally stabbed by Brutus Jones. At this point there is an abrupt cut to Jones, in prison garb, working at a stone quarry. He is ordered by the white guard to whip another black prisoner; he refuses and the guard begins whipping him. Jones picks up a shovel and kills the guard. (In the film we do not see him actually killing the guard; the Production Code would not allow the depiction of a black man murdering a white man.) Jones escapes from the prison and returns to his original girlfriend, Dolly, who helps him file the chain off his leg. Here occurs another abrupt cut, to Jones as a stoker on an oceanliner. The ship passes a remote island which his shipmates tell him is nothing but "trouble." "Trouble, here I come," he says—and jumps off the ship and swims to the island.

On the island he is greeted by gun-carrying natives, who take him to their king—a nonnative black man in tuxedo and top hat. In the palace he meets Smithers, who sees that Jones is quick-witted and wily and can be useful to him, so he takes charge of the prisoner himself. They begin their fraudulent trading deals; Jones becomes increasingly more important to the operation. Finally they are discovered in their fraud and the king orders that Jones be shot. The gun fired at him is loaded with blanks which Jones has planted in the gun (in the play the bullet simply misses him). Jones announces that his life is charmed and that only a silver bullet can kill him. The natives, in awe, immediately accept him as their new leader. Declaring himself the Emperor Jones, he redecorates his palace in pastiche rococo and fills it with mirrors. Soon follows a parade of Jones's cabinet ministers. At the meeting Jones announces drastic and overbearing tax increases. They are shocked and horrified at this. Further tax increases are later announced, until finally the natives revolt and his cabinet ministers desert him. Smithers comes to the palace and tells him that all his subjects have deserted him and that they are off in the mountains preparing magic charms to work against him. At this point Jones decides to flee, having well prepared himself for this inevitability. Forty-five of the film's total seventy-two minutes have gone by and we are just at the point where O'Neill began the play.

This rather detailed summary of the film's action serves to suggest the thrust and interest of this adaptation of O'Neill's play. While the film adaptation is quite radically different from the play, it does manage to translate into filmic terms some of O'Neill's themes and the power of the central character. Perhaps a more cinematically sophisticated version of the play could have worked in all of the past materials through the alteration of past and present times, which is common in the film medium. Rather than having Brutus's past unfold chronologically, as it does here, it might have appeared as fragments in flashbacks during the major action of the jungle flight.

Margaret Kennedy, in her essay "The Mechanized Muse," makes the interesting point that in adapting from stage to screen, unlike adapting from novel to screen, "expansion rather than compression is the problem." She suggests that in translating a novel to the screen the director must condense and compress an excess of knowledge about its characters, whereas in translating a play to the screen it is often necessary to expand the information given in the play's text. Her essay makes other points which have relevance to the restructuring of *Emperor Jones:*

> The task is to break up a form which hampers screen narrative. Scenes which, in the play, all took place in one room now more naturally occur in different places. Incidents which the dramatist has obliged to indicate as happening "off" must be brought back into the story, since very few things can be allowed to happen "off" screen.[6]

The process of expansion in the case of *The Emperor Jones* accounts for both virtues and flaws in the adaptation. So much has been expanded and, in fact, added or invented in the film version to augment and individualize Jones's character that the jungle flight—the heart of O'Neill's play—is diluted in impact. Nonetheless, many of the film's strongest images come from the expanded portions of the film.

A closer look at some specific details from various scenes will better indicate the modus operandi of the film. In the opening scene there is a general atmosphere of tawdriness in the Baptist church; Jones shuns this atmosphere and tries to keep himself aloof from it. He is in uniform and the camera lingers on the stiffly pressed fabric of the suit and especially the shining brass buttons. Jones, admiring himself in a mirror, is fascinated with and proud of the uniform, which represents to him an escape from the paltriness of his world. This scene connects visually with the scene much later in the film when Jones again gazes at himself in the mirror, now dressed in Napoleonic fashion, as the Emperor. Here again the camera lingers on the shining brass buttons. In a montage quickly cutting from shots of rapidly moving trains with superimposed place names and shots of Jones working in the train, we see him insinuating himself into more and more elite crowds. He accepts a lesser-paying job because it allows him to be in the "Presidential Car." He now wears a tuxedo and associates with businessmen, from whom he can better learn the secrets of success through exploitation. Jones already realizes a concept he will later express to Smithers: "For the little stealin' they puts you in jail, but for the big stealin' they makes you Emperor."[7] After an investment deal with one of the busnessmen, we see him in a luxurious hotel with Ondine. This atmosphere contrasts vividly with the environments in which we have seen him earlier.

The decor of the Emperor Jones's palace reveals a great deal about his character through Murphy's careful focusing on objects and details and Ernest Haller's excellent photography. In O'Neill's play the set of the first scene is stark and austere:

> A spacious high-ceilinged room with bare, whitewashed walls. The floor is of white tiles . . . a portico with white pillars. The room is bare of furniture with the exception of one huge chair made of uncut wood which stands at center. . . . It is painted a dazzling, eye-smiting scarlet. There is a brilliant orange cushion on the seat and another smaller one is placed on the floor to serve as a footstool. Strips of matting, dyed scarlet, lead from the foot of the throne to the entrances.[8]

The decor here is minimal, only the "eye-smiting scarlet" suggests the extravagant nature of the Emperor's tastes. The set for the palace in the film is altogether more elaborate. Being, of course, in black and white, the film could not rely on color to communicate Jones's opulent and garish taste. In the film, Jones's garishness is reflected in the mélange of styles and periods of the furniture. Most of the furnishings in the palace are roughly Napoleonic in style, as are the costumes of Jones and his cabinet ministers. The exaggerated elegance and showy grace of the style are in keeping with Jones's Napoleonic self-image. His throne is massive and prepossessing, as O'Neill described it in scene 1 of the play, but here it is much more ornate. On the day that Jones gets the information that his "Empire" has collapsed we see him sitting astride the arms of the great throne, looking like a child playing king—but the game is now about to end.

The last third of the film's action, Jones's haunted flight through the jungle, generally follows the structure of the play, except for the complete deletion of scenes 5 and 6. This last section of the film was generally and quite rightly the most severely criticized part of the screen adaptation. *Time* magazine said of it: "These sequences are the least convincing in the film . . . fading in pictures of the shapes that the Emperor Jones thinks he sees somehow makes the shapes less real, less frightening."[9] Richard Dana Skinner makes a similar point about the lack of convincingness in the final sequence:

> The lighting of the jungle scenes is too obscure, the use of double exposure to indicate the phantoms is too conventional, and there is a vague sense of repetition and monotony which never emerged from the original stage play.[10]

Skinner's criticism of this sequence suggests that even by the filmic standards of 1933 Murphy's treatment of the jungle scenes is visually pedestrian.

The last part of the film remains the weakest and the most problematic aspect of this adaptation. The reasons for this are twofold. First, the jungle sequence seems to have been overshadowed by the lengthy and vitally realistic prologue that has led up to it; and, second, so little has been made of the cinematic potential in the play for exciting visual treatment. One crucial problem, cinematically, is the lack of spatial realism of the jungle set (as suggested by Skinner above). the jungle looks all too much like a studio set, and lacks the physical realism of most of the earlier settings. The faulty and unconvincing nature of the set is assuaged only by Murphy's employment of purely filmic devices to involve the audience in Jones's plight. Most of this sequence is filmed in close-up or middle-distance shots. Because of the camera's ability to move in and focus only on essential details, the defects of the set become less distracting. Through close-ups we can enter more fully into the psychology of Jones than we could in the theater with its fixed point of view. With the increased proximity of spectator to performer, the acting becomes paramount. Robeson's performance here, as throughout the film, is superb, and the magnification of face and gesture enhances the power of the monologue he speaks as he is haunted by visions of his past. Robeson's acting manages to walk a tightrope between realism and stylization, which is necessary in this structurally altered film version of the play.

Even though the final sequences in the film are specifically rooted in O'Neill's play (while much of the first two-thirds of the film are not), there are several marked differences. There are some important changes in the treatment of the visions that Jones sees in the jungle. As mentioned earlier, surprisingly little is made of the highly visual expressionistic qualities inherent in these fantasy scenes, which are quite conventional in their use of superimposition. But this is partially justifiable in terms of the essentially realistic mode that the film has established from the beginning. The first vision that Jones sees in the play is the "Formless Fears"; these are materialized in the play as "black, shapeless, only their glittering little eyes can be seen. If they have any describable form at all it is that of a grubworm about the size of a creeping child." In the film version, which we might expect to make good horror material out of these "Formless Fears," they are not shown at all. Jones uses the first of his six bullets to shoot at "them." The fact that they are not seen at all focuses attention on Jones's mind rather than the visions that haunt him, and was perhaps intended to ease the transition from the realistic mode of the film (to this point) to the expressionistic mode that is to follow. The second vision is that of Jeff, whom we have earlier seen being killed by Jones in the film version. There are close-up shots of Jones's face, which is now scratched, making him look fiercer and more primitive. The figure of Jeff appears in a double exposure in the upper left corner of the screen. (All of the fantasies in the film are treated in this way—the two levels of reality are kept separate and distinct.) Jones now uses his second bullet to "kill" Jeff again. The third fantasy, as in the play, is that of the chain gang. This sequence is treated in the same mechanical and pantomimic way that O'Neill describes it. This time the double-exposed fantasy fills more of the frame and Jones seems to overlap it, unconsciously joining into the pantomime. The prison guard seems to approach him and he shoots at the guard, using his third bullet.

It is at this point that the film diverges from the play. In scene 5 of O'Neill's play Jones fantasizes a Southern slave auction. He is forced into it and is about to be sold when he shoots both the planter and the auctioneer. This scene is entirely cut from the film. In scene 6 of the play, Jones is part of a crew of slaves forced to row in the galley of a ship. This sequence is also deleted in the film. Of the two recently published books on blacks in American film which discuss *The Emperor Jones* (Peter Noble's *The Negro in Films* and Edward Mapp's *Blacks in American Film: Today and Yesterday*),[11] neither makes any mention of these changes from the original text. This change from stage to film version would seem to be critical in a treatment of the film in terms of racism and black stereotyping. The slave-auction scene and the galley scene in the play underline the atavistic process that Jones undergoes in his jungle flight. The profound fears that Jones feels during his attempt to escape through the forest set off a chain of psychological regressions—first, to fantasies of his own recent past (the murder of Jeff, his imprisonment, the murder of the prison guard), and second, to fantasies of his collective racial past (the slave auction and the slave galley). The film version deemphasizes the theme of atavism. Since the film has focused primarily on realistic events and situations, and Jones as a particular character rather than universal type, the atavisism of the play would be less appropriate in the film version. Because the film has dealt so completely with Jones's personal past, the fantasies of collective racial past would seem to have less revelance. Only the fantasies with specific referents in earlier actions in the film—such as the murder of Jeff and the prison guard—have, to this point in the film, been shown to reflect Jones's guilty fear.

The next fantasy further departs from the play while it relates back to the opening sequence in the film. The deeply terrified Jones now calls on the power of the Baptist church to save him from the guilts and fears that haunt him. There is a double exposure of the preacher and his congregation singing "Didn't My Lord Deliver Daniel?" This Negro spiritual is clearly appropriate to Jones's situation, and he joins in singing. (Several other songs have been added to the film because of Robeson's fame as singer as well as actor.) This scene clearly relates to the church scene at the beginning of the film, and the songs used in both cases are apt. At the opening of the film the chorus is singing the song "Prodigal Son," which related to Jones's departure from the flock. Now, in panic, Jones calls up a song of deliverance, and the song becomes an extension of Jones's thoughts.

The final vision in the film comes directly from scene 7 of the play. Here Jones sees a witchdoctor preparing for sacrifice, and a crocodile appears as if to devour him. Jones uses his fourth bullet to kill the crocodile. Although this vision culminates the atavistic process of the play (which had been substantially avoided in the film's dropping of scenes 5 and 6 of the play), it is retained in the film. But this final fantasy does work on a more general level of psychological fear than do the two visions dealing specifically with the black past and slavery. The ending of the film is precisely the same as the ending of the play. Jones, in his fear and panic, had come full circle to the place where he started, and he is shot by the natives he has exploited with the silver bullet they made to end his charmed life.

Edward Murray, in his book *The Cinematic Imagination,* argues that *The Emperor Jones* as a play, while borrowing elements from cinematic style, "proved to be too theatrically stylized for successful picturization,"[13] and he goes on to say that "a playwright's or novelist's use of cinematic techniques is no guarantee that the finished play or novel will prove any more viable for the screen than a noncinematic construction." How much O'Neill was specifically influenced by expressionism in cinema is questionable. It is known that he did see *The Cabinet of Dr. Caligari* in 1921, which, as he said, made "me aware of wonderful possibilities I had never dreamed of before."[14] But this would have been a year after the first production of *The Emperor Jones,* in November of 1920. It is much more likely that O'Neill's interest in theatrical expressionism, especially Strindberg's *Dream Play* and *Ghost Sonata,* and his reading of Gordon Craig's *The Theatre Advancing,* were more influential on the structure and dramatic mode of *The Emperor Jones* than expressionism in film.

Murray's thesis, simply stated, is that a playwright who is influenced by the cinema takes cinematic principles and theatricalizes them, making it difficult to retranslate them back into cinema. Most of his criticism of the film version of *The Emperor Jones* is based on this assumption. But, clearly, Dudley Murphy and DuBose Heyward significantly reworked the play for cinematic treatment. Murray considers the film totally unsuccessful because it fails fully to incorporate the cinematic elements inherent in O'Neill's scenariolike text. This criticism is partially true of the last third of the film, the jungle scenes, which, as he says, "are fluid and exciting in the theater, but static in the

THE EMPEROR JONES (1933) United Artists. Directed by Dudley Murphy. With Paul Robeson. (Jones with native woman soon after his arrival on island.)

film."[15] (But he fails to take into consideration the use of the close-up as a genuinely cinematizing and powerful device.) Moreover, most of the film is so different from the play that it must be judged in a different light. The film is primarily realistic in mode rather than expressionistic. The fantastical jungle sequence at the end seems almost tacked on as an afterthought. It is only through the acting of Robeson that the two distinctly different parts of the film are given any unity. The *Time* reviewer, noting the implausibility of the final sequence, suggests an accurate and interesting explanation:

> This may be partly because Paul Robeson, playing his first cinema role with effortless honesty, has in the earlier part of the story made the Emperor Jones a person so plainly and completely real.[16]

Robeson's acting does, indeed, have an intelligent blend of realism and stylized bravura which is necessary to make the Emperor Jones real on film.

O'Neill himself, as previously mentioned, had found Robeson to replace Charles S. Gilpin in the role of Brutus Jones after Gilpin, as O'Neill wrote, "began to play Emperor with author, play, and everyone concerned." Of his new discovery, Paul Robeson, O'Neill wrote:

> I've corralled a young fellow with considerable experience, wonderful presence and voice, full of ambition and a damn fine man personally with

real brains—not a "ham." This guy deserves his chance and I don't believe he'll lose his head if he makes a hit—as he surely will, for he's read the play for me and I'm sure he'll be bigger than Gilpin was even at the start.[17]

Robeson did prove a great success in the role on stage both in London, following its run on Broadway, and in the 1925 revival of the play in New York. The fact that he was chosen to play the Emperor on film in 1933, his screen debut, was logical and pleased O'Neill. Robeson, by 1933, was also highly acclaimed as a singer with a rich baritone voice. Heyward's screenplay made accomodations for Robeson's vocal ability, and four songs were added to the film that are not in the play. The songs are used effectively to reinforce the film's narrative line. He joins in singing "Prodigal Son" and "Jacob's Ladder" along with the congregation in the opening church meeting, and he later joins with them in the singing of "Didn't My Lord Deliver Daniel?" in the fantasy sequence. But the most important traditional Negro song used in the film is "John Henry"—the words of which are:

> This ol' hammer killed John Henry!
> But this ol' hammer won't kill me!
> Take my hammer to the walkin' boss
> Tell 'im I'm gone,
> If he asks you any questions
> You don't know, tell 'im you don't know.[18]

This song works well metaphorically during the chain-gang sequence in which Robeson first sings it, since Jones and the other convicts are chopping away with pick hammers at a stone mountain. It also foreshadows the fact that Jones is about to remove himself from this situation. "John Henry" is repeated during the jungle sequence. At this point in the film it foreshadows the following fantasy, of the black man, Jeff, whom he had killed, connecting the prison chain gang with the murder for which he was imprisoned. Given the importance of music in the film, it is curious to note that the one scene in the play which called for Jones to sing—scene 6, the slave-galley fantasy—is cut from the film, for reasons stated earlier. But this is more than adequately made up for in J. Weldon Johnson's excellent use of songs and background music throughout much of the film. The important sound effect of the tom-toms during the jungle sequence, however, do not have the relentless and accelerating (beginning at the normal rate of a heartbeat) rhythm that O'Neill intended, since their sound is interrupted by songs.

Like several other film adaptations of O'Neill's plays, *The Emperor Jones*, seems to have been somewhat more successful with critics than with general audiences. In this case, however, it is not because the film was too intellectually "highbrow," but because of the somewhat inflammatory nature of the subject matter. Peter Noble, in *The Negro in Film*, suggests that neither white nor black audiences of the time could be entirely satisfied with the film.

In discussing the place *The Emperor Jones* takes historically in the depiction of the black man on the screen Noble says that the film was

> remarkable in that it gave to a Negro actor a leading part in a film also featuring white actors, something never previously experienced. . . . To have a black man playing the star part in a film in which the white actors were of lesser importance was indeed something of a filmic revolution. Indeed it was enough of a social revolution to make the film a financial failure! Distribution difficulties were encountered, especially in the southern states.[39]

Critical reaction in exclusively black newspapers was mixed, some seeing the film as an advancement in the serious treatment of the black man on the screen, others focusing on the negative implications of Jones's character. Nonetheless, as Noble points out, "the film gave encouragement to many independent Negro producers who thereafter began to make their own films to be shown to Negro audiences. . . . It is a landmark in Negro film."

While historically important, the film is only a limited artistic success. The significant alterations and expansions on O'Neill's text, insufficiently blending realism and stylization, account for both virtues and flaws in the work. Heyward's reworking of the structure of the play, while successful in realistically fleshing out Jones's character, remains rather conventional and stereotyping. It is Robeson's tour de force performance that creates most of the excitement of the film; his Jones is dignified, tragically noble, and believable. But Robeson's performance alone cannot bridge the stylistic gaps that exist in this adaptation of *The Emperor Jones*.

NOTES

1. O'Neill's strained relationship with Gilpin is discussed fully in Sheaffer's biography, *O'Neill: Son and Artist* (Boston: Little, Brown and Company, 1973), pp. 34–38.
2. Edward Murray, *The Cinematic Imagination* (New York: Ungar, 1972), pp. 18–20.
3. Stanley Kauffmann, "Notes on Theater and Film," *Performance* 1, no. 4 (September–October 1972). Reprinted in *Focus on Film and Theatre* (Englewood Cliffs, N.J.: Prentice-Hall, 1974).
4. *Nine Plays by Eugene O'Neill*, p. 15.
5. Allardyce Nicoll, *Film and Theatre* (New York: Thomas Y. Crowell Co., 1936), p. 165.
6. Margaret Kennedy, "The Mechanized Muse," in *Film: An Anthology*, ed. Daniel Talbot (Berkeley: University of California Press, 1967), p. 97.
7. *Nine Plays by Eugene O'Neill*, p. 8.
8. Ibid., p. 3.
9. *Time* 22 (September 25, 1933): 31.
10. Richard Dana Skinner, *Commonweal* 18 (October 6, 1933): 532.
11. *Nine Plays by Eugene O'Neill*, p. 19.
12. Peter Noble, *The Negro in Films* (New York: Arno Press & The New York Times, 1970); Edward Mapp, *Blacks in American Films: Today and Yesterday*, (Metuchen, N. J.: The Scarecrow Press, Inc., 1972). Though both of these books were published at nearly the same time, Noble's is the earlier (a reprint of a dissertation written in the late 1940s). Most of the information on *The Emperor Jones* in Mapp's book is from the earlier one by Noble. Neither book, however, has a very detailed study of *The Emperor Jones*.

13. Murray, p. 24.
14. Sheaffer, p. 351.
15. Murray, p. 23.
16. *Time* 22 (September 25, 1933): 73.
17. Sheaffer, p. 36.
18. John W. Work, *American Negro Songs* (New York: Crown Publishers, 1940), p. 233.
19. Noble, p. 59.
20. Ibid., p. 58.

4
Ah, Wilderness! (1935) and *Summer Holiday* (1948)

O'Neill's bittersweet comedy *Ah, Wilderness!*, which he called a "comedy of recollection,"[1] was perhaps the most likely of O'Neill's works for screen adaptation, and it generated two screen versions. The first adaptation was directed by Clarence Brown, who had earlier done the sound version of *Anna Christie*. Brown's version of *Ah, Wilderness!* was released by MGM in the winter of 1935 and was chosen to be the Christmas show at Radio City Music Hall—a dubious distinction, perhaps, but one that is congruent with the tone and style of both the play and its adaptation. The second screen version, a musical directed by Rouben Mamoulian, was also produced at MGM, and was released thirteen years later, in the summer of 1948. Here again scheduling was shrewd—the film was released in late June in time for the Fourth of July celebrations, this being the day on which most of the film's action occurs. Mamoulian's musical version, shot in color, while based on the 1935 version's screenplay by Albert Hackett and Frances Goodrich, was retitled *Summer Holiday*. Both films are "family-fun films," filled with the spirit of nostalgia and Americana.

O'Neill himself viewed the play in much the same light as did Hollywood. Shortly after its premiere by the Theatre Guild in 1933 he commented:

> My purpose was to write a play true to the spirit of the American large small-town at the turn of the century. Its quality depended upon atmosphere, sentiment, and exact evocation of the mood of a dead past. To me, the America which was (and is) the real America found its unique

expression in such middle-class families as the Millers, among whom so many of my own generation passed from adolescence into manhood.[2]

This is precisely the kind of nostalgia that the film industry has been, and certainly still is, so fond of—a tender and sentimentalized backward glance at a little golden age of American life. It is interesting to note that O'Neill stressed atmosphere and exact subjective evocation of mood as the criteria by

AH, WILDERNESS! (1935) MGM. Directed by Clarence Brown. With Lionel Barrymore, Wallace Beery, Spring Byington, Frank Albertson, and Eric Linden. (Atmosphere and period qualities are suitably evoked in the Miller home.)

which the success or failure of the work must be judged. This is the realm in which the screen has decided advantages over the stage. Atmosphere and mood can be quite exactly evoked through a preponderance of readily datable physical objects and actual locations which are impossible to realize on the stage, and Brown's film version is particularly successful in this respect.

All of the exterior scenes of *Ah, Wilderness!* were filmed in the small Massachusetts town of North Grafton, near the town where its director, Clarence Brown, had grown up. The reviewer in *Newsweek* reported the effect of "the coming of the Hollywood caravan" on North Grafton: "It threw the little town of 7,500 into an uproar. Attic trunks flew open, leg-of-mutton sleeves and Irish crochet-trimmed numbers came out into the light they hadn't seen for three decades. The whole town went movie-mad, and everyone wanted to be a movie extra: two hundred got their wish."[3] O'Neill had based the setting of the play on the New London, Connecticut, of his own youth, but North Grafton, being smaller and less urbanized, would have preserved more of the period charm and atmosphere essential to the film.

Brown is masterful in the recreation of the milieu and physical characteristics of the period. Several critics reviewing the film after its premiere paid special attention to Brown's handling of ambience in the film. Otis Ferguson observed:

> What the screen really makes out of *Ah, Wilderness!* is a first class atmosphere piece. . . . It calls up more matters than it knows of but its sure reconstruction of the day-to-day life of the New England county in a time that is as dead but as vivid in the general memory as the smell of leaves burning in piles along the gravel walks, this fall or when you were a kid. Practically all of it that is good is background, in the way of local color. Not only the sets of stiff cluttered rooms, lawns, gas buggies (actually steam-run vehicles), picnics, but the incidental life of the place.[4]

Andre Sennwald, in his review in the *New York Times*, said of the film: "In its warm, sprawling and achingly reminiscent mood of story telling, it brings Mr. O'Neill's 'large small-town' into a new richness of life on the screen."[5]

Morton Eustis suggested that the film manages to go beyond mere surface details into the very heart of the life-style of the period. He says of the makers of the film:

> They went farther, they went somehow back to books and old natives . . . and reconstructed a frame of the locale, the life of the town within it—all things as strong and irretrievable as Mrs. Hixon's preserved ginger in the sitting room, as taffy pulls, sleigh rides, town-hall meetings, cantata, fairs. In the end the production goes beyond the meaning of the play, immersing all the business good or bad in a mood that is difficult to quarrel with. It is blurred with illusion yet inexorable in its details, tugging at silly heartstrings yet common enough."[6]

O'Neill had said that the play would stand or fall in its ability to evoke exactly the mood of a dead past, and the contemporary critical responses to the film version indicate, quite rightly, that it was amply successful in this respect.

Most criticism of the first film version does tend to focus on such superficial physical and atmospheric values of the film. O'Neill seems almost to have anticipated such comments in asking Lawrence Langner of the Theatre Guild shortly before the opening of the play: "Has it got something finer to it than its obvious surface value—a depth of mood of atmosphere, so to speak, that would distinguish it from another play of the same genre?"[7]

It isn't completely clear exactly what O'Neill meant by this question. If he is referring only to the stylistic qualities of mood and tone, then the film is certainly as successful as any stage production of the play could be. If by "depth of mood of atmosphere" he is referring to the darker qualities inherent in the play, clearer now since the publication of *Long Day's Journey into Night*, then the film is not so successful. The film adaptation tends to brighten further what, for O'Neill, is an unusually bright vision, but one with characteristic underlying tensions. Commenting on this dual nature of the play, Louis Sheaffer in his biography of O'Neill says:

> Here again is a sensitive youth at odds with his parents, an alcoholic ne'er-do-well, a regretful spinster and, curiously enough, considering that this is a genial play, the author's most realistic prostitute to date.[8]

Richard, the central character of the play and the one that O'Neill loosely based on some of his own youthful experiences, loses some of his bitterness and antisocialness in the screen version. (This fact becomes all the more obvious, almost to the point of ridiculousness, in the musical version starring Mickey Rooney as Richard. Rooney's portrayal of Richard is merely a slight variation on his famous screen role as Andy Hardy.) Many of Richard's lines of social criticism in the play are cut from both screen versions. The Hackett/Goodrich screenplay upon which both films are based makes some important changes in the pivotal character of Richard. He must subtly stand apart from the naively idealistic milieu of his family and his hometown. O'Neill described him in the stage directions as "definitely different from both his parents. . . . There is something of extreme sensitiveness added—a restless, apprehensive, defiant, shy, dreamy, self-conscious intelligence about him."[9] Richard's rebelliousness is adolescent, bookish, self-conscious, but it nonetheless reflects a genuine sense of disquieting alienation from people and values that surround him.

In both screen versions most of Richard's social criticism is compressed into a final paragraph of his valedictorian speech at the graduation ceremony. The graduation scene is not a part of O'Neill's original script; the passage is gleaned from certain speeches of Richard's in act 1. After Richard delivers the traditional eulogistic comments on "the quality of education" that all the students have received and has compared, in perfect cliché, the life of students to a brook that will now branch out into new streams, we see on the screen the next part of the speech that he won't deliver because his father stops him before he can proceed. The camera focuses on the text that was to continue: "But these are all lies, lies, lies; the world is run by dishonest Capitalists who suck the very life blood from the wage slave. My message to you is workers unite."[10] This is the scenario's principal example of the rebellious, political side of Richard's character. The following scene even further undercuts whatever serious implications his speech may have had: his father offers to let him drive the Stanley Steamer home from the graduation, and Richard is revealed as essentially a child with a new toy.

O'Neill's Richard requires a delicate balance of the would-be poet, the would-be anarchist, and the would-be romantic—yet both film versions tend to exaggerate his youthful, naive, idealistic, and romantic qualities to the virtual exclusion of his darker and more discontented side. Eric Linden as Richard in the original screen version captures many of the stiff, adolescent, socially uncomfortable aspects of Richard's character. His speech is declamatory and abrupt. His portrayal brings out the dichotomies and inconsistencies of Richard's role. But nonetheless the very sructure and tone of the film cast him decidedly into what can be seen as just another love story.

Looking at the overall structure of both play and film is revealing, since this accounts for the greatest changes in the transition from stage to screen. In O'Neill's text the first three acts of the play are set on the Fourth of July. In act 1 we meet the Miller family; Richard is the last to be introduced to us. At the end of act 1 he gets a letter from Muriel saying that she cannot see him again. Act 2 is the comical dinner scene; Uncle Sid is playfully drunk and Mr. Miller is the butt of several jokes concerning his obsessive dislike of bluefish, which he has been unknowingly eating all his life. Act 3 is made up of two scenes. The first is Richard's nocturnal escapades at the bar of the Pleasant Beach Hotel, including his encounter with the prostitute Belle. The second scene of act 3 has Richard returning home, drunk, to his very worried family, quoting from *Hedda Gabler*—"At ten he will come with vine leaves in his hair." The fourth act is made up of three scenes. In the first scene, the following day, we hear of the repercussions of Richard's conduct the night before. He receives a new letter from Muriel, saying that she still loves him and only shunned him because her father forced her to. At this, Richard decides to leave the house now in the early afternoon in order to meet Muriel that night at nine o'clock. It is not until the second scene of act 3 that we finally meet Muriel. The young lovers quarrel over his encounter with Belle and then, after much haggling and name calling, reach a reconciliation. In this scene O'Neill has Richard whistling the tune "Waiting at the Church" as he waits for Muriel. The final scene of act 4 is again in the Miller home and is made up primarily of the comically faltering and naive discussion between Nat and Richard about "the facts of life," marriage, and prostitutes.

The structure of the film is substantially different from that of the play. The film covers a longer period of time than does the play, and takes place in a greater number of settings. Several scenes are added to the film to both "open up" the play spatially, and to focus interest on the Richard/Muriel relationship. The added scenes—the dance, the graduation, the picnic, and outdoor concert—also expand the character of Mildred, and tend, unfortunately, to conventionalize the character of Richard.

The film does not open in the Miller home, as did the play, but at a pregraduation high-school dance. The first shot of the film is of the high-

AH, WILDERNESS! (1935) MGM. Directed by Clarence Brown. With Eric Linden, Wallace Beery, Lionel Barrymore, and Spring Byington. (Richard drunkenly returns home to his worried family.)

school seal followed by a zoom-back to reveal all the students dancing to the tune of "Glow-Worm." (Music is important throughout the film and will be discussed fully later.) Richard and Muriel isolate themselves from the other students to discuss their futures, now that Richard is to leave their small town for Yale. The primary romantic interest of the film is firmly established, introducing us into a world of teenage romance rather than domestic comedy as the play does. It is important to note that whereas in the play we do not meet Muriel until the third act, in the film we meet her in the first few minutes. The scenario's point of view toward Richard's character is limned in the brief scene with Muriel in which he interposes philosophic comments, poetry recitations, and comments on the cake being served at the dance. He is the typical adolescent, brighter and more literate than most, but still not to be taken too seriously. He is a child at heart, despite his quoting from Swinburne, Wilde, Nietzsche, and Carlyle, and the general thrust of his character is such that we may assume that this reading-thinking phase might well pass away with time and experience. This is not precisely what O'Neill had in mind for Richard's character.

Muriel, as played by Cecilia Parker in the 1935 film, is also more naive and literal-minded than she appears in the play. Two lines characterize Muriel in this scene. When Richard says that "man cannot live by bread alone," she responds that "there is also cake" to eat at the dance. When Richard says ponderously that he was "born a hundred years before his time," she responds: "I was born ten days before mine." Much new dialogue has been added to the film to fit situations not found in the play; the exchange cited above is but one example. The added dialogue in the screenplay tends to overemphasize the stereotypical qualities of Richard and Muriel. The predominant romantic quality of the film is further emphasized in the following scene in which Muriel and Richard walk home at dusk down a tree-lined street with shadows from the trees playing on their faces. Richard leaves Muriel at her house and continues home whistling the popular song "My Dearie," which becomes the romantic leitmotif throughout the film. It is only after the tone of these first scenes (and the centrality of the Richard/Muriel "love story" has been set) that we enter the Miller home and meet the family—the point at which O'Neill had begun the play.

Despite certain problems in the scenario itself, Brown's direction of the film is visually imaginative and effective. There is one silent sequence in the film that effectively communicates to us the isolation that Richard feels during his separation from Muriel. It also illuminates the romantic concept that governs the cinematic treatment. While everyone else is enjoying the holiday, Richard is off walking alone. It seems that everywhere he goes he meets young lovers together. He walks over a small bridge and sees a couple talking and enjoying each other's company. He walks along the bank of a river and sees another couple merrily rowing by in a boat. We see a close-up of his feet as he aimlessly walks along the railroad tracks and over large rocks in some isolated part of town. As he walks back home we see the shadows from fences getting longer and lower to suggest the passing of time through the change in the sun's position. This montage communicates, in purely visual terms, the dejection that Richard is experiencing, now made worse by the presence of other young couples who are joyful and harmonious. This sequence, of course, also underlines the romantic nature of the adaptation in general.

Brown's treatment of the graduation ceremony is also visually interesting and subtly comical, in its extensive cross-cutting from the paltry performances of high-school students in hackneyed recitations and bad vocal performances, to the bored responses of the families and townspeople in the audience; this captures visually the essence of the event and the innocent charm of the "large small-town" atmosphere. In a series of slow lap dissolves we see and hear the entertainment of the day: an emotionless recitation of "Friends, Romans, countrymen," a nervous young lady's description of her trip through Switzerland, an atrocious flute performance, a sing-song recitation of "Bells, Bells, Bells," and finally a strident soprano version of "My Lady Sweet Arise." Intercut with these performances are the antics of the audience: Tommy

(Richard's kid brother) making a telescope and looking around the room (seen subjectively through circular masking on the camera lens), Arthur and Muriel playing a word game with the letters of their names, little Mildred sticking chewing gum on the pigtail of her enemy, and the forcedly proud expressions on the faces of the parents of the performing youth. There are also pan shots of the chorus and other members of the audience that visually describe the nature of the town and its inhabitants. The final dissolve from the girl singing "My Lady Sweet Arise" to Richard's valedictorian speech is the slowest of the sequence. Both figures are superimposed for several seconds, which ironically emphasizes Richard's separation and aloofness from this banal event. Brown's direction of this sequence is stylish and clever; it is comically effective without resorting to caricature. (Mamoulian's directorial method in this same sequence in the later adaptation, *Summer Holiday*, we will see is quite different.)

Clarence Brown's work with actors throughout his career, including silent and sound films, has often been noted as excellent. (His success with Garbo in three films—*Anna Christie, Conquest,* and *Anna Karenina*—is now legen-

AH, WILDERNESS! (1935) MGM. Directed by Clarence Brown. With Lionel Barrymore, Spring Byington, Eric Linden, Aline McMahon, and Cecilia Parker. (The idealized Miller family in their new Stanley "Steamer.")

dary.) Kevin Brownlow, in *The Parade's Gone By* . . ., suggests a reason for Brown's great success with actors. Brownlow said that as well as being a "great technician," Brown also had "a warm feeling for people in his handling of players, and of situations; he achieved a naturalism that, even when stylized, was always convincing."[11] Brown's handling, and the casting of the Miller family is superb. Lionel Barrymore, as Nat Miller, is excellent in the role that George M. Cohan had made famous on stage in the original production. Barrymore, in appearance, manner, and gesture, is well suited to the idealized father figure—gentle, kindly, and wise—that O'Neill had created. Spring Byington is also well cast in the role of Mrs. Miller. She is eminently maternal in aspect and has all the warmth and charm, with just a touch of spunkiness, that O'Neill wrote into the character. Barrymore and Byington are suitable Hollywood counterparts of O'Neill's idealized family, based partly on an exemplary family named the McGinley's that he had known in his youth in New London. The eight-year-old brat-child, Tommy, useful for many comic bits, is played by the thirteen-year-old Mickey Rooney, who curiously enough, at the age of twenty-five, would play the role of Richard in the second Hollywood version, *Summer Holiday*. Rooney is more appropriate in the role of Tommy than he will be later in the role of Richard.

Wallace Beery's performance in the role of the jovial, weak, and comically pathetic Uncle Sid seems much better at a distance in time than it did to contemporary critics of the film. Sennwald, in the *New York Times*, said of him: "Mr. Beery's mannerisms are getting pretty routine, and his comic horseplay is generally at odds with the quiet and rueful mood of the work."[12] Otis Ferguson disparagingly refers to Beery as the "all-time Muggenheim Fellow."[13] At a perspective of forty years from the release of the film, and without many recent Beery stereotypic roles in mind, he seems eminently suited to the role of Sid. His "comic horseplay," far from being at odds with the mood of the work, is essential to it and to Uncle Sid's place in the play. Aline MacMahon, who plays the prudish and slightly neurotic cousin Lily, is also well cast. (This becomes more obvious when one compares her performance to that of Agnes Moorehead in *Summer Holiday*.) MacMahon is physically perfect for the role, statuesque and refined; she invests the role with suitable melancholy and nervousness.

As is so often the case in O'Neill's plays, music plays an important part in *Ah, Wilderness!* Herbert Stothart's use of songs and scoring for the film version is particularly noteworthy. Whereas O'Neill's text mentions seven songs, which are heard at different times during the play, Stothart's score reduces this to only two songs, which recur, in different contexts, throughout the film. To these are added several standard patriotic songs not in the play, owing to the vastly expanded Fourth of July celebration in the screen version. Of the several songs that O'Neill suggested in the text, Stothart uses only the romantic "My Dearie" and the rollicking "Bicycle Built for Two." These become leitmotifs which either emphasize the dominant emotion of the scene or ironically comment upon it.

The song "My Dearie" works as a kind of love theme throughout the film. It is often played as background music to scenes involving Richard and Muriel. Arthur sings it, to amuse and distract Mrs. Miller on the evening that Richard is out too late at the bar with Belle. The same song is used romantically at the end of the film when Nat Miller comments to his wife that "we are surrounded by love." At this point it is Aunt Lily who sings "My Dearie" as she sits on the porch swing with Sid, to whom she has been "engaged" for some fifteen years. Associating the song at this point with Lily and Sid as well as with the young lovers may also act as an ironic commentary on both the naive romanticism of Richard and Muriel, and the underlying pathos of Sid and Lily's relationship. Earlier in the film there has been a visual analogy made between these two pairs of lovers, by placing Sid and Lily in the same romantic setting in which we have just seen Richard and Muriel.

The song "Bicycle Built for Two" recurs frequently throughout the film. It is first heard as the children go off on bicycles to the Fourth of July picnic for the young people. It becomes the musical theme associated with the frivolous and carefree qualities of youth. In the bar scene in which Richard ineptly tries to deal with the "swift" and sophisticated big-city girl, Belle, the song is heard playing on the player piano. It now has a cheap honky-tonk quality, and in this new context underlines Richard's essential childishness and lack of sophistication. He is out of his element, out of his world—trying to be something he is not. The song reminds us that he is more like the young children riding off to the picnic than he is like Belle and the world she represents. There are a series of sound-overlap cuts from the scene in the bar with the player piano version of "Bicycle" to the Miller home with Arthur singing "My Dearie." This is appropriate since Richard is hopelessly obsessed with romantic notions of Muriel, with whom this song has been associated, while trying to play the part of the rake with Belle. In terms of both sound usage and crosscutting, this is one of the strongest sequences in the film.

The film's final scene, between Richard and Muriel, which is most patently Hollywood in its romanticism, again uses the song "My Dearie" as an integral part. This theme is heard in the background throughout the scene and the music swells and diminishes as the emotions of the scene rise and fall. Visually, this final scene is almost comic in its romantic excess. We see Richard and Muriel in a park (not along the seashore, as in the play), and the scene is one of moonlight and magic. The young lovers quarrel about Richard's escapades of the night before, each threatens to leave, and then there is the inevitable reconciliation. Richard and Muriel are seen facing each other and in the background is a lovely New England church. It is a long shot and the church is beautiful in the moonlight. They move closer together and the shot tightens with the church perfectly framed by their silhouettes. They

AH, WILDERNESS! (1935) MGM. Directed by Clarence Brown. With Eric Linden and Cecilia Parker. (Richard and Muriel before their final romantic reconciliation.)

move closer together and the shot tightens again, now with only the church spire visible above them, they kiss, and at precisely that moment the church bells chime! All of this, combined with the love theme in the background, is pure Hollywood romance, the tone established from the first scene of the film.

The musical score is congruent with the overall romantic concept of the picture. From the very beginning of this film we have been immersed in a world of teenage love. Clarence Brown's direction is subtle and extremely successful in cinematially evoking the atmosphere and nostalgia that O'Neill's period piece required. But the main problem of the film rests squarely with the scenario, which through its shift of emphasis from the family to Richard and Muriel substitutes sugary romance for O'Neill's bittersweet *déjà vu* of family life, of which he said: "For me it has the charm of a dream of lost youth, a wistfulness of regret, a poignant melancholy."[14] The refocusing of certain key dramatic elements in the play tends to diminish much of the underlying melancholy and tensions among the characters. The character of Richard, an admittedly lightweight but nonetheless real prototype for Edmund in *Long Day's Journey*, suffers the greatest reduction in force in the transition from stage to screen. However, Brown's earnest screen version of *Ah, Wilderness!* remains far closer to the truth of the play than the later 1948 musical "adaptation of an adaptation" would.

When Rouben Mamoulian, newly hired by Arthur Freed of MGM Studios, undertook the task of directing the second film version of *Ah, Wilderness!*, a 1948 color musical retitled *Summer Holiday*, he had long been a distinguished stage and screen director. Mamoulian's varied, imaginative, and exciting stage productions included *Porgy* (1927), O'Neill's *Marco Millions* (1928), the Schönberg opera *Die Glückliche Hand* (1930) at the Metropolitan Opera House, *Porgy and Bess* (1935), *Oklahoma!* (1942), and *Carousel* (1945). His screen work, no less varied, creative, and technically innovative, included *Applause* (1929), *City Streets* (1931), *Dr. Jekyll and Mr. Hyde* (1931), *Queen Christina* (1933), *Becky Sharp* (1935), and *Blood and Sand* (1941). Familiar with the mechanics, dynamics, advantages, and problems of both media, Mamoulian was asked to write an essay for *The Screen Writer* positing some essential distinctions between the stage and screen, apropos of his working on the new adaptation of O'Neill's play. This little-known essay sets down many interesting theoretical distinctions between working for the stage and the screen, and illuminates the reason for certain of Mamoulian's radical changes in adapting *Ah, Wilderness!* Mamoulian emphasizes the differences rather than similarities between the two media: "They are like two beautiful trees growing out of the same soil but bearing different fruits," he observes. "Stage and screen are two separate arts, subject to different laws and entirely sufficient unto themselves." Mamoulian states further at the end of the essay that: "I think the hope of both Stage and Screen lies in their divorce. The further they get away from each other, the purer and more significant their achievements will be. Theirs are different roads."[15]

Mamoulian is insistent on the primacy of the visual image in film, but notes that both "the theatre and the stage were born speechless" and can work without words, although theater rarely does.

> Stage and Screen are basically the arts of telling a story through visual dramatic action, and the words, no matter how significant, are of secondary importance. This is the common ground of the two mediums which otherwise are completely different in the techniques and final artistic achievement.[16]

The most important difference in medium, according to Mamoulian, is the intervention of the camera between the dramatic performance and the audience's perception of it. He says that "the eye of the camera becomes the eye of the audience. Thus, the camera combines within itself the creator and the ideal spectator."

Speaking more specifically of the problems of adaptation from stage to screen, Mamoulian suggests:

> One must have imagination and courage to translate or rather transform that play into film-terms. The result must be faithful to the author's conception, it must retain the truth of the story, his characters and his words, yet at the same time relate all these in pictorial and emotional terms which are the Screen's own.[17]

Of his current endeavor, the adaptation of O'Neill's *Ah, Wilderness!*, he goes on to say: "A fine play like this must be either transformed into a new form, that glows with a beauty of its own, or else be respectfully left alone."[18] Mamoulian's ideas on adaptation are certainly sound and appear to be eminently respectful of the original author's intentions. Maumoulian, in fact, went to see O'Neill in Boston in 1946 to discuss his plans for *Summer Holiday* with him. Hugh Fordin, in his book *The World of Entertainment: Hollywood's Greatest Musicals*, reports the episode:

> Mamoulian told O'Neill that he was about to do a musical version of *Ah, Wilderness!* O'Neill shrugged his shoulders and asked, "How can you?" "Loving the play as I do, loving you as I do, and revering you as I do," Mamoulian said, "I would like to make a lot of changes. It sounds paradoxical, but I can add new values with music and color . . . !" At the conclusion of their meeting O'Neill was very excited by the idea. "He understood that what I was trying to do was out of admiration, and he agreed with anything I wanted to do after that."[19]

But, contrary to the suggestion of the above incident and to Mamoulian's insistence on the necessity to "be faithful to the author's conception . . . his characters, his words," Mamoulian's musical is clearly based on the scenario of the earlier 1935 adaptation rather than being a new and direct adaptation of O'Neill's play. It utilizes all of the structuring and focal changes made in the Hacket/Goodrich scenario. Mamoulian has indeed done some superb things with the screenplay that was already on hand at MGM, but the fact remains that it is less an adaptation of O'Neill's play than a twice-removed creation— an adaptation of an adaptation.

Considering the title change from O'Neill's (and the 1935 film version's) *Ah, Wilderness!* to *Summer Holiday*, we might expect greater changes from both the original play and the first film adaptation. But this is not really the case; it is essentially the first film version, pleasantly retitled for popular appeal (remember also that the film was released during the summer), with music and color added. Robert Hatch, in his review in *The New Republic*, put it this way:

> For the book of *Summer Holiday*, M.G.M. has adapted the original screen adaptation of O'Neill's *Ah, Wilderness!*, set it to music, tinted it with Technicolor and turned it over to Mickey Rooney. It is so far removed from the source that the credit line is no more than a pleasant gesture and comparisons become ill-tempered.[20]

The overfaithfulness to the scenario on hand and infidelity to O'Neill is only the first of the film's major problems. The second, and perhaps, greatest is Mickey Rooney, who further diminishes the already diminished character of Richard. Bosley Crowther, commenting on the film generally and Rooney in particular, in his review in the *New York Times*, said: "It is plainly lacking in the poignance and the delicate charm of the original," and it "has been stripped down to a vehicle for Mickey Rooney."[21] Of Rooney's performance Crowther says: "He is given to clowning in his familiarly impish way. He makes puppy love with burlesque shyness, he wears his clothes in exaggerated styles and he acts the big cheese in his household, exactly as Andy Hardy does."[22] At this time Rooney had seven Andy Hardy films behind him, with an accumulation of mannerisms from the role that are unmistakably present in *Summer Holiday*. Richard's character becomes merely clownish as portrayed by Rooney. It is all but impossible to believe that he is the type of intellectual young man who would read, and be influenced by, writers such as Shaw, Wilde, Carlyle, Nietzsche, and Omar Khayyám. When he quotes from these authors it seems just as silly as all the rest of his clowning in the film.

In his book on the films of Mamoulian, Tom Milne excuses the box-office-minded miscasting of Rooney as Richard as something more than a mere financial matter:

> His cheerfully strident interpretation of the role as a minimal variant on Andy Hardy works remarkably well, despite the anachronism of his enthusiasms for Swinburne, Omar Khayyam, and Carlyle's French Revolution, and despite the fact that he seems hardly likely to develop into the

SUMMER HOLIDAY (1948) MGM. Directed by Rouben Mamoulian. With Mickey Rooney. (Rooney is broad and clownish in his impersonation of Richard.)

writer-poet envisaged by O'Neill. The yearning arrogance of adolescence, after all, doesn't change all that much from generation to generation; and with so much built-in sentiment present in the settings, songs and dances, his stridency is probably useful as a door-stop to prevent the film from succumbing to the ever-present danger attendant upon nostalgia: sentimentality.[23]

The chief problem with this justification of Rooney's performance as Richard is that the "anachronisms" that Milne lightly extenuates should be an essential element in the fabric of Richard's character. While, as Milne suggests, adolescent behavior "doesn't change all that much from generation to generation," it remains that the character of Richard is a particular adolescent, brighter, better read, and more susceptible to the ideas in the books he reads. And while it is true that the earlier screenplay that Mamoulian used had already deemphasized this aspect of Richard's character, Rooney's clownish impersonation of the character reduces him to an inexplicably clever buffoon. To use a theatrical metaphor, Rooney "upstages" rather than plays Richard. The audience seems forced to be more aware of Rooney as a personality and performer than with the character he portrays.

The structure of *Summer Holiday* precisely follows that of the 1935 film version of O'Neill's play, including both visual and verbal repetition. The musical version has the same sequence involving the graduation ceremony, using precisely the same language as the earlier screenplay. There is the same sequence involving the car that Richard is allowed to drive after the ceremony, and the same slow fade-in to the firecrackers and rockets on the morning of the Fourth. In both versions the last two acts are necessarily telescoped owing to the long and elaborate outdoor sequences that are in the film but not in the play. The treatment of the character of Muriel is much the same in the second screen version; she is again introduced at the very beginning of the film, and her part is conspicuously enlarged. Sid's return from his new job after being fired and the scenes between Lily and Sid are also treated in the same way, using the same additional dialogue that was written for the earlier screenplay. There are, however, some important sequences in which Mamoulian deviates from the 1935 screenplay by Hackett and Goodrich, and these are most indicative of Mamoulian's creative method in his musical adaptation.

The use of color film becomes an important element distinguishing this film from its predecessor, and it is important to the entire conception of the film. Mamoulian's ideas about the quality of color in the film were quite precise; he said: "I didn't want any contrasting colors—just tints within a very narrow chromatic range—various degrees of yellow, beige and green. This I considered to be the colors of 'Americana'—like Thomas Benton, John Curry and Grant Wood."[24] These experimental ideas about the use of the color in the film at first caused some controversy at MGM—the film's art director, Cedric

Gibbons, warned Mamoulian that Mayer, who wanted "to see bright colors on the screen," would never "buy" the idea.[25] Mamoulian telephoned Arthur Freed, and the matter was soon settled. Mamoulian did get his way, fortunately, since the color quality of the film is important to its overall atmosphere and dynamics (especially in relation to the several *tableaux vivants* of famous American paintings such as those by Benton, Curry, and Wood, whom Mamoulian mentioned above, which will be specifically discussed later).

The outdoor sequences, with the addition of music and color, become even more spectacular in *Summer Holiday* than they were in the *Ah, Wilderness!* film. Mamoulian relies more heavily on these sequences to evoke tonal qualities; they become vaster, grander, more elaborate. There are expanses of very green lawns, flowers of muted colors, and extraordinarily bright sunlight. We see Richard and Muriel, in a long shot, in the first scene, dancing through a splendid park (this sequence and the picnic sequence were filmed in Anheuser-Busch Gardens, a state park outside Pasadena) to the tune of the opening song, "It's Our Home Town." The Fourth of July activities, the men's, women's, and children's, become very elaborate affairs in which Mamoulian uses extreme long shots, the vastness of the space, and fluid cinematic choreography to capture the high-spirited nature of the events. The final scene between Richard and Muriel in the park becomes much more fantastic in setting than was the analogous scene in the earlier screen version. In all of these scenes Mamoulian aimed at creating vivid and picturesque images of a utopian past, where beautiful and harmonious natural settings evoke the spirit of past and better days in American life. These scenes, which might have been mawkishly oversentimentalized, are effective because of Mamoulian's visual style and wit.

For example, during the graduation ceremony Mamoulian presents us with a series of visually and comically effective *tableaux vivants* of famous and popular paintings which celebrate the image of "Americana." He cuts from a pan shot of grim-faced women in the audience at the graduation to a recreation of Grant Wood's *Daughters of the American Revolution*. The live enactment of the painting acts as commentary on the audience at the graduation. This is followed by Grant Wood's *Woman with Plant*, Wood's *American Gothic*, and finally Benton's *Reaper*. These images all come from Midwestern American paintings of the 1930s, hence seem anachronistic in the 1906 New England setting of the film. But in the context of the extremely banal graduation event they take on a comic and parodic edge. Another element of subtle burlesque in the scene occurs with the bank president, Mr. Peabody, a former valedictorian who introduces the new recipient of this, as he says, "immortal honor." Mr. Peabody, as played broadly and blusteringly by Howard Freeman, is a pompously silly man who first reminds the audience that he owns a bank whose assets are "three and one-half millions of dollars," and then forgets the name of the person he is to introduce.

Mamoulian is at his best when he deviates from, or cleverly improvises on, the format of the 1935 scenario. An important sequence not in the earlier film version is the highly stylized triple picnic sequence referred to above. The sequence opens at the men's picnic with another cinematic allusion to a famous American painting. We see a close-up of a motionless trumpeter and then there is a quick zoomback to reveal the entire *tableau vivant*, precisely depicting *The Spirit of '76* by A. M. Willard. The sequence continues with a shot of rows of beer kegs—a fast pan to men childishly playing in trees—a fast pan to a drinking contest—a fast pan to circle dance, and finally a long shot of the frenzied and chaotic movement of the men. The film then cuts to the extremely formalized order of the women's picnic. A long shot reveals the elegantly white-clad women playing croquet (reminiscent of a Winslow Homer painting), all the tables are arranged in meticulous order, and the arrangement and positioning of the women is highly stylized. The rigidity and stuffiness of the women's activities is visually contrasted to the rough abandon of the men's. The film then cuts to the activities of the children. The transition from the women to the children is typical of Mamoulian's fluid editing. One of the women hits a croquet ball off the field and the camera follows it until it stops in the midst of the children's festivities. Here we find some of the youngsters swimming in a pond and others involved in square dancing. We then cut back to the men's picnic and witness the end of the beer-drinking contest. Besotted Uncle Sid is, unfortunately, the winner, and this leads right into the following scene at dinner, in which Sid is both comically and pathetically drunk.

The interior or studio sequences in *Summer Holiday*, however, do not work so well as in the earlier film version. The dinner scene is a good example of the musical's shortcoming in this regard. Uncle Sid, as played by Frank Morgan, is not so comically effective as Wallace Beery had been in the earlier film. Morgan looks too old and frail for the part. He seems old enough to be Lily's (Agnes Moorehead) father rather than would-be husband. The dinner scene, a comic highpoint of O'Neill's play and the 1935 adaptation, is here very much abridged and its pace and comic values are greatly reduced. Most of the studio sequences are drastically cut in the same way. The actors in *Summer Holiday* tend to become caricatures rather than characters. With Mamoulian's great emphasis on the visually dynamic outdoor musical sequences, there is little time left to explore the more subtle aspects of the Miller family as O'Neill's play does. Walter Huston and Selena Royle seem less charming and credible than their counterparts, Barrymore and Byington, in the earlier screen version. The youngest and highly annoying Miller child, Tommy, as played in *Summer Holiday* by Butch Jenkins, also degenerates into caricature and exaggeration. Gloria De Haven, as Muriel, is "pretty enough," as Bosley Crowther mentions in his review of the film; however, she is little else but pretty and vivacious, and Mamoulian apparently had a great deal of trouble directing her. Rooney's Richard, as mentioned before, is probably the film's greatest flaw, if we take seriously Mamoulian's statement that an adaptation

SUMMER HOLIDAY (1948) MGM. Directed by Rouben Mamoulian. With Mickey Rooney and Gloria De Haven. (Richard and Muriel at the graduation ceremony.)

must "be faithful to the author's conceptions . . . his characters, and his words."[26] Rooney's bouncing, boyish, "impish" portrayal of Richard reduces the character even further than it had been in the earlier screen version.

There is one studio sequence, however, that works exceptionally well owing to Mamoulian's imaginative direction and a clever expressionistic use of color to reflect psychological states; this is the "bar-room scene" between Richard and the prostitute Belle. Mamoulian wrote a memorandum to the set designers asking for a set that would "be very flexible both in design and color, so it can reflect the series of moods which Richard undergoes, as the scene progresses. Possible use of transparency. Colored lights, smoke, diffusion. This is a very important set!"[27] This sequence, the last one to be shot for the film, took eight days to complete and "involved several costume, hair and make-up changes for Marilyn Maxwell,"[28] as pointed out by Hugh Fordin. Fordin also quotes Walter Plunkett's (the costume designer for the film) description of the sequence as Mamoulian wanted it:

At the start Marilyn was in a pale, washed-out, pink dress, that blended with the indoor complexion of the customers. As Mickey drank a little more her dress changed into a stronger shade of pink, better made and more stylish. As he kept drinking and the bar became hazy with smoke she kept changing ever so subtly until she was in a bright red dress, looking absolutely radiant.[29]

This sequence has enormous visual power and Marilyn Maxwell's performance as Belle is adroit. Unfortunately, the visual strength of Mamoulian's direction is not matched in the banal lyrics of the song Belle sings.

Generally, the music in the film is weak and rather uninspired, and this seems to be its chief problem as a musical. The music and lyrics, by Harry Warren and Ralph Blane, are neither distinguished nor memorable. Warren and Blane seem to be trying to recapture the style of the songs they had done earlier for Freed's 1944 production of Minnelli's *Meet Me in St. Louis*. *Summer Holiday* is derivative of Minnelli's film in another way. Curiously echoing Minnelli's ideas concerning the use of music and song to further the plot in *Meet Me in St. Louis*, Mamoulian said:

What we are trying to do with it is a new type of musical film wherein no singing, dancing or music is used unless it adequately replaces pages of the play's dialogue and consistently advances the story. There is no room here for "numbers," "choruses" or "specialties." Singing and dancing must be interwoven and integrated with speech. Speech must range from everyday prose to rhythmic, cadenced sentences, and to rhyming verse written to music. Dancing must be a poetic and emotional extension of dramatic action.[30]

This is neither totally original (having been done earlier by Minnelli) nor totally true of Mamoulian's use of songs in *Summer Holiday*. Seven songs are included in the musical score for *Summer Holiday;* they are "It's Our Home Town," "Afraid to Fall in Love," "All Hail Danville High," "The Stanley Steamer," "It's Independence Day," "Weary Blues," and "I Think You're the Sweetest Kid I've Ever Known." Mamoulian said, in the passage quoted above, that songs and dances should only be used when they adequately replace "pages of the play's dialogue and consistently advance the story." If we view *Summer Holiday* as an adaptation of O'Neill's original *Ah, Wilderness!*, this presents some problems, since four of the seven songs in the film occur in scenes with no reference in O'Neill's play. The song "Our Town," the graduation song, the "Stanley Steamer" song (which, by the way, is a direct but pale copy of the "Trolley Song" in Minnelli's *Meet Me in St. Louis*), and the "Independence Day" song are actually "numbers" and "choruses" that musicalize scenes added to open up O'Neill's play in the 1935 version. This is not to suggest that the film should slavishly follow the structure of the play from which it is drawn (as Mamoulian himself suggested, this is often quite the wrong thing to do), but to point out that the general overreliance on the earlier scenario rather than original play leads to this seeming contradiction, as well as other problems that weaken the film both in itself and as an adaptation faithful in spirit to O'Neill's play.

Moreover, the situations and characterizations that were somewhat oversimplified in the first screen version now become even more simplified and broadened in the second adaptation. The delicacy of tone of O'Neill's play, much of which is retained in the 1935 adaptation, is now replaced with the broadness and caricature quality of comic strips. Rooney and De Haven become comic-strip versions of Richard and Muriel, and, in *Summer Holiday*, we are in the world of comic-strip romance.

Summer Holiday is an uneven film. Mamoulian has done some very clever things with the camera; the film's editing is fluid and slick; and there are clever touches of ironic humor as in the *tableaux vivants* and the choreography of the picnic scenes. (Unfortunately, what was considered by many to be one of the most charming and visually effective sequences in the film—a fantasy built around the song "Omar and the Princess," in which Rooney and De Haven were magically transported to a Persian garden—was cut from the final release print of the film.)[31] Overall, however, it suffers from the corporate structure of the film industry. The director of the film, after all, had to work from a previously filmed screenplay since MGM had one on hand for this revival of a previous success. The lyrics of the songs by Harry Warren are essentially banal and too cute. O'Neill used popular songs from the period in which the play was set to evoke the tone and atmosphere of the period. This practice, with only slight changes, was followed in the 1935 adaptation quite successfully. In *Summer Holiday* the songs seem to be at odds with the rest of the dialogue in the film (even though there are attempts at aligning them with the dialogue through recitative preludes and through the use of some rhyming dialogue before and after the songs). O'Neill most likely would have shuddered had he seen or heard the lyrics from *Summer Holiday* and known that Mamoulian had told his lyricist that "they should sound as if they were O'Neill's—lyrics O'Neill could write if he would or if he could."[32]

Summer Holiday was ultimately, as noted by Fordin, "a failure both critically and commercially." He points out that the film, when it was completed, had gone almost $500,000 over its budget and that the MGM financial reports indicated a loss of nearly a million and a half dollars.[33] Its critical and artistic failure, despite several flashes of brilliance by Mamoulian, seems mainly to lie in its uninspired music, and the fact that it was derivative of both the earlier screenplay for MGM's *Ah, Wilderness!* and Minelli's *Meet Me in St. Louis*. In the late 1940s, MGM was riding a crest of musical successes and *Summer Holiday* was but another attempt at formula success— and one that failed. But it, like Minnelli's earlier film, *Meet Me in St. Louis*, helped to change and sophisticate the Hollywood musical, through the integration of songs and dances into the story line of the film.

NOTES

1. Barbara and Arthur Gelb, *O'Neill* (New York: Harper's, 1960), p. 762.
2. Ibid.
3. *Newsweek* 6 (December 14, 1935):38.
4. Otis Ferguson, *New Republic* 85 (December 25, 1935): 198.
5. Andre Sennwald, *New York Times*, December 25, 1935, p. 30.
6. Morton Eustis, *Canadian Magazine* 85 (February 1936): 38.
7. Gelb, p. 769.
8. Louis Sheaffer, *O'Neill: Son and Artist* (Boston: Little, Brown and Co., 1973), p. 404.
9. Eugene O'Neill, *Ah, Wilderness!*, in *The Later Plays of Eugene O'Neill* (New York: Random House, 1967), p. 14.
10. Lines transcribed from viewing of the film, not O'Neill's text.
11. Kevin Brownlow, *The Parade's Gone By . . .* (New York: Balantine Books, Inc., 1968), p. 158.
12. Andrew Sennwald, *New York Times*, December 25, 1935, p. 30.
13. Otis Ferguson, *New Republic* 85 (December 25, 1935): 199.
14. Sheaffer, p. 406.
15. Rouben Mamoulian, "Stage and Screen," *The Screen Writer* 11, no. 10 (March 1947): 1–2.
16. Ibid., p. 2.
17. Ibid., p. 14.
18. Ibid.
19. Hugh Fordin, *The World of Entertainment: Hollywood's Greatest Musicals* (Garden City, N.Y.: Doubleday and Co., 1975), p. 193.
20. Robert L. Hatch, *New Republic* 118 (June 28, 1948): 28.
21. Bosley Crowther, *New York Times*, June 12, 1948, p. 8.
22. Ibid.
23. Tom Milne, *Rouben Mamoulian* (Bloomington, Ind.: Indiana University Press, 1970), p.143–44.
24. Fordin, p. 189.
25. Ibid., p. 190.
26. Mamoulian, p. 14.
27. Fordin, p. 196.
28. Ibid., pp. 201–2.
29. Ibid., p. 202.
30. Mamoulian, p. 14.
31. Fordin, p. 200.
31. Fordin, p. 200.
32. Ibid., p. 190.
33. Ibid., p. 202.

5
The Long Voyage Home

(1940)

John Ford was certainly the perfect director to bring O'Neill's early one-act sea plays to the screen. Ford, like O'Neill, had had experience on the sea, and his Irish-American background was similar to O'Neill's. The film *The Long Voyage Home* is a combination of four of O'Neill's early sea plays—*Bound East for Cardiff, The Moon of the Caribbees, In the Zone,* and *The Long Voyage Home,* the last of which was wisely chosen as the film's title because of its poetic appeal. Ford, in many of his films, was interested in precisely the same dramatic tension that O'Neill was exploring in these early one-acters. In an interview with Ford in 1955, Jean Mitry asked Ford why so many of his films have the same theme—that of "a small group of people thrust by chance into dramatic or tragic circumstances." Ford replied:

> It enables me to make individuals aware of each other by bringing them face to face with something bigger than themselves. The situation of the tragic moment forces men to reveal themselves, and to become aware of what they truly are. The device allows me to find the exceptional in the commonplace.[1]

O'Neill's four one-act plays presented Ford with an ideal situation of men brought "face to face with something bigger than themselves"—the sea, and all of the related problems of the lonely sailor's life.

Although the four plays upon which the film is based were not meant to be sequential, they had been successfully performed together, under the title *S.S. Glencairn,* by the Provincetown Players in 1924. The four plays share many of the same characters and the cargo ship *Glencairn* is used for the main setting. O'Neill found that "they went together in great shape"[2] after seeing the first performance in Provincetown. The film version with Dudley Nichols's superb screenplay, which takes some liberties with the plays in order to integrate them more fully, creates a complete and satisfying, if episodic, whole. O'Neill, generally critical and skeptical of Hollywood, fully enjoyed the film and called it "the best picture made from my stuff."[3]

The success of the film is due to several winning combinations of Hollywood professionals. Walter Wanger (producer), John Ford (director), and Dudley Nichols (screenwriter) had been a most successful trio in several other films, notably *Stagecoach*, produced just a year before. Wanger's excellence in casting, combined with Dudley Nichols's intelligent and synoptic abilities in screenwriting, and Ford's often extolled "muscular realism"[4] and attention to details of mood and atmosphere all blended together to create a film that perfectly captured O'Neill's wistful feelings toward the sea, and the camaraderie, pleasures, and pains of its shipboard inhabitants. The film's photographer, Gregg Toland (who had also worked with Ford in other, earlier films and who was to become most famous a year later for his camera work on *Citizen Kane*) rounded out this crew of superb Hollywood first-raters. The richness and toning of Toland's photographic style is, in fact, responsible for much of the unity of the total work. A cast of fine ethnic character actors also contributed to the convincing realism of the film: Thomas Mitchell as the robust and belligerent Irishman, Driscoll; Barry Fitzgerald as the cantankerous and appropriately named Cocky; Ian Hunter as the alcoholic and embittered former officer, Smith; John Qualen as the lumpen but sweet-natured Yank; Mildred Natwick as the inveigling prostitute, Freda. The most surprising casting in the film is that of John Wayne as the young Swede, Ole Olson. Wayne, in fact, gets top billing in the film although his part is one of the smallest and generally least important. Since he was one of Ford's most successful stars and one of Hollywood's most lucrative properties, it is not surprising that Wayne, rather outrageously, was given top billing. His Swedish accent (he actually says little other than "I yust vant yinger beer") is somewhat comical and weakens the naturalism so strongly maintained by the rest of the fine cast. But Wayne is physically well suited to the role and lends a certain charm to the likable character of Ole.

The release of the film was preceded by a great deal of pomp and circumstance. Walter Wanger launched a bizarre and unprecedented pre-release advertising campaign which involved nine prominent American artists. At a cost of $50,000, he brought artists Grant Wood, Thomas Benton, Raphael Soyer, George Biddle, James Chapin, Ernest Fiene, George Schreiber, Robert Phillip, and Louis Quintanilla to the studio where much of the film was being shot, and each was to choose his favorite image from the film and paint it. There was much coverage by the press of the event, and soon after the film's release *Life* magazine did a fully illustrated article on the film and the artists' works that sprang from it.[5] The paintings were also circulated to thirty-five museums in major cities of the country while the film was having its first run, creating a certain amount of popular interest in the film before and during its initial run.

Critical response to the film was generally favorable. Bosley Crowther hailed it as a "modern odyssey" and went on to say that it was

> a stark and tough fibered motion picture which tells with lean economy the never-ending story of man's wanderings over the waters of the world and search of peace for his soul . . . harsh and relentless in its revelations of man's pathetic shortcomings, . . . one of the most honest pictures ever placed on the screen.[6]

Theatre Arts magazine highly praised it, saying that the film showed

> a movie man with imagination, who can go straight to the source from which the playwright drew, and can play his own understanding upon the original material as well as on the stage version, and then, most important of all, can transcribe the material into filmic terms, can make a great film.[7]

The key point in the above remark is the suggestion that Ford and Nichols have completely and viably translated these plays into a successful cinematic whole.

Since the film was made from four short plays that are connected only by setting and the repetition of a few main characters, there would appear to be problems of structuring the film. Each of O'Neill's four plays is built around a central situation. Nichols's screenplay joined the four plays together smoothly and coherently, but much of the episodic quality inherent in the plays themselves remains. Reviewers in both *Commonweal* and *Time* criticized the film for its lack of "sustained plot." But Bosley Crowther more aptly pointed out the film's episodic nature as a virtue, essential to the mode and feeling of the film. He argues that

> the very essence of the film lies exactly in its inconclusiveness, in deliberate fumbling toward a goal which is never reached, toward a peace which is never attained. . . . This is the endless story which Mr. Ford has told with magnificent sharpness.[8]

Crowther's point seems precisely appropriate to the nature of both O'Neill's plays and Ford's film. As the title of the film suggests, it is all about "the long voyage home," the long voyage that never ends; there are false starts and aborted attempts, but not one of the characters ever escapes his own bondage to the sea. This title, like the title of *Long Day's Journey into Night*, uses a metaphor of movement through space to suggest a process which is at once aimless, self-revealing, and self-defeating. (In the play *The Long Voyage Home*, the young Swede, Ole Olson, who is finally to go home, doesn't make it;

he is highjacked aboard the starvation ship *Amindra*. In the film, Ole does get to go home but, in his stead, the rough and likable Driscoll is shanghaied aboard the *Amindra*.)

In order best to suggest how director Ford and screenwriter Nichols have substantially and very wisely altered the plays for screen treatment, I will summarize the major actions (and visual elements) of the film with reference to the corresponding scenes from O'Neill's plays. Following the film's titles there is a narrative title card which summarizes the action of the film:

> Men who live on the sea never change—for they live in a lonely world apart as they drift from one rusty tramp steamer to the next, forging the life-lines of nations.

Nowhere in O'Neill's plays do these lines appear; they are Nichols's own introduction to the mood and tone of the plays. The first shots of the film are on land in the West Indies. The S.S. *Glencairn* is "at anchor off an island in the West Indies"—as O'Neill describes the setting in the beginning of *The Moon of the Caribbees*. Advantageously employing the cinematic potential of fluid treatment of space, the film can begin on land rather than on the boat as O'Neill began this play. The shots on land establish the tranquil, warm, and sensual feelings that the men of the S.S. *Glencairn* nostalgically associate with the land. There is a long, continuous panning shot of languorous women sitting and standing by trees in the moonlight. These opening shots are highly romantic, suggesting the idyllic qualities that men of the sea associate with land. The romantic feeling is heightened by the song "Harbor Lights," heard in the background. O'Neill throughout *Moon of the Caribbees* suggests that "a mournful" or "melancholy" tune be heard from the shore—in the film this becomes the apt "Harbor Lights." The tranquil tone established by the shots on shore is quickly replaced by the frenzy on the ship and the loud reporting of war news on the ship's radio. (Whereas O'Neill's plays were set during World War I, the film version has changed this to World War II, which, in 1940, gave the film greater contemporary appeal.) All of the major characters of the film are now introduced in purely visual terms. The captain is suspicious of an intruder aboard the ship, and with the aid of police who have just come aboard, the ship is searched by flashlight. The beam from the flashlight passes by the faces of all the men; few words are spoken and no music accompanies this scene, only the natural sounds of the movement of the officers and the waves hitting the sides of the boat. This scene, not suggested in the play, is added to the film for the sake of a visually interesting introduction to the men of the S.S. *Glencairn*. After this fruitless search for an intruder, the men resume their work and wait for the women from shore who will bring them contraband rum.

The arrival of the women and the troubles that follow bring the film to the point of the major action of *Moon of the Caribbees*. This sequence—the arrival of the women, the acquiring of rum, the dance that follows, the pairing off of couples, and finally the fight that breaks out among the men—is based directly on the play. These actions are all edited quickly and are shot mainly from low angles with a wide (24mm) lens. Cameraman Gregg Toland had just begun experimenting with the short-lens, low-angled photography that would become so important an element a year later in his work on *Citizen Kane*. There is one significant alteration in the text during this sequence. All direct references to the women as prostitutes are cut from the film version, owing to the stricter enforcement of the Production Code after 1934.

The film's action drawn from *The Moon of the Caribbees* focuses, as does the play's, on the character of Smitty. Smitty is an aristocratic young Englishman who is trying to fight off his addiction to alcohol. His refined manner makes him suspicious to the rest of the seamen. At this point in the film he submits again to his craving for alcohol; this will become more important in the section of the film taken from *In the Zone* in which Smitty's past is revealed because of his fellow crewmen's suspicions that he is a German spy. Nichols's screenplay has expanded Smitty's character, making the most of dramatic possibilities inherent in the treatment of him in O'Neill's play. At the end of the section from the *Caribbees* play, we see Smitty trying to escape from the ship, which is nowhere suggested by O'Neill. But Smitty's alcoholism has been shown as a sign of general weakness throughout the film, and his attempted escape is also an opportunity for filmic excitement. He runs beside the hulk of the ship in a shaft of very bright light that comes from in front of him. Police chase after him and finally return him to the ship, which now slowly pulls away from the dock. All the men stand by the side of the deck and pass by the camera's vision as the ship leisurely pulls out of harbor. Ford has done this scene also without dialogue, and only the whistles from the ship and the sound of waves accompanying the motion of the ship are heard, which underlies the sense of entrapment that the seamen feel on the voyages.

The next two shots telescope time—we see the prow of the ship at night and then a slow dissolve reveals the prow of the ship in daytime. (Devoted to realism and authenticity of detail, Ford rented the S.S. *Munami* at Wilmington Harbor, California, where much of the film was shot.) In these two shots the ship has moved to a different location, where it is to pick up ammunition to be delivered to England. The idea of the ship being an ammunition carrier is suggested by dialogue from *In the Zone*, but the film will at this point pick up on the central action from *Bound East for Cardiff*, which is the death of Yank. In the play it is intimated that Yank's injury was due to a careless fall from a ladder; Ford elaborates on this by having Yank injured in a violent storm at sea. The storm (created quite convincingly by intercutting rear projection and actual location shooting) becomes an exciting visual element which contrasts with the slow and static scenes to follow.

The most striking feature of the filming of the storm sequence is again Gregg Toland's low-angled, short-lens photography. The camera is positioned at

THE LONG VOYAGE HOME (1940) United Artists. Directed by John Ford. With Thomas Mitchell and Barry Fitzgerald. (Ford and Toland's visual evocation of atmosphere is always impressive, as in the storm sequence.)

deck level and the waves are seen crashing over the sides of the ship. The water rushes along the deck squarely into the lens of the camera, putting the viewer (through this use of subjective camera) into the storm along with the seamen on deck. Yank is finally thrown by an enormous gush of water and hurled against the side of the ship, breaking a rib and suffering internal bleeding. The film quickly cuts to below deck and the vigil attending the slow death of Yank. This scene is taken directly from the play, but Nichols has synoptically pared down the dialogue. The reviewer in *Theatre Arts* found this to be the one scene in the film which is weak because it belies its theatrical background, and said that "it ran too long for comfort." But Ford has certainly employed cinematic resources to give this scene visual power, using close-ups of the faces and reactions of the men involved emotionally in the death of Yank. His dying forces each of them to face his own mortality, and the tough exteriors of the men soften in fear. The dying of Yank also renews their feelings of nostalgic longing for the land and renews their hatred for "the ol' davil sea," as O'Neill called it in *Anna Christie*. Throughout this sequence the ominous sound of the foghorn is heard and is associated with Yank's death. (There is an interesting parallel to this in the way that O'Neill used the mournful sound of the foghorn in *Long Day's Journey into Night*.) Ford skillfully employs this sound effect all through the scene; this sound and the accompanying image of mist become metaphors for death. There is one small detail in this section of the film characteristic of Ford's attention to precise and revealing details. One of Yank's final actions before he dies is to take a puff from an offered cigarette—when he exhales he blows a perfect smoke ring. Earlier in the film, when Yank was introduced to us, he did the same thing. This becomes a visual equivalent to the pretended nonchalance with which Yank tries to face death and perfectly underscores the forced joviality and poignant banality of his dying words (he is telling his friend Driscoll to give a gift to a girl he once liked in the West Indies).

Nichols and Ford depart from O'Neill's text again in the following sequence, which depicts the burial of Yank at sea. Whereas the play ended with his death, the film follows this action to its conclusion. Yank's body is thrown into the sea on a cold, bleak, and windy morning. Ford uses sound most effectively in this scene. All the men stand around Yank's body as the captain reads the prayers to accompany sea burial—his words are almost entirely obscured by the sounds of the wind and the waves crashing against the sides of the boat. We are reminded of the inexorable forces of nature that have brought this man to his death. The camera angle is again low and the sequence is shot with a wide-angle lens in order to magnify the elemental forces that surround the men and the ship, small and insignificant when seen against the

THE LONG VOYAGE HOME (1948) United Artists. Directed by John Ford. With Thomas Mitchell, Ward Bond, John Wayne, and John Qualen. (Below deck after the storm.)

larger context of sea and sky. The power of the visual image, as happens so often in this film, renders words unnecessary.

The following episode in the film is taken, for the most part, directly from *In the Zone*. The central dramatic action of the play is the men's suspicion of Smitty, the refined but alcoholic Englishman, as a German spy. Ford, for the sake of cinematic action and excitement, has added a sequence of aerial attack by enemy planes (discussed more fully later). Typical of Nichols's adroit screenplay, both material from the play and the new material added to the film are cleverly integrated by expanding the character of Smitty and making him central to both of these events. This section opens with a bright interior shot of the ship as the men are painting the portholes black to avoid detection by planes and submarines. The brightness of the scene contrasts with the bleak grayness of the previous sequence of Yank's burial. Suspicion of Smitty begins when his porthole window is discovered to open and close quickly (he has merely forgotten to lock it and it blows open and shut with the wind); the men think that he might be using this as a coded signal to the enemy. Suspicion grows when Axel reads a newspaper article about a German posing as an Englishman to infiltrate enemy ships and report their positions and strategies. He notes that the German spy used letters written in code to inform his government, and Smitty happens to have a black box of letters that he jealously guards. The men of the *Glencairn*, boyishly caught up in this spy game, see all the clues pointing to Smitty as an enemy agent. Smitty returns below deck as his shipmates are about to go through his trunk and examine the box of letters. His hysterical protests cause them to tie him up and gag him, and Driscoll begins to read the letters. As they are slowly read, the drama of the scene is heightened through the use of many close-ups of Smitty's pained face. The letters do not prove him to be a spy, but sadly reveal the unpleasant facts of his past, his alcoholism, the loss of his commission, and the undying love of his wife, Elizabeth, who penned the letters.

Nichols in his screenplay has substantially altered the content of the letters that Driscoll reads, making the situation all the more poignant and pathetic. In O'Neill's play, the letters are from a girl to whom Smitty was engaged, rather than his wife, and reveal that he was hopelessly lost to drink. In Nichols's treatment, they are from his wife, who laments that he has deserted her and their children in order to protect them from his own weakness, and they reveal the crucial fact that through this weakness he has lost his commission. As Driscoll reads the letters, he is photographed from a low angle, emphasizing his size and power in the scene. Smitty is photographed from a high angle to suggest his helplessness. The repeated use of close-ups on Smitty involves the audience sympathetically in his plight and effectively works to intensify the emotions of the situation. Nichols's changes are effective because they are an integral part of reworking of O'Neill's plays for film treatment. The revelations gleaned from the letters in the play would seem to fall rather flat after the extraordinary build-up given to them in the film. By changing Smitty into a married man with children and a former officer, Nichols has given Smitty's character more weight and dramatic intensity.[9]

The highly acclaimed sequence that follows—the bombardment by German planes—allows for further psychological expansion of the character of Smitty. Having been forced psychically to relive and reassess the disasters of his past, Smitty seems able to reassert himself and to act decisively and courageously during the bombardment. He now acts as the officer he was trained to be and takes command of the other men, who become weak and frightened during the bombardment. Nichols's reworking of Smitty's character makes it psychologically appropriate for him to reestablish his former position as a leader. Now that the past, which he has been trying to forget and to hide, has been brought to the surface, it liberates what was previously strong and good in him. In his bravery, however, he is killed, but one feels that his death as a hero is superior to his life of self-deprecation and self-loathing. By integrating O'Neill's four plays, Nichols has turned the character of Smitty, which was fragmentarily interesting in the plays, into a fully realized and developed personality in the film.

What is filmically most interesting about the treatment of the bombardment sequence, however, is Ford's avoidance of the cliché of cross-cutting from the planes to the ship. The enemy planes are never seen, we see only the bombs falling into the sea, and the bullets hitting the deck, cabins, and portholes of the ship. And in one moment of tension, bullet holes seem to outline the body of a seaman huddled on a tarpaulin on the deck. Ford, an established master of action filming, here has used all the devices that cinema has to offer to make this an intense and exciting visual experience. The editing is very fast, and the chaos of the scene is reinforced by loud sound effects and by the use of rapidly alternating camera angles and tense diagonal shots. The frenzy of the situation ends with the death of Smitty. Here Ford has created another fine metaphor for death: after Smitty is killed, a white tarpaulin is blown over his body by the wind. The attack is over, and the sentimental Axel says, "Smitty got home" (a line not in O'Neill's play but wonderfully in keeping with his style and the suggestion of "home" as death, the sea, or final destiny as in the title *The Long Voyage Home*).

The following brief scene in the film is another that was not in the play, and one that is cinematically very effective. We see Smitty's family leaving the boat after picking up his possessions. This takes place in a courtyard by the London pier where the ship is docked. The streets are dark and glazed with rain, and this visual imagery is suggestive of death. This short sequence also serves as a transition into the action of the play *The Long Voyage Home*, and it foreshadows the death of Driscoll and the sense of fatality at the end of the film, which takes place in the same locale. Whereas in the play the action of *The Long Voyage Home* is entirely set in "the bar of a low dive on the London waters,"[10] in the film the transition to this setting is spatially expanded. In several superb atmospheric shots by Toland we see the men wander idly through the foggy, shadowy, and deserted streets of the London waterfront in search of drink and entertainment. They are at the same time mindful of their duty to get the young Swede Ole (John Wayne) to his ship bound for home. They soon meet the sleazy pimp Nick, who solicits sailors to "Joe's Place"; once there, they begin drinking toasts to Ole's safe return home, and soon forget him as he is highjacked to the starvation ship *Amindra* (only to be rescued later). The action of the play *The Long Voyage Home* is expanded in the film, taking up about a third of the total running time.

We are again reminded of war, and the action of *In the Zone*, as the men pass by newspaper signs that read "Nazis Invade Poland" on their way to Joe's Place. Once the action reaches the bar, there are several important changes in and expansions on O'Neill's text. John Baxter describes very well the atmosphere in this section of the film:

> As an exercise in tension this section bears comparison with *The Informer*, which in playing, appearance and photographic style it resembles. Ford peoples his phony London with twenties' grotesques; J. M. Kerrigan's sly and falsely amiable tout, Mildred Natwick, superbly raddled and maudlin as the prostitute who drugs Ole in an attempt to shanghai him, a blind violinist who plays "Shenandoah" for the sailors, and thugs and barmen who would not have been out of place in *The Threepenny Opera*. Plainly at home in this setting, Ford responds with the film's liveliest and most atmospheric scenes.[11]

Much of the success of this sequence is owing to the superb performance by Mildred Natwick as the bedraggled prostitute, Freda, who feigns Swedish ancestry to win Ole's naive affection in order to drug him in preparation for his kidnapping. (As in the earlier scene with the women from the island, all direct suggestions of Freda or the other women as prostitutes are cut from the screenplay because of censorship. Women characters as prostitutes are prevalent not only in this play but in many other of O'Neill's plays; this is especially true of the plays adapted to the screen.)[12] Natwick captures both the lubricity and the pathos of Freda's character; she is both very much a part of and also trapped within this corrupt world of London low life. By omitting one small detail from the play, Nichols had made her character less cold and slightly more sympathetic. In the play, after Ole has been drugged and passes out, Freda quickly goes through his pockets and steals his wallet. In the film she doesn't do this, but rather shows some signs of sympathy for the plight of the young Swede.

The ending of the film is quite different from the ending of the play. In the play, Ole is successfully shanghaied aboard the *Amindra*, and his friends never learn of this. In the film they discover the plot and go to rescue him from the accursed ship. A fight breaks out between the two groups of seamen; Ole is taken off the ship, but the rough and tough Driscoll is injured and passes out on the deck of the ship. Before the others realize that he has not returned to the dock, the *Amindra* launches out to sea, taking Driscoll with her. Ole does get to his ship bound for Sweden and, unlike Ole in the play, will get home. The final, highly poetic scene in the film depicts the return of the men to the *Glencairn*. All but one, Donkeyman, had refused to sign up again in advance, thinking that this time they would remain on land and perhaps get home. Now, bedraggled, wasted by drink, tired, and penniless, they reluctantly return to the ship for yet another "last voyage" and a chance to earn enough money to get home. It is a bleak, gray, and windy morning—as it was on the day Smitty was buried at sea. The scene opens with a shot of the empty courtyard and a gust of wind blows dust and some old newspapers across the cobblestones—a fine metaphor for the sense of doom and desolation in this scene. Sound is also used to intensify the imagery; the loud whistling of the wind is heard, and the melancholy strains of the song "Harbor Lights" are heard quietly in the background. The recurrence of "Harbor Lights" at this point in the film is poignant in its ironic counterpoint to the despondency and hopelessness of the situation.

The melancholy and fatalism of the end of the film are heightened by one last superb detail in Nichols's screenplay: Donkeyman stands on the deck of the ship and looks at a newspaper which announces that the ship *Amindra* has been torpedoed and that all of its crew have been killed. He silently shows this to the other crewmen and then drops the newspaper into the sea. Their great friend Driscoll has been killed! The following shot is remarkably effective in its imagery and sums up the theme and atmosphere of the film. The newspaper floats along the surface of the water with sludge washing over it. As the newspaper begins to sink slowly, a second image is superimposed—that of water rapidly passing over it suggesting that the ship has set to sea again. This superimposition transposes the film from a realistic to a metaphorical level and prepares for the title that ends the film:

> So men like Ole come and go
> and the Driscolls live and die
> and the Yanks and Smittys leave their memories—
> but for the others the long voyage home never ends.[13]

Both the opening and closing titles are original to Nichols's screenplay and are adroitly in keeping with O'Neill's attitude toward the sea and its hypnotic power over those who succumb to its attraction.

As suggested by the above analysis of the film, Ford's treatment of O'Neill's unconnected one-acters certainly transcends both the limitations of the plays themselves and the problems of integrating them into a successful artistic whole. From O'Neill's rather motley assortment of characters and ethnic types, Nichols and Ford have created several fully realized and believable characters whose actions are consistent throughout the film. In expanding several of the most important characters, Nichols has improved on the sketches we get in the plays. The success of the film also depends, to a great extent, on the cinematography of Gregg Toland. Toland is generally considered among the best Hollywood cameramen of the period. He is a master at creating tone and atmosphere through precisely the right lighting, camera angle, and lens to evoke the exact visual equivalent to the theme and dialogue of each sequence. John Baxter pays tribute to Toland's work:

> [His] camera work is a unique excursion into visual imagery and the alternation of textures. Heavily-filtered high-contrast stock, hard side lighting and a relentless observance of the correct angle in the face of dramatic and narrative necessities make the film an essay in pictorial counterpoint. . . . To see *The Long Voyage Home* in a good copy, with the bronze texture and deep blacks of nitrate print, is to realize again that Toland was one of supreme visual stylists of the cinema.[14]

Baxter's tribute is in no way excessive. One is struck by the extraordinary rightness of all of Toland's chiaroscuro style in the film. Several images, owing to the richness of Toland's black-and-white photography, remain hauntingly implanted in one's memory after the film is over: the sensuous writhings of the native women at the beginning of the film, the fury of the sea during the first storm sequence, the sea burial of Yank, the looming hulk of the *Amindra*, and the final shot of the newspaper headline mentioned above. Baxter, extolling the appropriateness of Toland's photography to the tone of the drama, points out that "hard shapes dominate every shot, even those of the sea and the sky, water glinting like crushed glass, clouds clipped out of copper, the moon hard as a coin." Toland's pioneering use of the 24mm lens, as suggested by James Scott in *Film: The Medium and the Maker*, may have been adopted to "relieve the filmed plays he shot for Ford and Wyler of their theatrical look. At least this could be said of *The Long Voyage Home* and *The Little Foxes*."[15] The wide 24mm lens does work well in cramped interiors, expanding the space and allowing for more interesting visual compositions. This is important in *The Long Voyage Home* since most of the action of the film takes place in the confining cabins of the ship. Peter Bogdanovich, in his book *John Ford*, asks the director why the film is so claustrophobic, being a story about the sea, and Ford answers: "We purposely kept it in confined space—that was what the story called for. Life on a ship *is* claustrophobic, but you get accustomed to it."[16] Again there is a parallel to *Long Day's Journey into Night*; both screen adaptations require a sense of physical claustrophobia, but both are substantially relieved of visual claustrophobia through the use of the wide-angled lens.

Toland, in an interview given in 1942, explains his use of the wide-angle lens in two other ways.[17] He said that the greater compositional space afforded by the lens allowed more freedom and fluidity in the shooting of long takes with several actions taking place at the same time. A scene of dramatic tension would not have to be broken up by many direct cuts because the whole action could be shown in a single shot through the use of the wide-angle lens. (The film versions of *Long Day's Journey* and *Iceman Cometh* would later use the same technique for very much the same purpose.) Toland also stresses the importance of movement or "the dynamism" within each shot, and he explains that the wide-angle lens allows greater freedom of movement within any shot. Toland's camera work in *Long Voyage Home* makes it clear that spatial confinement need not necessarily diminish compositional interest of a shot or the visual quality of a film. (Hitchcock's *Lifeboat* is another example of visual and dramatic effectiveness within highly confined space and contains striking visual parallels to Ford's film.)

Lindsay Anderson, in an intresting article published in the summer 1950 issue of *Sequence* magazine, makes an astute point about Ford's method as a director and his particular kind of cinematic poetry:

> Ford has always found his true image of reality in this world. Not in the deliberately fashioned symbolism of a literary invention. His symbolisms arise naturally out of the ordinary, the everyday; it is by familiar places, tradition and themes that his imagination is most happily stimulated.[18]

The imagery of *The Long Voyage Home*, harshly austere and powerful, yet strangely beautiful, seems to evoke precisely the feeling toward the sea that O'Neill strove to create in words throughout his career. The sea is the "ol' davil" in *Anna Christie*; it seems to entrap and hypnotize its victims in *The Long Voyage Home*, making it impossible for them ever to return to "normal" or "happy" life ashore. But the sea also represents romance, escape, adventure, and imagination, as it does in *The Long Voyage Home*, *Mourning Becomes Electra*,[19] and *Beyond the Horizon*.[20] It is a means for man to go beyond himself, beyond the confines of the known facts and ways of life—indeed, beyond the horizon. Edmund, in *Long Day's Journey into Night*, says he would have preferred to be a sea creature rather than a man,[21] and O'Neill himself often talked about ending his life by swimming out to sea until he drowned.[22] O'Neill was obsessed with the profound poetry of the sea, in both its romantic and its brutal aspects, and Ford's film captures these qualities both verbally and visually. It is no surprise that O'Neill liked *The Long Voyage Home* very much and considered it the best film made from his work. He especially liked "the talkless parts"[23] of it, most likely finding expresssed in its visual images a kind of concrete poetry that his own words never fully expressed.

NOTES

1. Jean Mitry, "Interview with John Ford," *Cahiers du Cinema* 45 (March 1955), trans. Andrew Sarris and reprinted in his book, *Interviews with Film Directors* (New York: Avon, 1967), p. 195.
2. Louis Sheaffer, *O'Neill: Son and Artist* (Boston: Little, Brown and Company, 1973), p. 149.
3. Sheaffer, p. 546.
4. Bosley Crowther, *New York Times*, October 9, 1940, p. 30.
5. *Life* 9 (November 11, 1940): 83–84.
6. Crowther, p. 30.
7. Hermine Rich Isaacs, *Theatre Arts* 24 (December 1940): 867.
8. Crowther, p. 30.
9. A different point of view is taken toward Nichols's screenplay by John Baxter in his book, *The Cinema of John Ford* (New York: A. S. Barnes & Company: 1971). He argues that Nichols's screenplay oversentimentalizes certain dramatic incidents in O'Neill's original script.
10. Eugene O'Neill, *The Long Voyage Home*, in *Seven Plays of the Sea* (New York: Random House, 1946), p. 57.
11. John Baxter, *The Films of John Ford* (New York: A. S. Barnes & Company, 1971), p. 115.
12. O'Neill's view of women in general is a large and complex study which is beyond the scope of this book. But it is interesting to note that in almost all of the plays adapted to the screen, women are not portrayed in a very flattering light. Women as prostitutes figure importantly in most of the plays. Anna Christie was a prostitute in Minneapolis before the play begins. There is also the "wharf-rat" Marthy in *Anna Christie*. Nina Leeds of *Strange Interlude* prostituted herself after the death of Gordon. The prostitute Belle is important in both *Ah, Wilderness!* and *Summer Holiday*. All of the women in *The Long Voyage Home* are prostitutes. Several of the women are schemers, such as Nina Leeds in *Strange Interlude*, Abbie Putman in *Desire* (Anna in the film), and Mildred in *Hairy Ape*. The third type of female image is that of the obsessive, overprotective, or even incestuous mother: Abbie in *Desire*, Nina in *Strange Interlude*, Christine in *Mourning Becomes Electra*, and Mary in *Long Day's Journey*. It is interesting to note that Hollywood was interested in plays dealing with such subjects even though the negative implications of these female characters had to be toned down in all of the films except *Mourning Becomes Electra* and *Long Day's Journey*. Lavinia in *Mourning Becomes Electra* is an especially complex personality who combines the schemer, the neurotic, the incestuous and in a certain sense (from suggestions of her activities on the island), the prostitute.
13. The tendency for film versions of plays to simplify or, perhaps, overexplain thematic material is evident in many other film adaptations, notably Pascal's film adaptation of Shaw's *Pygmalion*, which opens with a title card explaining the background of the story in order to clarify Shaw's theme. The tendency is well explained by Donald P. Costello in *The Serpent's Eye: Shaw and the Cinema* (Notre Dame: Notre Dame Press, 1965), pp. 74–76.
14. Baxter, p. 113.
15. James F. Scott, *Film: The Medium and the Maker* (New York: Holt, Rinehart and Winston, 1975), p. 47.
16. Peter Bogdanovich, *John Ford* (Berkeley: University of California Press, 1968), p. 78.
17. As quoted in James F. Scott, *Film: The Medium and the Maker*.
18. Lindsay Anderson, "The Method of John Ford" as reprinted in Lewis Jacobs, *The Emergence of Film Art*, (New York: Hopkinson and Blake, 1974), p. 239.
19. In *Mourning Becomes Electra* the sea clearly represents romantic yearnings of escape from the stifling restrictions and conventions of life on land. The sea is the means of escape from the prison of land to the "blessed isles" of adventure and fulfillment.
20. *Beyond the Horizon*, written shortly after the four one-act plays which make up the film *The Long Voyage Home*, clearly expresses O'Neill's rhapsodic attitude toward the sea. It depicts tragic consequences for the poetical young man, Rob, who, unlike the crewmen of the S.S. *Glencairn*, does not heed the call of the sea, and whose life is ruined by remaining on land.
21. Eugene O'Neill, *Long Day's Journey into Night* (New Haven, Conn.: Yale University Press, 1956), p. 153.
22. Sheaffer, p. 638.
22. Sheaffer, p. 638.
23. Sheaffer, p. 546.

6
Mourning Becomes Electra

(1947)

Mourning Becomes Electra, the seventh of O'Neill's films to be adapted to the cinema, was reverentially brought to the screen in 1947, written, produced, and directed by Dudley Nichols, whom O'Neill highly respected for his earlier screenplay for *The Long Voyage Home* (1940). O'Neill's trilogy, written in imitation of Aeschylus's *Oresteia*, occupies a rare and hallowed position in American theatrical history, and its own theatrical history has some bearing on the film version that would later emerge. The play premiered at the Theatre Guild in October of 1931. It was immediately accepted by most critics as a peak in both O'Neill's career and in the American theater.[1] Both the size of the work, requiring over five hours for production, and its attempts to Americanize one of the most durable of Greek tragic legends assured it of very serious consideration by critics and intelligent theatergoers concerned with American drama. It was received with the greatest enthusiasm that O'Neill would enjoy in his lifetime.

The history of *Mourning Becomes Electra*'s long journey to the screen is interesting and reveals changes in both O'Neill's attitude toward the film industry and changes in the industry itself. It was first considered for the screen by Theresa Helburn, who wanted Katharine Hepburn as Lavinia. Miss Helburn went to Louis B. Mayer with the idea. "Over my dead body,"[2] Mayer replied in what seems almost clichéd Hollywood philistinism. Mayer's attitude, however, should be viewed in light of the fact that MGM had unsuccessfully produced *Strange Interlude* only three years before. Neither was O'Neill himself interested in the project, although he liked the idea of Hepburn playing Lavinia. He feared that *Electra* would become the same "dreadful hash of attempted condensation and idiotic censorship"[3] that *Strange Interlude* had become on the screen. With the Hays office in full power enforcing its own Motion Picture Production Code, written five years earlier, 1935 was a far better year for Hollywood to produce the uncontroversial *Ah, Wilderness!* than the volatile *Mourning Becomes Electra*.

It was not until 1946 that O'Neill was finally convinced to sell the rights to *Electra* for screen treatment. A condition of O'Neill's agreement was that Dudley Nichols not only write the screenplay but produce and direct it as well. Nichols was already a distinguished screenwriter, whose credits included *The Informer, Mary of Scotland, Stagecoach,* and *The Long Voyage Home,* among

MOURNING BECOMES ELECTRA (1947) RKO. Directed by Dudley Nichols. With Nancy Coleman, Kirk Douglas, and Katina Paxinou. (Orin returns from the Civil War to his mother Christine and fiancée Sarah.)

others. Nichols was to work in conjunction with the Theatre Guild, which had first performed the play on stage. Katharine Hepburn, earlier considered for the part of Lavinia, was unable to accept the role and it was given to Rosalind Russell. The role of Christine Mannon was offered to Greta Garbo, but Garbo flatly refused to come out of retirement. She gave the reason that it would be inappropriate for her, at the age of forty-two, to play the mother of Rosalind Russell, aged thirty-nine. We can only wonder what the ineffable screen personality of Garbo might have contributed to the success or failure of the film. Nichols then chose Katina Paxinou, a noted Greek stage actress with limited screen experience, for the role of Christine Mannon. Curiously enough, Paxinou was then only forty-three years old, just a year older than Garbo. Michael Redgrave, the distinguished English actor, made his American film debut in the role of Orin Mannon, and Raymond Massey played the cold and stiffly puritanical father, Ezra Mannon. Kirk Douglas was chosen to play the minor part of Peter Niles; this was only the fourth film of his Hollywood career.

Dudley Nichols, profoundly respectful of O'Neill and the text play, conferred with the author at length on the changes and deletions he would make in the screenplay, and got O'Neill's approval. Nichols's screenplay is indeed faithful to the play. No new dialogue was added—something rare among film adaptations, and the play is generally well synopsized. Nichols's film version runs just under three hours while the original play runs closer to six hours. Many of the scenes involving the townspeople, whom O'Neill conceived of as a kind of chorus to comment on the Mannons and to set their actions against a larger social context, are cut from the film version with no real loss to the narrative line. Essential actions and their implications are retained.

Reception of the film was mixed, but as Robert L. Hatch put it in *The New Republic:* "No one can pretend it isn't culture."[4] Much of the criticism stressed the film's "importance," just as most of the reviews of the play had after its premiere sixteen years earlier. William Rose Benét said that it was "one of the most remarkable moving pictures I have ever seen." He went on to say that, while viewing the film, "one is in the presence throughout of massive tragedy, and, most certainly, of real greatness of the creative mind."[5] Hermine Rich Isaacs, writing in *Theatre Arts*, ended her review by saying: "This film will remain without precedents, perhaps without successors, but secure in its own indomitable presence."[6] To the contrary, Phillip Hartung complained that it was "static and talky,"[7] and Bosley Crowther argued that the fidelity to the original was "one of the major reasons for the film's exhausting tedium."[8] Phillip Hartung made the trenchant point that "those who see *Mourning Becomes Electra* for the first time will be surprised to see the material for a thriller without the action of a thriller."[9]

Much of the negative criticism of the film actually faults the source of the adaptation and cites flaws inherent in O'Neill's play. *Mourning Becomes Electra* is a peculiar combination of classical tragedy and sensational melodrama. It vacillates between highly stylized formality and prosaic realism. This dichotomy becomes even more apparent on the screen. Nichols's faithfulness to the original underlines some problems already in the theatrical work, and the style of the film itself seems to waver somewhat uncomfortably between realism and formalism. Another problem stemming from the source of the film, as noted by most contemporary critics, is the language of the play, which Nichols has kept unaltered. With the exception of certain flashes of

MOURNING BECOMES ELECTRA (1947) RKO. Directed by Dudley Nichols. With Raymond Massey and Rosalind Russell. (Ezra and Lavinia accuse—with their eyes—Christine of murder.)

brilliance in dialogue, the prosaic language seems to be at odds with the grandiose nobility of its tragic themes. Nichols's directorial approach to the work nonetheless emphasizes formal and thematic elements of the original and manages successfully to focus cinematically much of the dramatic power of the play.

Following the mode of O'Neill, who in turn was imitating that of Greek tragedy, Nichols has aimed at grandeur and simplicity in the film. The facade of the house, with its Greek revival architecture, as in the play, suggests a classical context for the action. The film is shot in high-contrast black and white, giving the whole a chiaroscuro quality appropriate to the tragic nature of the subject. The alternation of light and shade is anticipated in O'Neill's stage directions:

> Behind the driveway the white Grecian temple portico with its six columns extends across the stage. . . . The white columns cast black bars of shadows on the gray wall behind them. The windows to the lower floor reflect the sun's rays in a resentful glare. The temple portico is like an incongruous white mask fixed on the house to hide its somber gray ugliness.[10]

The white portico is here envisioned as a mask that hides the guilt and ugliness within the house. O'Neill uses this as a metaphor for the Mannons' very existence. Nichols evokes the same feeling for the house. Lighting on the front of the house is generally bright and glaring; this is true even in night scenes, which stretches the film's credulity somewhat, but lighting does effectively create the entrapment image that O'Neill had suggested.

The exterior of the Mannon house becomes a leitmotif that recurs throughout the film to remind the audience of the inevitable doom of its inhabitants. The film opens with the titles superimposed over shots of the open sea, with the song "Shenandoah" sung in the background. When the titles end, the shot of the sea fades out and a long shot of the facade of the Mannon house fades in. The image of freedom, motion, and expansive space is replaced by the stark and static image of the house. The obvious studio set used for the house is unconvincing in terms of realism, but on the level of image or metaphor it works well, and Nichols uses these shots in a clearly stylized way. Similar ponderous long shots of the portico will punctuate the major actions of the rest of the film. Upon Ezra's return there is a fade-out from the scene of the family leaving the railroad station to a slow fade-in of the house, which prepares us for Ezra's fate. After the murder of Adam Brant, there is an abrupt cut to the gloomy facade, as Orin and Lavinia return with the news. The curse of the "Mannon House" does not end with the first generation of Mannons. When Lavinia and Orin return from their trip to the South Sea islands the facade is again ominous, reminding us of the fearful fate in store for them. The handling of their return is visually interesting: in a long shot we see them drive up in a carriage and it seems not to be the children, but the Mannon parents, arriving. The shot is deliberately ambiguous, setting up the idea that henceforth Orin and Lavinia will relive the lives of their parents; they will become them both physically and psychically.

Nichols continues this pattern of light and dark imagery: Lavinia, now emotionally liberated by the death of her mother, seeks happiness with Peter Niles, to whom she has been engaged for many years. Their reunion, after her trip to the islands, is filmed in bright sunlight suggesting joy and hope. At the end of this scene there is another fade-out and fade-in of the facade of the accursed house, again reminding the viewer of the impossibility of happiness for the Mannons. Sometime later, after Orin's suicide, Lavinia is seen sitting outside the house in the shadow cast by one of the large columns. Christine had been seen in precisely the same position twice before in the film, on the night of Ezra's return and on the night that she is told of the death of her lover. The thematic pattern of unhappiness conforms to the visual patterning of shade and light. Lavinia's fate is visually related to that of her mother and to the general curse of the Mannons. The last shot in the film again establishes the connection between the Mannon fate and the house itself. Lavinia enters the house after ordering the servant Seth to nail all the shutters closed. Her life and the Mannon fate are to be literally sealed up within the house. The camera pulls back farther and farther as Seth is seen closing and nailing the shutters.

Just as the many shots of the portico are used in a formalized way to underscore thematic patterns, so is a portrait Ezra Mannon formally framed in many shots to emphasize psychological relationships. The portrait of Ezra in judicial robes becomes an important visual and compositional element in several of the film's key scenes. Nichols is essentially following the suggestion of O'Neill's stage directions and merely amplifying on a basic stage convention. Portraits are often important and prominent parts of stage settings, as in this and other plays of O'Neill (or as in Ibsen's *Hedda Gabler*, where the portrait of General Gabler, centered on the backdrop, is crucial to the actions of the play and to the audience's understanding of Hedda). In *Mourning Becomes Electra* the portrait of Ezra is prominently displayed at rear center of the set. O'Neill described him in the portrait as

> a tall man in his early forties, with a spare, wiry frame, seated stiffly in an armchair, his hands on the arms, wearing his black judge's robe. His face is

MOURNING BECOMES ELECTRA (1947) RKO. Directed by Dudley Nichols. With Rosalind Russell and Kirk Douglas. (Lavinia and Orin remain haunted by their father in effigy.)

handsome in a stern, aloof fashion. It is cold and emotionless and has the same strange semblance of a life-like mask that we have already seen in the faces of his wife and daughter and Brant.[11]

In both the play and film the portrait of Ezra is associated with guilt and punishment—he is the aloof and omniscient judge, watching and judging the actions of others. The importance of the image of Ezra as judge is underlined by O'Neill in his setting one pivotal act in each section of the trilogy in Ezra's study, with its formal air and the prominence of the judge's portrait. These are act 2 of *The Homecoming*, in which Lavinia confronts Christine over Brant; act 3 of *The Hunted*, in which Lavinia proves Christine's guilt, shocking her mother into hysteria by putting the lethal pillbox on the stomach of the dead man; and act 2 of *The Haunted*, in which Orin announces that he is writing a history of the Mannon crimes, and in so doing has discovered that he and Lavinia are reliving the lives of their parents.

In the film, these same scenes, as well as others, take place in Ezra's study. Nichols can further emphasize the importance of the portrait by its positioning in each individual shot, and by isolating only a part of it, in close-up, to underline Ezra's power. Often we see only the hand in the portrait at the very top of the shot, with one or more characters standing beneath it. For example, early in the film when Peter Niles asks Lavinia to marry him, we see her standing below the portrait with her father's hand seeming to reach down between them. Even when Ezra is away, his power over the rest of the family is felt, and communicated to the audience visually by the close-up detail from the portrait.

Several shots in the film are arranged around the portrait in full view in the background. Here Nichols is blocking the action much as it might be on the stage, but the limited vision of the camera can further emphasize the meaning of the compositions. When Adam Brant and Christine discuss the possibilities of continuing their relationship upon the return of Ezra, they are seen separated by the portrait over the mantle. Much later in the film, in a scene that parallels the one above, Lavinia and Orin discuss the possibilities of her marrying Peter Niles, and they are now separated by the painting of Ezra above them. The strict paralleling of these two shots visually emphasizes the idea that Orin and Lavinia are reliving the past. The curse, or fate, of the Mannons does not disappear with the death of Ezra; and we are reminded of his continued control through his portrait.

Similarly, several other kinds of significances result from the arrangement of characters within the compositional frame of the film. Lavinia, for example, is very often alone in the shot, usually standing in a doorway, suggesting her isolation from the rest of the characters. To emphasize Lavinia's malicious dominance over others in the family, she is often photographed from a slightly low angle. This is especially true in scenes involving Lavinia and Orin; she physically and emotionally towers over him because of the angle at which each

MOURNING BECOMES ELECTRA (1947) RKO. Directed by Dudley Nichols. With Rosalind Russell. (Lavinia recreating the image of her dead mother.)

is filmed. Nichols retains the structural formalism of O'Neill's play in the visual formalism of the arrangement of characters on the screen. The characters in each shot are grouped according to psychological and emotional alliances; for example, Lavinia and Ezra are seen on one side of the screen with Christine separated from them, or Orin and Christine together and Lavinia apart, or Adam Brant and Christine together and Lavinia off to the side of the shot. This formalism in arrangement of characters on the screen is also used to articulate the film's themes more effectively. For example, the similarities between Lavinia and Orin and their parents are stressed, in the latter part of the film, by placing them in exactly the same positions that Christine and Ezra had been in earlier. Lavinia and Christine, in parallel shots, are each seen sitting in deep shadows cast by the pillars of the portico as each is thwarted in her romantic desires. This same kind of positioning of characters would, of course, also be possible on stage, and Nichols has generally followed O'Neill's stage directions in these blockings. Nonetheless, these spatial relationships can be more selectively focused on by the camera than they could be on stage.

In 1943 Nichols wrote an essay called "The Writer and the Screen," which argued a point relevant to his handling of *Mourning Becomes Electra*. He said:

> Unthinking people speak of the motion picture as the medium of "action"; the truth is that the stage is the medium of action while the screen is the medium of reaction. It is through identification with the person *acted upon* on the screen, and not with the person acting, that the film builds its oscillating power with an audience. At any emotional crisis in a film, when a character is saying something which profoundly affects another, it is to this second character that the camera instinctively roves.[12]

The idea was not original with Nichols. René Clair, the important early French director, had pointed out the same idea eighteen years earlier. Making observations on the first two years of sound films, Clair wrote in 1929:

> Already in the films we are shown at present, we often feel that in a conversation it is more interesting to watch the listener's rather than the speaker's face. In all likelihood American directors are aware of this, for many of them have used the device quite often and not unskillfully.[13]

Nichols does focus his camera on the listener in several key scenes in the film. During the confrontation between Lavinia and her mother over Adam Brant, the camera focuses its attention mainly on Christine's reactions to Lavinia's scathing attack. As Lavinia's remarks become more vicious, the camera moves into a tighter and tighter close-up of Christine's face. We do not see Lavinia very often as she speaks, but we hear her words and see their effect on Christine. Similarly, the camera studies Orin's responses in two scenes, one with Lavinia and one with Christine, as he learns of the affair between his mother and Adam Brant. Orin's obsessive love for his mother and the dangerous implications of this latent incestuous affection are visually revealed by the extravagance of his response. Perhaps the most striking use of this method of shooting occurs when Christine is told of the death of her lover, Adam. She stands outside the prison-like Mannon house; Orin and Lavinia give her the news. She says nothing—only listens to them and then begins to moan pitifully. Her face is, as O'Neill described it, "like a tragic mask, devoid of expression." The pathos of the situation is indeed heightened by focusing our attention on Christine the reactor, rather than Lavinia and Orin, the actors. Unfortunately, examples of such effective use of this technique are all too rare in this adaptation.

All of the scenes examined so far have taken place either in the house or on the portico and have been closely based on scenes from the play. There is only one sequence in the film that departs from the original in an attempt to open up the adaptation. It is a sequence in which Lavinia secretly follows her mother to Boston, where Christine will meet her lover Adam Brant. It is a quickly edited series of shots, without dialogue and accompanied by rather ponderous music. This sequence is made up of twenty-two shots and takes less than four minutes of running time. The sequence is worth noting in detail; a close study of the film reveals the following shooting and editing techniques:

> Christine leaves her father's house. Close-up of Christine in her carriage. Close-up of Lavinia in her carriage. Lavinia's carriage follows Christine's. Long-shot of street scene. Christine's carriage stops. Shot of street. Lavinia's carriage stops. Close-up of mail box with name Adam Brant on it. Close-up of Lavinia's face—anxious expression. Lavinia searches house for Brant's room. She looks out of the window and sees Christine and Adam kissing. Lap dissolve to Lavinia and Adam kissing by the seashore. Housekeeper comes in. Lavinia hides, and then hurries down the stairs. Lavinia goes off in carriage. Long shot of Mannon house, cast in heavy shadows. Christine walks up the stairs of house carrying a candle which casts dark barlike shadows on the walls. The shadow of Lavinia is seen passing under the locked door. Close-up of doorknob turning. Close-up of Lavinia's face. Superimposition of Lavinia's face and flashback of her and Adam kissing by the shore.[14]

This is the most routinely cinematic sequence in this adaptation, which is generally more formally stylized; nonetheless, it serves several functions quite effectively. It is our introduction to both Lavinia and Christine; the parallel close-up of each in her carriage, each dressed in a dark dress and large hat with a veil, sets up the physical similarity that will become much more important later on. Also the air of mystery and secrecy in Lavinia's actions establishes a fundamental aspect of her character, which will be fully developed later in the film. The two flashbacks to Lavinia and Adam Brant kissing by the seashore, juxtaposed with the romantic liaison between Christine and Adam, firmly establish the romantic/sexual rivalry between mother and daughter. The shot of the exterior of the Mannon house cast in dark shadows, in conjunction with the shadows cast within the house by the candles Christine carries up the stairs, visually underlines the idea of the house as a prison for its inhabitants. Although this episode is concise, visual, and cinematically sound, it remains generally out of keeping with the style of most of the film.

There is only one other episode in the film that is done with similar spatial fluidity and edited so quickly—this is the murder of Adam Brant by his lover's son, Orin (from part 2, act 4 of the play). This murder is one of the melodramatic highpoints of the film, because of Orin's unnatural love for his mother and feeling of sexual rivalry with Brant. The melodrama is intensified by the frenetic style of the cutting and unusual camera angles in the sequence. It involves a great deal of crosscutting from Christine and Adam inside the boat to Orin and Lavinia atop the boat looking down through a window hatch. The extreme overhead shot, from the perspective of Orin and Lavinia, is one of the few striking camera angles in the film. An outline of the cutting of the sequence is as follows:

> Long-shot of Brant's ship—*The Flying Trades*. Lavinia and Orin enter onto the dock. Brant comes out of the ship. Close-up of Orin's pistol. Brant looks around suspiciously, also carrying a gun. Cut to Lavinia and Orin. Brant shouts, "Who's there?" Christine appears on the dock. Brant and Christine meet and embrace. Orin and Lavinia go to cabin door of the ship. Brant and Christine talk as Lavinia and Orin listen to them. Brant and Christine enter the cabin. Overhead shot as Lavinia and Orin watch them. Four crosscuts from Brant and Christine talking to Orin and Lavinia listening. They kiss. Close-up of Orin's expression of repulsion. Christine and Brant leave the ship. Lavinia and Orin steal into Brant's cabin. Brant reenters the room where Orin is hiding behind a door. Orin steps out and shoots Brant in the back. Lavinia returns to the Mannon house; it is again cast in dark, heavy shadows.

The editing is unusually fast in contrast to the general pace of the film; there are some thirty-five shots occupying only ten minutes of running time. The murder of Brant and the sequence depicting Lavinia following her mother stand out dramatically from the rest of the film, which is paced much more slowly—averaging about one shot per minute. These two sequences, while effective in several ways, seem obtrusive and are essentially inconsistent with the style of most of the film.

There are other inconsistencies that weaken the overall effectiveness of the film. The styles of acting of the main characters do not sufficiently blend to create strong ensemble playing. Katina Paxinou, primarily a stage actress, gives a strong performance as Christine, yet her manner is the most highly stylized of the film. She plays Christine with a grandness of gesture suitable to Greek tragedy, which is generally incompatable with the acting styles of the others. (Part of the problem rests with the nature of O'Neill's character.) Also, Michael Redgrave plays his role as Orin in a more typically theatrical manner than does Rosalind Russell as Lavinia, or several of the minor characters in the work. Redgrave is often poignant and convincing as the "haunted" and "hounded" Orestes figure in O'Neill's mythic recreation, yet there is too often an edge of exaggeration in his performance. (Again, part of this problem is written into the character.)

Rosalind Russell as Lavinia and Raymond Massey as Ezra Mannon tend to work in a more realistic style, and the ensemble work is thrown further off balance. Russell's portrayal of Lavinia captures the obsessive dominance of the character—her need to control the fates of others—yet it lacks the deeply neurotic underpinnings of Lavinia's psychology. The realistic bent of Russell's portrayal of Lavinia sometimes makes the character more petulant than tragic. Raymond Massey is suitably and typically saturnine in his portrayal of Ezra Mannon, yet the essentially realistic style of his performance necessarily clashes with the style of Paxinou in their several important scenes together. There is generally a kind of inflated style to most of the acting in the film owing to the mystique of the play itself, which had long been something of a cultural institution. Part of the problem of the inconsistencies of the performances also rests with the original work, which, as suggested earlier, wavers between realism and stylization.

While there is much of value in this adaptation of O'Neill's play in terms of Nichols's careful attention to compositional details, which are used to articulate thematic patterns of the original work, the film is finally only a limited artistic success. There are certain stylistic inconsistencies, such as the jarring contrast between the two opened-up and spatially fluid sequences and the formalized nature of the predominant studio style. There are also discrepancies stemming from the acting in the film as discussed above. Such problems tend to underline the hybrid film/theater nature of the adaptation itself and call attention to difficulties inherent in the original play.

The film was a modest success critically, but was a financial failure, losing much of the $2,250,000 invested in it. Dudley Nichols had hoped that the film would become a "road show with Theatre Guild backing"[15] (prefiguring the phenomenon of the American Film Theatre of the 1970s). But this did not happen. The film was not given any particular support by the Theatre Guild, and it rather quickly sank into oblivion. Nonetheless, its distinction and validity as a judiciously abridged filmed record of O'Neill's important, if ponderous, work is unquestionable. It is further significant that the subject matter and themes of the play could be so closely followed in a Hollywood film. The controversial theme of incest and psychosexual malaise that dominate the play are cogently kept intact. Whereas the controversial elements in *Strange Interlude* had been so bowdlerized in 1933 as to make its film adaptation rather trivial, it is significant that by 1947 *Mourning Becomes Electra* could be filmed without dilution. It is something of a tribute to both Nichols and Hollywood that O'Neill's play could be brought to the screen with its thematic material compressed but essentially unaltered.

NOTES

1. Louis Sheaffer, *O'Neill: Son and Artist* (Boston: Little, Brown & Company, 1973), see pp. 387–90.
2. Barbara and Arthur Gelb, *O'Neill* (New York: Harper's, 1960), p. 857.
3. Sheaffer, p. 547.
4. Robert L. Hatch, *New Republic* 117 (December 8, 1947): 37.
5. William Rose Benét, *Saturday Review* 30 (November 29, 1947): 41.
6. Hermine Rich Isaacs, *Theatre Arts* 32, No. 29 (November 1957): 31.
7. Philip T. Hartung, *Commonweal* 46 (November 28, 1947): 175.
8. Bosley Crowther, *New York Times*, November 20, 1947, p. 38.
9. Hartung, p. 175.
10. Eugene O'Neill, *Mourning Becomes Electra*, in *Nine Plays* (New York: Random House, 1953), p. 687.
11. Ibid., p. 711.
12. John Gassner and Dudley Nichols, *Twenty Best Film Plays* (New York: Crown Publishers, 1943), "The Writer and the Film," by Nichols, p. xxxiii.
13. René Clair, "The Art of Sound," reprinted in *Film: A Montage of Theories* (New York: Dutton, 1966), p. 42.
14. This, and the following chronological listings of shots, is not taken from the film's shooting script, but transcribed from viewings of the film.
15. *Time* 104, no. 24 (November 24, 1947): 103.

7
Desire under the Elms

(1958)

O'Neill's *Desire under the Elms*, the ninth of his plays to reach the screen, was released in 1958, four years after his death. It was produced by Don Hartman, Paramount's executive producer, and directed by Delbert Mann, who had achieved fame for his film *Marty* in 1955, winning the Academy Award for best director. Unfortunately, Mann's treatment of *Desire* lacks the subtle direction and excellent casting of his first and most famous film. The casting of the film was both daring and problematic. Burl Ives, either a jovial and rotund or a sinister and rotund singer-actor, was cast as the gaunt and hard bastion of New England puritanism, Ephraim Cabot. Ives had recently had screen success in the film adaptation of Tennessee Williams's *Cat on a Hot Tin Roof* in the pivotal role of Big Daddy, a role that was more ideally suited to Ives's style and talents. Sophia Loren, the Italian beauty recently imported to Hollywood, was cast in her first serious dramatic role as Cabot's youthful third wife. The play had to be changed to accommodate Miss Loren in the role of Anna (originally Abbie Putman, a New England woman, in O'Neill's play); the New England woman is changed to an Italian immigrant for the film version. But this change is in keeping with a revision that O'Neill had made himself in 1927 in preparing a film scenario of *Desire under the Elms*. O'Neill had changed Abbie into Stephanie, a young and unfortunate immigrant from Hungary. (O'Neill's scenario will be discussed more fully later.)

In the pivotal role of Eben, Cabot's youngest son, who plays Hippolytus to Anna's Phaedra, Tony Perkins was cast. Perkins, like Loren, was a relative newcomer to Hollywood; this was his fourth film and, as one critic suggested, he had been "polished into stardom."[1] It is curious in retrospect to note that Perkins has played the Hippolytus role twice in film, in *Desire* and in Jules Dassin's *Phaedra*, and it becomes even more interesting when his psychotic Oedipal role in Hitchcock's *Psycho* is added to the list. Perkins's image has

DESIRE UNDER THE ELMS (1958) Paramount. Directed by Delbert Mann. With Sophia Loren, Tony Perkins, and Burl Ives. Publicity still from *Desire*—Ephraim observing his new wife Abbie and his son Eben together.)

undeniably been affected by his career subsequent to *Desire;* thus, it is impossible to look at him with the freshness (or naiveté) of the contemporary critics of the film. Perkins's performance was generally lashed by most critics, as were those of the two other principal players in the film. These performances will be looked at in closer detail later.

As mentioned earlier, O'Neill had prepared a scenario of *Desire* for the screen in 1927. In the mid-1920s O'Neill had been interested in and intrigued by Hollywood. The advent of the "talking pictures" made the cinema even more appealing to a dramatist, and later in 1927 O'Neill sent his scenarios of both *Desire* and *The Hairy Ape* to Richard Watts, Jr., of the *New York Herald Tribune* for comments and criticisms and gave Watts permission to discuss them in his column. Watts was most enthusiastic "Regarding Mr. Eugene O'Neill as a Writer for the Cinema,"[2] the title of his article. He called O'Neill's two scenarios "the most important acquisition the motion pictures have made in recent ages." He added that, in O'Neill's reworking of the two plays for film, he has "seriously considered its problems, its potentialities, its requirements, and its limitations" and had rewritten them for "a new field of creative expression." Unfortunately these scenarios are lost, probably burned by O'Neill and Carlotta late in his life when he destroyed many of his works. Both the Sheaffer and the Gelb biographies refer fleetingly to these works, but they only duplicate the information given in Watts's article (i.e., that O'Neill had changed the role of Abbie from a New Englander to a Hungarian immigrant).[3]

According to Watts, O'Neill had made even greater changes in the play for the anticipated screen version. In the play, Abbie, married to the old man Cabot, falls in love with Eben and eventually has a child by him that her husband considered to be his own; she then kills the infant to prove her love for Eben, and both are delivered to justice in the end. In O'Neill's screen treatment, he changes Abbie into the Hungarian immigrant Stephanie, but she does not marry the old man. She merely works as a housekeeper, and plays the three Cabot men off against one another for her love. There is a large mortgage on the farm and Stephanie will marry none of them until he can afford to pay the mortgage. The two older brothers go off to California in search of gold, in hopes of winning the farm and Stephanie. The brothers eventually become rich and kill each other in greed for the other's gold. Left alone with Ephraim and Eben, Stephanie sets the son against the father and finally convinces the youngest son, Eben, to kill his father. In a reversal of the last scene of the play, she finally gives herself up to justice along with her active partner in the crime. Sheaffer, in *O'Neill: Son and Artist,* suggests that in both this screenplay and in *The Hairy Ape* O'Neill aimed at making both the heroines stronger, more culpable, and (quoting O'Neill) "more bitchy."[4] This idea seems slightly to miss the mark. It does not seem that the female protagonist of *Desire* could be seen as stronger, more culpable, or "bitchy" if she has not (1) married the old man for his money; (2) had incestuous relations with her stepson, and (3) killed her own child to prove her love for her stepson/lover.

It seems more likely that O'Neill, fearing the censor's shears and the mass film audience's shock, decided to soften his own psychologically nightmarish play (the plot of which he said came in a dream[5]), which involved both incest and infanticide. Whatever the reasons may have been, it is clear that O'Neill decided to deemphasize the Oedipal theme for the film medium. His instincts seem to have been right, for even as late as 1958, with the Hartman/Mann production of *Desire*, most of the dialogue that stresses the mother/son relationship between Anna and Eben is cut from the film.[6] Both the *Newsweek* review and Stanley Kauffmann in *The New Republic* cite the O'Neill scenario in their pieces on the Mann film of *Desire*. Kauffman says that O'Neill certainly "prettied up the story"[7] and the *Newsweek* reviewer suggests that O'Neill changed Abbie into a "foreigner, apparently feeling that the enchantress's behavior would be more believable to a mass audience which associates New England with Puritanical conduct."[8] Both of these suggestions seem quite right; it is unquestionable that O'Neill felt that his original play was too volatile for film audiences of the late 1920s.

O'Neill's scenario for *Desire* never did reach the screen despite the efforts of Kenneth Macgowan, one of the "triumvirate" of the Greenwich Village Theatre, who, along with O'Neill and Robert Edmund Jones, presented the original production of *Desire* in 1924. Macgowan, in his review of the film version in *Theatre Arts* magazines, mentions that he had tried to interest RKO studios in O'Neill's screen version of *Desire* in 1933.[9] Obviously nothing came of Macgowan's attempts in 1933, just as nothing had come of O'Neill's scenario back in 1927 when he prepared it. Incidentally, this was the only time in O'Neill's career (discounting youthful hack attempts at screenwriting to make money, examined in the introduction of this study) that he ever seriously reconsidered and rewrote any of his own works for the screen. This early shunning by Hollywood probably accounts for some of O'Neill's later hostility toward the film industry.

The film version of *Desire* released in 1958 met with almost unanimous critical rejection. The only positive thing that most critics could say about it was that it was generally faithful to the plot of the play, but even this idea seems to be exaggerated. When one closely compares the film and the play several significant differences emerge. It is, indeed, changed more drastically, both in plot and mood, than one is led to believe from reading the reviews and essays on the film. Reviews in *Time, The New Republic, Newsweek, Theatre Arts, The Nation, Commonweal,* and the *New York Times* all suggest that Irwin Shaw's screenplay alters O'Neill's play only in minor ways. The most obvious changes from the play were noted by most—the addition of a prologue that shows Eben as a child with his mother, both secretly watching old Cabot bury his money (the money that rightfully belongs to Eben's mother); the return of the brothers Simeon and Peter with their wives during the christening celebration; and a suspenseful scene in which Cabot nearly catches the young lovers hiding in the barn. But there are even more important changes made in the transition from stage to screen. Almost all of O'Neill's attempts at creating poetry and local color through dialect are removed from the film (with a few incongruous exceptions to be mentioned later).

The film is set, unexplainably, in 1840 (according to a title at the beginning of the film) rather than in 1850 as O'Neill set it. Changing the period of time to 1840 makes all the references to gold in California absurd since the California gold rush did not begin until 1849. Since there is no possible explanation for the fact that the time is changed to 1840, one might assume that someone simply misread the date of the play. Four characters are added to the film— Min, the widow whom all four of the Cabot men have shared sexually, Florence and Lucinda, the wives of the two older Cabot brothers, and old Cabot's previous wife, whom we meet in the prologue. The "love story" between Anna and Eben is changed, in essence if not in outline, and their romantic escapades are vastly expanded in the film. Although the romantic aspects of Eben and Anna's relationship are expanded, the important sense of the spiritual presence of Eben's real mother and her eventual replacement by Anna are cut from the film.

Finally, the enormous elms of the title have become scrawny studio props, or else are only seen in the photographs of the farm that punctuate the film to suggest changes in the seasons. O'Neill described the elms—the central metaphor of the film—in the following stage direction:

> Two enormous elms are on each side of the house. They bend their trailing branches down over the roof. They appear to protect and at the same time subdue. There is a sinister maternity in their aspect, a crushing jealous absorption. They have developed from their intimate contact with the life of man in the house an appalling humanness. They brood oppressively over the house. They are like exhausted women resting their sagging breasts and hand and hair on its roof, and when it rains their tears trickle down monotonously and rot on the shingles.[10]

Of course, all these qualities are not really manifestable either on stage or on the screen; O'Neill here, as in many of his stage directions, indulges in highly metaphoric rather than realistic scene depiction. Given the vaster spatial scope (not to mention vastly higher budget for scenic design) in films than in the theater, it is odd that so little has been made of the possible imagery of the elms. They are, if anything, less imposing than they would be in a small stage production of the play. The potentially expressive quality of the elms is ignored, their oppressive and menacing aspect cast aside, in favor of using the trees in a much more romantic context. The only time the elms appear at all

Desire under the Elms (1958)

DESIRE UNDER THE ELMS (1958) Paramount. Directed by Delbert Mann. With Sophia Loren and Tony Perkins. (Abbie and Eben in a disproportionately romantic setting.)

real and imposing is in a scene that was added for the film. Following the drastically cut scene between Anna and Eben in the parlor, the room associated with his mother, there is a scene in which Anna and Eben frolic in a meadow and picturesquely stand beneath a magnificent old elm. The outdoor scene is romantic in a visually routine way incongruous with the general nature of the relationship between Anna and Eben, and is at odds with the studio style of most of the film.

All of the shooting for the film was done on a sound stage, with the exception of one day's shooting on location on a ranch outside Santa Monica; and the location and studio scenes are not carefully matched. The attempts to open up the play for filmic treatment, with these infrequent location shots, do not succeed because they merely emphasize the lack of intelligent filmic treatment of the bulk of the film. The necessity of opening up plays for the cinema, as examined in the introduction and in discussions of several other O'Neill adaptations, is at best a shaky proposition. Merely to expand physical space is not necessarily to make a dramatic work more filmic. Either the whole work must be treated in terms of fluid film space, as in *The Long Voyage*

Home, or the confined physical space of the drama must be dynamized through entirely filmic devices (such as camera angle, flatness or depth of field, camera movement, effective close-ups), as in *Long Day's Journey into Night*. This film version of *Desire under the Elms* is too obviously hybrid to be cinematically effective. In this respect it seems stylistically a regression to the style of Nichols's *Mourning Becomes Electra* (1947) or even Brown's *Anna Christie* (1930), but neither of these earlier adaptations had as great problems in dealing with space as does the film of *Desire*.

The reviewer in *Time* magazine suggested that the central problem with the film was that "the vast space of the screen dissipated the atmosphere."[11] The space of the film is not all that vast, but the dramatic and tragic atmosphere is certainly dissipated or conventionalized. While most reviewers primarily faulted the actors, it seems that most of the faults of the film lie with the director. Everything is so conventionalized that, as Hatch pointed out, "there is something wrong at the center of it."[12]

Much of the poetry and tragic dignity of the play has been removed in Irwin Shaw's screenplay, and there is very little else to replace them in the new scenes added to the film. The added scenes—most prominent among them the rather conventional prologue showing Eben and his mother several years before the action of the film begins (which also stresses the Oedipal relationship, later to be abandoned in the film); the return of old Cabot, who nearly discovers his wife and son in the hayloft; the highly romanticized exterior scene between Anna and Eben "in love" beneath an elm tree in a meadow; and the absurdly coincidental return of the elder Cabot brothers on the very day of the christening of their new brother/nephew—all rank as structural and cinematic clichés, attempts to open up the play that serve very little function in the drama. These new scenes, rather than adding to the power of the story itself, become distractions. Contemporary criticism of the film focused on two central problems—its casting and, to a lesser degree, the obvious lack of realism in the sets. But the performances of the three main actors in the film, Ives, Perkins, and Loren, were seen to be the essential cause of its failure. Burl Ives, in particular, was singled out as the greatest weakness in the film. Bosley Crowther struck a note which resounded in most of the other reviews:

> There is something curiously missing . . . something that, by its absence, causes the whole ambitious project to fall flat . . . something that should charge with electricity the terrible events of this drama and give force to its obvious tragedy. . . . That something is the feeling of a menacing and unrelenting fate, suggesting the hardness of nature, that should emerge from the character of the old man.[13]

Stanley Kauffmann damned Ives even further, saying, "He can't act, he only poses."[14] Arthur Knight said that Ives was "weak and doddering, incapable of

Desire under the Elms (1958)

the hard tenacity that the part demanded."[15] John McCarten attacked Ives on his accent, saying that he seemed "just to have come from Missouri."[16] And echoing Crowther's criticism of Ives's stagey style, Phillip Hartung said that he was "mannered and theatrical."[17]

Physical characteristics, as critic John Simon has often maliciously pointed out during the past decade, are immensely important to an actor's success or failure in a film role. Ives is simply physically wrong for the role of Ephraim Cabot. O'Neill described Cabot in the stage directions as

> seventy-five, tall and gaunt, with great, wiry concentrated power, but stoop shouldered from toil. His face is as hard as if it were hewn out of a boulder. His eyes are small, close together and extremely short-sighted, blinking continually in the effort to focus on objects, their stare having a straining, ingrowing quality.[18]

Quite obviously, to anyone who has seen him, Burl Ives has none of these physical characteristics. Ives, forty-eight years old when the film was made, showed no signs of Cabot's advancing years. He was quite the opposite of

DESIRE UNDER THE ELMS (1958) Paramount. Directed by Delbert Mann. With Burl Ives and Sophia Loren.

"gaunt" and "wiry" and showed none of the effects of a life of hard work. Physically Ives was soft and flabby, in conradiction to Cabot's obsession with images of hardness and toughness as the ultimate value in life. This is not to say that physical characteristics can totally determine one's success or failure in a film role, but they certainly are of great importance as filtered through the indomitable and magnifying eye of the camera. Not only were Ives's physical characteristics unsuited to the role, but his acting was out of keeping with both the character he portrayed and with the other actors in the film. Ives was acting in a broad, stylized, and theatrical manner while Loren and Perkins worked in a more intimate, more subtle, more cinematic style. Loren and Perkins, in a sense, played to the close-up, while Ives played to the long shot. His performance seemed oblivious to the camera; it was all played with an exaggeration that would be effective in a large theater, even to people in the back of the house.

Ives, despite the above criticism, does have one moment of partial glory in the film, in a scene that well suits his overall interpretation of the role. During the christening party for the son that Cabot believes he fathered (act 3, scene 2 of the play), he tried to provoke all of the guests to dance in appreciation of his hospitality. Cabot leads the dance as a proof of his strength and vigor. Interspersed with his avowals of physical prowess—boasts of defeating an Indian tribe with an arrow in his back, promises to live to be a hundred years old, and claims of being the only "man in the county"—he dances an absurd and frenetic dance. O'Neill had described Cabot's dance as showing "tremendous vigor . . . he begins to improvise, cuts incredible grotesque capers, leaping up and kicking his heels together . . . like a monkey on a string."[19] Ives certainly captures all of these qualities, but the scene in the film becomes so overplayed and visually busy that it tends toward comic exaggeration. Cabot swings on the beams of the porch of the house; he swings women around by their waists and drops them; he turns cartwheels; and finally, overcome with exhaustion and a hint of the ridiculousness of the whole affair, he goes to the barn to find peace with the animals. This scene, perhaps more than any other, reflects all that is right and wrong with Ives's performance as Cabot. He has the brio and bravura that Cabot demands as a character, but the exaggeration in Ives's capers lessens his effectiveness as the serious, tragic figure that O'Neill has envisioned.

Sophia Loren, in her fourth film during the first two years she spent in Hollywood (which reflects her box-office success), was surprisingly good and fared far better than did Ives with the film's critics. In 1961, three years after the filming of *Desire*, Loren was recognized by the Hollywood establishment as a fine actress, receiving an Academy Award for *Two Women*. But at the time that Mann made *Desire* she was considered merely a sultry Italian beauty. Disregarding such stereotyping, several critics found her to be the best performer in the film. Among them was Stanley Kauffmann. In his review Kauffmann said that Loren is "quite convincing as a woman who has been used harshly by men and who means to be revenged on the world through this marriage, but who is confounded by falling in love."[20] Bosley Crowther saw Loren's performance as capturing both the scheming and feeling sides of the character. He said that "she is initially the spitfire who can tempt the wild young man with cogent wiles. Then she dissolves into a woman who is raptly and recklessly in love."[21] Arthur Knight, on the other hand, suggested that Loren's performance, while "admirably controlled," was inadequate since it suggested neither "a schemer plotting to acquire old Cabot's acres for herself, or a frantic, love-starved woman," but "a femme fatale of innumerable Italian movies, the woman who attracts all men in spite of herself."[22] This criticism seems unfair to Loren's performance, since during the first half of the film she is every bit the selfish schemer, and Simeon, Peter, and Eben clearly recognize this and hate her for it. Loren's Anna is transparently deliberate and conscious in exciting feelings only when they are to her own advantage. Kenneth Macgowan, who would have been most familiar with the play, having been involved with its original production in 1924, makes a simple but astute point about Loren's performance in his *Theatre Arts* review. He points out that Loren's performance is not "maternal" but that she "isn't asked to be motherly." He goes on to say that "the script demands a great deal else of her, and she gives a fuller, deeper performance than she has ever achieved."[23] Macgowan's point is an important one. The film version has indeed removed most of the lines that suggest that Anna will symbolically take the place of Eben's own mother; hence, Loren does not, and need not, project the same maternal qualities that are present in the play. Another significant fact here is that in the film version Anna is presented as twenty-five years old, whereas in O'Neill's play Abbie is thirty-five. This ten-year difference is enough to demand significant modifications in the relationship between Eben and Anna.

Physically Loren is very well suited to the character O'Neill describes in the stage directions of the play. He said that the young woman is

> buxom, full of vitality. Her face is pretty but marred by its gross sensuality. There is a strength and obstinacy in her jaw, a hard determination in her eyes, and about her whole personality the same unsettled, untamed desperate quality which is so apparent in Eben.[24]

Director Mann has emphasized and exploited Loren's youthfulness (she was twenty-four years old when the film was made) and beauty throughout the film. All of her costumes emphasize the contours of her body; during the scene in which she first tries to seduce Eben she wears a see-through lace blouse which seems anachronistic to the period of 1840. She never shows any visible signs of her pregnancy, and a week after the child is born she is again wearing a tightly cinched dress. Her role in the film is generally glamorized and romanticized, especially in her relationship with Perkins. Yet, despite this romanticizing, Loren succeeds in manifesting much of the single-purposed

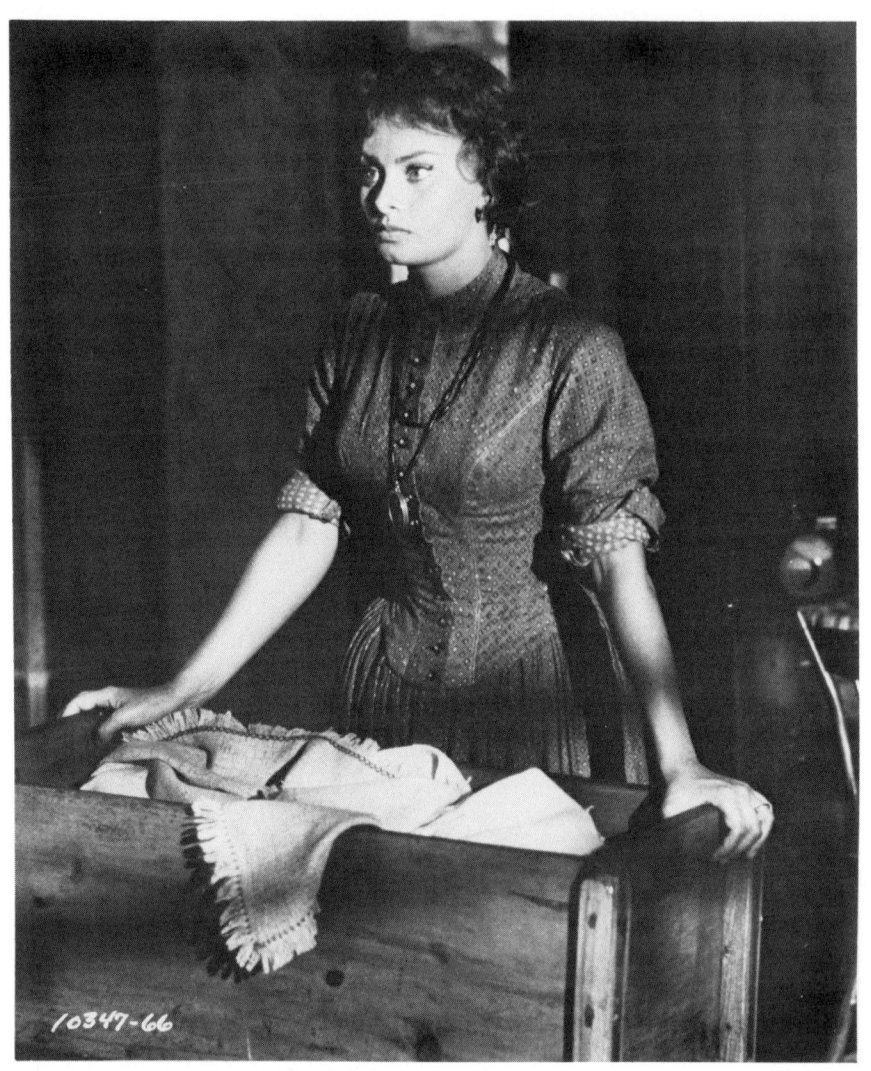

DESIRE UNDER THE ELMS (1958) Paramount. Directed by Delbert Mann. With Sophia Loren. (Abbie contemplates the murder of her child.)

Desire under the Elms (1958)

greed which is necessary for the credibility of her role. Typical of Mann's rather heavy-handed direction of Loren is the visual business she is made to do during her first attempt at seducing Eben. As she stands on the porch of the farmhouse, talking to Eben about the sun and "the forces of nature," she fondles and caresses a pillar that supports the roof of her porch. The effects of these gestures, with their obvious sexual implications, have often evoked the laughter of audiences seeing the film. The power of the language (taken almost directly from act 1, scene 4 of the play) is greatly dissipated and the speech becomes ludicrous because of the cliché-ridden nature of the visual business. Loren's triumphs in the film occur in the most poignant and quietly dramatic scenes, such as her fearful announcement to Eben that she has killed the baby, and the following scene, in which she tells Cabot that the baby is dead. In both scenes she emerges as a profoundly confused, hopelessly passionate, and guilt-ridden woman. Her acting in both cases is skillfully suited to the intimacy and magnification of the camera.

Tony Perkins, in the role of Eben, is also physically well suited to the role. O'Neill described Eben as

> twenty-five, tall and sinewy. His face is well formed, and good looking, but its expression is resentful and defensive. His defiant dark eyes remind one of a wild animal's in captivity. . . .There is a fierce repressed vitality about him.[25]

Perkins, twenty-six when the film was made, embodies all of the physical traits that O'Neill has ascribed to Eben; he is "tall and sinewy" and does have a resentful and defensive quality about him. Perkins, later famous for his neurotic and psychotic roles, succeeds in emphasizing the nervous and repressed qualities of the character. What he lacks, however, is much of the strength and determination of Eben, a point of criticism suggested in several reviews of the film. Perkins lacks Eben's single-minded and obsessive greed. Nonetheless, Perkins's performance is generally subtle, sensitive, and strongly individualized. Perkins and Loren are reasonably successful in the picture, while Ives is not, mainly because they are working in a style more appropriate to the cinema, and because they are better suited physically to their roles.

In general, the chief problem with the acting seems to lie with the director rather than with the performers. There is too much discrepancy and inconsistency in the styles of performance in the film. Loren's and Perkins's style is incompatible with that of Ives. The older brothers, Simeon and Peter, as played by Frank Overton and Pernell Roberts, are also acted in a broad and stagey style, their lines declaimed rather than spoken. The inconsistencies become even more pronounced when we add to the list the wives of the two brothers (who return to the farm with them in a scene which is added to the film). Rebecca Welles and Jean Willia, who play the Cabot wives, Lucinda and Florence, are radically out of keeping with the acting styles of the other performers. They have neither the presence of Ives (or Overton or Roberts) nor the subtlety of Loren and Perkins. They also seem quite anachronistic to the period of 1840 in their clothing, hairstyling, and general manners. The incongruities grow when, during the christening party, some of the neighbors speak in New England dialect and some do not. Finally, the sheriff, who comes to take Eben and Anna to prison, speaks the last line of the play—"It's a jim-dandy farm, no denyin' it—wish it was mine"—in a strict New Englandese such as has not been heard anywhere else in the film. The mélange of acting styles and accents make it almost impossible for the viewer to take the grim tragedy seriously.

The problems with the conflicting acting styles in the film are characteristic of more central problems—those of spatial inconsistency and the lack of pictorial realism. The film is neither shot on appropriate locations to give it spatial realism, nor is it entirely done in a studio to underline the stylized quality of the play; instead, Mann has settled on a compromise. The compromise results in what Arthur Knight called "studio realism—always antiseptic, sparkling, and singularly unconvincing."[26] The hybrid quality of the film's space is palpably presented right from the opening sequence of the film. The film begins with the titles superimposed over a full-screen photograph of the Cabot farm in autumn. The stylization of the still photograph might be acceptable were it not for the "real" leaves which we see falling in front of the photograph. This discrepancy sets the tone for similar problems throughout the film.

Most of the exterior scenes are shot in a studio with painted backdrops for the mountains and trees that surround the farm. The bogus quality of the backdrops is further underlined by attempts at spatial realism (rocks, gravel, grass, etc.) in the foreground of the scenes. Other attempts at realistic details of farm life, such as the occasionally seen horses and cows in front of the farm and in the barn, merely emphasize the lack of convincing realism in the sets that surround them. The interior scenes in the film share some of the same dificulties as the exteriors. Scenes that take place in the kitchen, the bedrooms, or the parlor of the farm are lighted in ways that are obviously more appropriate to the stage than to the screen. Several times, in fact, we will see characters casting two distinct shadows where there is, realistically, only one light source in the room. In an essentially realistic film, attention must be paid to details of space and lighting and disregard of these details demonstrates the visual carelessness in Mann's film. One inexcusable realistic lapse occurs in the third scene in the film. The Cabot sons are piling rocks and discussing the farm and its future ownership; at two points in the scene the microphone is seen clearly bobbing down into the top of the frame. Another indication of the lack of attention to details of space occurs in a barn scene toward the end of the film. Eben is confronting Anna, accusing her of using him only to get a son to inherit the farm. Emotionally, it is a highly charged scene (in this scene

Anna decides to kill the baby to prove her love for Eben). As Anna and Eben are emotionally lashing away at each other, a cow, in the background of the shot, decides to lie down. The movement of the cow within the frame is not only irrelevant and distracting, but it also creates an unintentional bit of comic undercutting to the drama going on in the scene. Doubtless this is a small point, but it gives an obvious example of other similar, if less evident, flaws in the film's attention to details of space and effective imagery. Another scene weakened by visual business is the one that functions as a prelude to Anna's seduction of Eben. Early in the film Anna is newly arrived at the Cabot farm and is feeding chickens, significantly throwing seeds of grain from the clutched lap of her skirt; she discovers Eben, shirtless, chopping wood—the obviousness of the sexual imagery lessens rather than enhances the drama of the scene.

The filmically clichéd nature of these sequences, along with the generally pedestrian quality of Daniel Fapp's photography and the highly exaggerated melodramatic music of Elmer Bernstein, tend to lessen the dramatic and emotional power. Bernstein's music, large and symphonic, is self-consciously overused in the film. Nearly all the moments of tension and suspense are orchestrated, and too much of the dialogue is accompanied by background music. The soundtrack, like the screenplay and the general direction of the film, tends to overemphasize the melodramatic qualities already present in O'Neill's text. It is ultimately the broadness and heavy-handedness of the treatment of the story along with the incongruities in the styles of acting and treatment of space that account for the film's failure. The whole film is rather like the bizarrely manic dance that old Cabot does during the christening scene—potentially powerful, but exaggerated ludicrously.

NOTES

1. Robert Hatch, *Nation* 186 (April 5, 1958): 304.
2. Richard Watts, Jr., *New York Herald Tribune*, November 7, 1927.
3. The information given in Watts's article is repeated in the Sheaffer biography, *O'Neill: Son and Artist* (Boston: Little, Brown and Company, 1973), p. 352; and in the biography by Arthur and Barbara Gelb, *O'Neill* (New York: Harpers, 1960), p. 718.
4. Sheaffer, p. 352.
5. Gelb, pp. 538–39.
6. Another example of the removal of Oedipal implications from the film is the revision of act 2, scene 3 of the play. In O'Neill's scene Eben dresses in his "best Sunday clothes" before going to the parlor to meet Abbie (this room is associated with his mother and was, in fact, the room where her body was laid out). The film, in cutting Eben's dressing for the encounter, removes the implication that Eben is profoundly remembering his mother as he goes to meet his stepmother.
7. Stanley Kauffmann, *New Republic* 138 (April 7, 1958): 23.
8. *Newsweek* 51 (March 17, 1958): 106.
9. Kenneth Macgowan, *Theatre Arts* 42 (April 1958): 81.
10. Eugene O'Neill, *Desire under the Elms*, in *Nine Plays* (New York: Random House, 1954), p. 206.
11. *Time* 71 (March 17, 1958): 106. The film was shot in a process called VistaVision, which was Paramount's answer to Cinemascope. VistaVision is a nonanamorphic process that allows distributors to

choose their own ratio of projection—either 4 × 3 or 2 × 1—this meant that no essential action should be included in either the top or the bottom of the frame. The *Time* review, in commenting on the vastness of space, implies that the film was originally shown in the simulated Cinemascope proportions of 2 × 1; prints of the film in 16mm have the usual proportions of 4 × 3. Some of the spatial problems of the film may be due to the limitations of VistaVision.

12. Hatch, p. 304.
13. Bosley Crowther, *New York Times*, March 13, 1958, p. 13.
14. Kauffmann, p. 22.
15. Arthur Knight, *Saturday Review* 41 (March 18, 1958): 55.
16. John McCarten, *New Yorker* 34 (March 22, 1958): 95.
17. Phillip Hartung, *Commonweal* 67 (March 22, 1958): 734.
18. O'Neill, *Nine Plays*, p. 155.
19. O'Neill, *Nine Plays*, p. 187.
20. Kauffmann, p. 23.
21. Crowther, p. 24.
22. Knight, p. 55.
23. Macgowan, p. 80.
24. O'Neill, *Nine Plays*, p. 155.
25. Ibid., p. 137.
26. Knight, p. 41.

8
Long Day's Journey into Night

(1962)

That *Long Day's Journey into Night* should ever have been adapted to film is something of a wonder, considering the unusual history of its publication. According to O'Neill's directions upon depositing the sealed manuscript of the play with Bennett Cerf at Random House in 1945, it was not to be opened or looked at until twenty-five years after his death. At that time the play could be published, but never, according to O'Neill's wishes, was it to be performed on stage.[1] Only three years after his death the play was both published and being performed on stage in New York; and only nine years after O'Neill's death his work, "written in blood and tears' as he wrote in the dedication to his wife, Carlotta, was being shown nationally in the mass medium of film, which he had never much respected. O'Neill understandably felt so close to the characters in this painfully autobiographical work that he could not even imagine actors impersonating them on stage. Ironically, the adaptation that O'Neill most likely would not have allowed to be made became one of the most artistically successful film versions of his work.

The Ely Landau–produced, Sidney Lumet–directed version of *Long Day's Journey into Night* is something of a rarity among American films. Unlike most other Hollywood films, it was made at the surprisingly low cost of $435,000, and it was shot in sequence during a thirty-seven-day shooting schedule, after a three-week rehearsal period. These facts would be less noteworthy if it were merely a filmed stage play, but it decidedly is not. While it has much in common with the static and spatially confined elements of the filmed stage play, it manages to transcend these limitations and, in fact, works toward questioning the validity of commonly accepted theories about the process of adaptation.

Criticism of the film was sharply divided. Most critics either liked it totally or disliked it totally. Only three of the fourteen reviews I have surveyed had substantially ambivalent feeling about the film. Reactions to it seem to be dependent on the critics' previous notions of what is and is not acceptable or "cinematic" in a film adaptation of a play. A look at a sampling of the negative reactions to the film is enlightening in this regard. Moira Walsh boldly says that "it is not a motion picture at all. Rather it is a faithful screen transcription of a play which would seem, on its face, to be peculiarly unsuited to the screen."[2] Jay Jacobs says that it is "oblivious to the unique demands of the film medium and is a crashing three-hour bore."[3] Jacobs's "unique demands" of the cinema are not clear, but they seem to have to do with the primacy of the visual over the verbal element in film. He says that "the dynamics [i.e., verbal elements] are not transferrable to the screen when the static physical structure of the stage is maintained." This seems to suggest that any film involving essentially only one locale cannot possibly be a good film, which is not to take into account the particular film and its own particular dynamics.[4]

Jacobs compares the film to a beached whale that "stretches out at grotesque length, gray, and inert . . . hauled bodily from its natural element." Jacobs may have been influenced by the same image used earlier by Stanley Kauffmann. Kauffmann said, "This theatrical whale has been stranded on the beach of another medium."[5] Kauffmann didn't like either the film or the play very much. He criticizes the play because of its factual errors, objecting to the author's telescoping of events that took place over a long period of time into a single day. This seems to be a too literal-minded approach to drama and one that would discredit many fine theatrical works, including most of Greek tragedy. Kauffmann goes so far as to say categorically that the play is "unadaptable to film," implying that there are types of plays that are clearly "adaptable" and those that are clearly "unadaptable" to film.

The single locale of the film, often referred to as the static spatial quality, was considered a great flaw. There seems to be some confusion between the element of space (in the ordinary physical sense of locale) and filmic space, which is the total compositional area within the frame in which the camera and actors can move.[6] Robert L. Hatch seems to confuse these two notions of space "The camera has nothing to do in such small space and jitters about looking for 'interesting' shots."[7] This would suggest an almost direct proportion between the amount of space available and the aesthetic quality of its use, which certainly has been disproven by filmmakers such as Dreyer, Ozu, and Bergman, for example. Hatch goes on to make the curious assertion that "it is the essential nature of the camera to follow people through doors and about town."[8] There are ample opportunities for this in *Long Day's Journey*: Edmund's visit to the doctor, Mary's trip to the drugstore for morphine, and Jamie's visit to the bordello, but these excursions away from the house would break the essential continuity of the work, which is built upon the emotional clashes between characters. It is, of course, easier in film than on the stage for the director to "follow people through doors and about town," but this certainly is not absolutely essential to film dynamics.

The question of opening up the play for film treatment is an essential consideration in most stage-to-screen adaptations. As discussed elsewhere in this study, it should not be axiomatic that to move outside the restrictions of confined physical space is necessarily to improve a work cinematically. The treatment of space ought rather to depend on the nature and themes of the work being adapted. The cinematic viability of spatial confinement is central to an understanding or analysis of *Long Day's Journey*, a work dependent on the dynamics of the struggle among individual characters, wills, and egos within the house that seems to imprison them. For this reason only the first scene of the film takes place outdoors. Lumet has said that his was "not the usual movie thing of 'breaking it out,'" but rather a visual way of intensifying the subsequent progression, or journey, into darkness. The titles are, in fact, superimposed over a blindingly overexposed shot of the sun to contrast further with the subsequent development of the film. The physical brightness of the first scene of the film underscores the tone of the sequence: it is the lightest and most jovial encounter among the Tyrones that we will see in the film. From this point on all of the action takes place within the confines of the house, and Lumet not only uses this confinement to his advantage but emphasizes it thematically with a series of images, suggesting the idea of entrapment.

Throughout the film Lumet insists that the four characters are not only confined but metaphorically imprisoned within the walls of the house and within their own problematic egos. He manages to present this idea in visual terms through the set design and by the way in which the interior of the house is photographed. The interior of the house is incredibly cluttered with objects, which seem further to confine the characters. Whereas O'Neill's stage directions suggest only a few essential pieces of furniture and props, Lumet has filled the space with tables, chairs, books, bric-à-brac, and the like, and the set is convincingly realistic. Lumet uses architectural details of the house to reinforce visually the idea of entrapment. The filigree work that surrounds all of the doorways and arches in the house is frequently photographed to create the image of prison bars.

The stairway leading to the second floor, with its closely set and ornate stair railings, is often photographed to create another image of entrapment. The preponderance of wicker furniture (with its crisscross weaving) and the beaded curtains in several doorways again contribute to the sense of imprisonment. A key example of this use of imagery occurs when Mary is left alone in the house: she is sitting on the first stair landing and says pitifully, "Oh God, why do I feel so lonely?"[9] (act 2). As she says this, we are watching her from behind the bars of the stair railing, emphasizing the fact that she is not only alone but trapped in this loneliness, trapped in the house, and trapped within herself. During the later scenes in the film, when Mary is upstairs (in the "spare room," where she keeps her morphine hidden), the three Tyrone men are downstairs wondering and worrying about her. Whenever there is a noise from upstairs, they turn toward the stairs, and the camera frames in on the

LONG DAY'S JOURNEY INTO NIGHT (1962) Embassy Pictures. Directed by Sidney Lumet. With Ralph Richardson, Dean Stockwell, and Katharine Hepburn. (Architectural details visually reinforce the idea of entrapment.)

bars of the stair railings; they, as well as Mary, are imprisoned within the house and within themselves, and the bars separating Mary from the rest of the family emphasize the isolation between them.

Lumet further accentuates the theme of imprisonment in the way several of the windows in the house are used in the composition of shots. O'Neill had envisioned the windows in the set as important metaphors for the action of the play. In his opening stage directions he notes that there are two sets of triple windows on either side of the Tyrone living room. As the play moves from the first act to the fourth, the light from the windows diminishes and the density of the fog increases. (Briefly, the stage directions indicate: Act 1: 8:30 A.M., bright sunlight streams in each window; Act 2: 12:45 P.M., light softened by slight haze; Act 3: 6:30 P.M., early dusk owing to fog; Act 4: midnight, a wall of fog, denser than ever.) O'Neill has carefully worked out lighting effects that mirror the emotional and psychological movement of the action of the play; the movement to darkness and the increase of the fog represent the progressive darkness of the psyches of the characters. By setting the first scene of the film outdoors, this sequential light imagery is augmented, and the windows in the house become an important metaphorical element. As in the play, the changes

Long Day's Journey into Night (1962)

in light seen through the windows suggest psychological changes in the characters; and, in addition, the windows are used further to underscore the imagery of imprisonment.

At moments of key emotional crisis during the first half of the film, Lumet shoots the scene with the camera facing one or more of the windows of the house. For example, during the first direct confrontation between Edmund and Mary over the fact that he may indeed be suffering from consumption, the camera frames both Edmund and Mary in front of a pair of windows in the background. Edmund tries to force his mother to realize the fact that he may have to go to a sanitorium. His leaving would be a kind of freedom from the immuration in the Tyrone house, but at the same time he feels trapped by the disease, which at this point he considers to be fatal. During several encounters between Mary and either James or Jamie about her return to the use of morphine, the characters are photographed against the windows, ironically underlining the fact that Mary is trapped within her own habit and habitation.

Byron Bentley made an insightful point about the confined space of the film. He suggested that the success of the film adaptation of this play would depend

LONG DAY'S JOURNEY INTO NIGHT (1962) Embassy Pictures. Directed by Sidney Lumet. With Jason Robards, Jr., Dean Stockwell, Katharine Hepburn, and Ralph Richardson. (Jamie, Edmund, and Mary confront the penny-pinching Tyrone.)

on the "extent to which the director heightens the illusion of inescapable reality." He goes on to point out:

> Just as O'Neill telescoped the events of months into a single day, so Lumet has compressed a whole world of anguish into one house and a patch of garden. We catch glimpses of the city beyond . . . but we only see these things in relation to the suffocating tensions of the house itself.[10]

As suggested above in the discussion of the effective visual imagery, it need not necessarily follow that confined physical space is uncinematic. Lumet, in a lengthy 1971 interview in *Film Quarterly*, elucidates the highly deliberate filmic nature of his adaptation. He says that he and his photographer, Boris Kaufman, concentrated on creating precise visual equivalents for the theatrical dynamics of O'Neill's play through the exact lighting control, careful selection of lenses with the appropriate depth of field, subtly differing camera angles, and editing rhythms appropriate to each character. These four important elements suggest the scrupulousness of Lumet's rethinking and reworking of the play for film, even though the effects are subtle and there is an apparent lack of technique. A brief summary of these ideas will suffice to demonstrate the ways in which he completely thought through the production for film.

Lumet said that lighting is "one of the key ways in which one extracts the meaning of the drama." Whether the director chooses to use key or filter lighting is integrally related to the mood and dramatic tension of a given scene, and he suggested that a great deal of the success of the film is due to the ability of the photographer, Kaufman, "to translate dramatic situations into the gray scale." He said that he created a "lens plot" for the film, and each character was filmed according to a preplanned progression in lenses. For example, in filming Katharine Hepburn as Mary, he used increasingly longer and longer lenses (i.e., telephoto), and the corresponding loss of depth of field (or clear focus of objects in the background) worked further to isolate her in her own world. With the characters of Jamie and Tyrone, wider and wider lenses were used as the film progressed. The greater depth of field achieved in the filming of these two characters suggests that they, in Lumet's words, "have more life to them." The increasing width of the lenses used also worked in another way, because of the distortion produced by wide-angle lenses. During the argument between Jamie and Tyrone near the end of the film, for example, an 18mm lens was used and the slight distortion it produced worked to underline "an increased hostility, an increased violence, and increase in the change of emotions the two characters were feeling." With the character of Edmund, the fewest lens changes were used, in order to keep him "objective," since he felt that Edmund "tries to play the observer but is, in actuality, the victim in many instances."[11]

Lumet's manipulation of space through technical means clearly illustrates the fact that even within a confined physical or realistic space, the cinema director can energize (or "dynamize," in Panofsky's phrase) the spatial element of the film. Filmic space can also be dynamized by the use of altering camera angles. Lumet gives only two examples of this in his treatment of *Long Day's Journey*. He points out that Mary is filmed from increasingly high angles, that Jamie and Tyrone are filmed from increasingly low angles, and that Edmund is filmed from a generally consistent eye-level point of view. He does not, in the interview, explain the significance of these points of view, but it would seem to go along with the ideas of each character that he suggested in his selection of lenses. Photographing Mary from higher and higher angles would tend to diminish her size on the screen as she becomes more and more lost within her own world. Photographing Jamie and Tyrone from lower and lower angles would tend to magnify their size and to magnify the nature of their conflicts. Low-angle camera shots generally tend to give a character a hostile or menacing quality, and it is important to note that Jamie is most often photographed from the lowest angle of all, especially in the scenes from the fourth act of the play.

Finally, in regard to the film's editing, Lumet pointed out that its cutting basically followed the sequential shooting, and that no structural alterations were necessary. More significantly, a particular cutting rhythm for each character was decided upon before beginning filming. Mary was filmed almost exclusively in long takes, and her speeches in the film are rarely interrupted by reaction shots, since he considered her character "legato." Jamie and Tyrone, on the other hand, are seen as "staccato." Jamie, Lumet said, "interrupts, and wants to be interrupted, wants conflict—he lives staccato."[12] Such consideration of editing—as well as of lighting, compositional perspective through lens changes, and camera angles suited to each character, as mentioned earlier—would seem to suggest clearly the ways in which *Long Day's Journey* was reworked into filmic form, employing devices intrinsic to the medium.

Long Day's Journey is a work built around the profound, complex, and painful tensions that exist among the four Tyrones. In successfully adapting this play to the screen, it is essential that the director find visual equivalents for the dramatic tensions. Lumet's direction of the film evidences several ways in which these tensions have been made palpable. One such way is the compositional arrangement of characters and objects within the image. A point overlooked in the criticism of this film generally is the fact that Lumet has emphasized diagonal lines in the composition of the film. An unusually high percentage of shots are actually done with the camera slightly tilted from the vertical. Diagonal compositions or slightly tilted camera angles in this film, as well as many other films, generally suggest tension, friction, or disharmony. (This same technique was used quite effectively, if somewhat more obviously, by Welles in *Citizen Kane*, Reed in *The Third Man*, Ray in *Rebel without a Cause*, and by Kazan in both *East of Eden* and *A Streetcar*

Named Desire, to cite just a few comparisons.) Three examples will illustrate Lumet's use of this diagonal compositional arrangement for emotional effect.

During the first confrontation between Edmund and Mary over her return to the use of morphine, Edmund is in the bottom left corner of the screen while Mary is in the upper right corner. The diagonal thrust of the shot underscores the tension and disjunction of both characters. One scene, between Mary and the maid, Kathleen, alone together while the three men are out, is likewise interesting in terms of compositional values. The scene begins lightheartedly as Mary reminisces about her past and her romantic first encounter with James Tyrone (from act 3 of the play). As they talk they both become increasingly inebriated from straight gin. Mary's fond reminiscences become more and more painful in their glaring contrast to her present situation. The shots become more and more diagonally composed and less conventionally symmetrical. The film alternates between shots of Mary in foreground right and Kathleen in background left and vice versa. At one point toward the end of the conversation, we see only Kathleen's arm in the extreme foreground holding a glass of gin, and Mary in the background in the opposite corner of the screen. The shooting of the scene becomes more and more askew, and finally Mary falls off the chair she has been sitting on and sprawls diagonally across the screen.

A final example of Lumet's highly dramatic use of space occurs in the final confrontation between Jamie and Edmund (act 4), in which Jamie drunkenly confesses his uncontrollable hostilities toward Edmund. Jamie and Edmund are seen lying on the wicker couch with their heads at opposite ends, and the couch is photographed so that it crosses the screen diagonally, and the camera is slightly tilted from its vertical axis. At the climactic moment of Jamie's speech, when he admits that a part of him would like to see his brother die, Edmund jumps up and stands on the couch; and the camera follows this movement from a high angle with an extreme tilt to the shot. The rest of the scene is photographed in this unusually asymmetrical way. Again, the diagonal structuring of the compositions and the unusual tilts of the camera contribute to the emotional impact of the scene.

In keeping with the above-described functional use of camera positioning is Lumet's equally appropriate use of camera movement. This was one of the most seriously criticized aspects of the film among its first reviewers. Those who did not like the film found the camera movement excessive; Hatch observed that "the camera . . . jitters about looking for 'interesting' shots."[13] John Simon declared that the "camera paces relentlessly" and Stanley Kauffmann suggested that Lumet "tries to supply missing cinema motion with camera motion."[14] Such attitudes seem unjust when one examines more carefully the functional quality of the camera's movement in the film. Neither is the camera movement so overused as suggested above, since many entire sequences are photographed from a static position with no movement at all.

Graham Petrie, in an article on Lumet in *Film Quarterly*, makes some

LONG DAY'S JOURNEY INTO NIGHT (1962) Embassy Pictures. Directed by Sidney Lumet. With Dean Stockwell, Ralph Richardson, and Jason Robards, Jr. (The Tyrone men united briefly by alcohol and books.)

important general points about the camerawork in the film. Contrary to critics who found the camerawork too busy, Petrie argues:

> The camera moves freely when required, but is not afraid to film many speeches from a purely static set-up, with the result that the camerawork is never a distraction from the vigor and meaning of the language. . . . Instead Lumet uses the camera to underline the emotional tone of the dialogue, isolating the characters from one another through close-ups, joining them together for brief moments of harmony and understanding, distancing them and studying them dispassionately during the pauses of drained and exhausted vitality which . . . punctuate the series of emotional clashes which constitute the structure of the film.[15]

The camerawork in the film, as Petrie suggests, is anything but frenetic. Most of the cutting of the film is done in rather long takes, longer than most film audiences are used to. As Lumet explained in the *Film Quarterly* interview, the cutting of the character of Mary is done with the longest takes of all, but even with the more "staccato" characters (such as Jamie), the cutting is seldom frenetic. Each character in the play (and film) has his or her moments of power, of psychological triumph over one or more of the other characters, and the long speeches, which generally accompany these moments, are filmed with correspondingly long takes and basically static camera positioning. There is undoubtedly a great deal of camera movement in the film, but most of it is extremely slow, at times almost imperceptible; and, upon close analysis, one finds that the camera movement is essential to the rhythms of the film and to the overall pace of its editing.

Lumet and Boris Kaufman use camera movement as a significant means of blocking or grouping characters on the screen. Many shots involve very slow tracking, panning, or zooming movements, which either change the balance of the shot or, through the movement and change in perspective, exclude one or more of the characters previously in the shot. In such shots the camera movement serves a double function: there is first of all the intrinsic visual interest of the slightly altering perspective within the confined space and, second, the dramatic focusing of the center of interest of the shot. Several times during the filming of Mary's long speeches, the camera very slowly zooms in to a close-up of her, thereby removing the listening characters from our vision. Isolating Mary within the frame of the shot serves to emphasize her isolation from the rest of the family. In a scene from act 3 of the play, in which Mary reminisces about her past to the servant Kathleen, as Mary speaks the camera zooms in remarkably slowly, cutting Kathleen out of the shot and focusing on the complexities of Mary's emotions during the reminiscence. The slowness of the zoom seems to draw us deeper and deeper into her mind, while we are almost unaware that this change in perspective is happening.

Similarly, as Edmund muses to his father about his glorious past days at sea (in Edmund's most lyrical and moving long speech in the play, the one in which O'Neill, incidentally, speaks most compellingly of his own wistful feelings toward the sea), the camera slowly zooms in, framing Edmund's face into a tighter and tighter close-up. Here again, the listener—Tyrone—is removed from the shot and from our concentration. It is only the speaker who is of importance in these moments of deep self-absorption and self-revelation. While both of these long speeches are addressed to someone else, they become almost soliloquies, as each character searches for understanding of his own life. The camera can focus and intensify such moments.

James Tyrone's profoundest moment of soul searching comes toward the end of the film, when, aided by the mellowing effect of alcohol, he tries to explain and justify his life to his son Edmund and to himself as well. The scene, as superbly played by Ralph Richardson and heightened by the way it is shot, is worth looking at in detail. Tyrone is trying to communicate to his son the hard lessons that life has taught him about "the value of a dollar," rationalizing the fact that his career as an actor has been an artistic failure, although financially successful. The past becomes alive in Tyrone's mind in this scene; he fondly recalls the praise that he once received from Edwin Booth, and looks back nostalgically at the fact that he might have been one of the "greatest actors of his lifetime." As the scene begins, we see Tyrone combing an old theatrical wig on a wig form, nowhere suggested in the play's stage directions; this visual business works very well as the scene develops on film.

The old wig becomes a metaphor for the dead past and the lost promises of Tyrone's artistic life as an actor. Throughout his speech, Lumet intercuts shots of Tyrone combing the wig as he speaks, and the action reinforces the verbal content of the scene.[16] It also clearly presents to us visually the image of Tyrone, as O'Neill described him in the opening stage directions to act 4: "a sad, defeated old man, possessed by hopeless resignation."[17] He is trapped within the contradictions of his own nature. He is profoundly questioning the desire for money that has ruined his career. His dreams and ambitions of the past are alive, yet at the same time he is unable to refrain from turning out the light bulbs in the lamp over the table to save money. The visual structuring of this scene is noteworthy.

Tyrone had earlier turned on three lights above the table, vainly attempting to prove his generosity. Minutes later, at the end of his speech on the value of a dollar, his compulsive miserliness resurfaces, and he says he must turn the lights out because the glare hurts his eyes. He must awkwardly stand on a chair to shut each of the lights. The scene is shot from a high angle, tilting down on Tyrone and the light fixture. "No, I don't know what the hell it was I wanted to buy," he says as he turns off the first light. "I'd be willing to have no home but the poorhouse if I could look back now on having been the fine artist I might have been," Tyrone continues, ironically, as he turns out the remaining two lights. Edmund cannot resist responding to the absurd irony of the situation and laughs. Tyrone is hurt and asks what he is laughing at. "Not at you, Papa. At life. It's so damned crazy."[18] The down angles and close-up shots of Tyrone during these moments of self-revelation are compelling, and lighting further contributes to the effect. As Tyrone switches off each bulb, his face, seen in close-up, becomes darker and darker, reinforcing the hopeless absurdity of the situation.

Effective visual imagery such as the examples give above is subtle and unobtrusive in Lumet's handling of the film, and this is certainly appropriate to his design in the entire film. Lumet, as mentioned earlier, said his greatest achievement, and that of the photographer Kaufman, was that the "art of the film is . . . that no techniques ever show." This is generally true but for two important and controversial sequences in which Lumet uses deliberately obtrusive techniques. The first is a 360-degree panning shot which follows Mary as she paces round and round the living room after Edmund has suggested the family's suspicion that she is using morphine again. She feels that she is being spied upon by the rest of the family and caged within her own house. Katharine Hepburn plays the scene with intensity and urgency, as she paces frenetically around the room, saying:

> If there was only some one place I could go to get away for a day, or even an afternoon, some woman friend I could talk to—not about anything serious, simply laugh and gossip and laugh and forget awhile—your father goes out. He meets his own friends in barrooms or at the Club. You and Jamie have the boys you know. You go out. But I am alone. I've always been alone.[19]

The continuous 360-degree panning shot following her around the room serves to reinforce the sense of entrapment that she feels in the house. She also feels the guilt associated with her drug taking, and she is embarrassed that the others have found her out. She tries to repel her own guilty feelings by changing the subject and counterattacking, a pattern that all of the characters in the film variously follow. Here the frenetic camera movement mirrors the psyche of the character and visually underlines the emotional dynamics of the scene.

The final sequence of the film, in which Lumet switches from a naturalistic to an expressionistic style, is the second exception to the overall simplicity of the style of the film. The last several minutes of the film are made up of Mary's long, final "monologue," or, as O'Neill puts it in the stage directions, "She speaks aloud to herself, not to them." By the end of the play Mary is entirely lost in the past; her closing lines retrace her years at the convent school, her aspirations to become a nun, her initially happy marriage to James Tyrone, and her subsequent loss of religious faith and any sense of meaning to life. For the first minute or so of her speech we see her in tight close-up. Her hair is by now completely disheveled (Lumet follows very carefully O'Neill's use of the degree of the disarray of Mary's hair as a metaphor for her psychic disintegration).[20] She speaks very much in the voice of a young girl, and uses adolescent mannerisms. The camera then begins very slowly to pull back higher and higher above the table at which all four are sitting. Mary talks of being urged to leave the convent for a year to insure the firmness of her vocation.

As the camera pulls back farther and farther, the characters at the table become isolated in a single shaft of light; the entire space surrounding them becomes black, except for the lighthouse lights slowly flashing across the windows of the room. The effect here is deliberately artifical. The naturalistic mode of the rest of the film has been abandoned here for the sake of a purely metaphorical and poetic ending. The four Tyrones become totally isolated within their own suffocating world; all that seems to exist is the table around which so much of their conflict has taken place. The light that passes from window to window and the sound of foghorns may suggest either boats passing or the light from the lighthouse, but the effect remains eerie and unnatural. The light and sound effects (the foghorn and melancholy notes of the piano) at this point are strangely unsettling to the viewer, who has been, like the Tyrones, confined in the limited space of the house itself, mindless of the world outside. The image of the four seen from above at great distance, with blackness totally surrounding them, visually reinforces the idea both of their isolation from the world, and of their confinement with each other. Very near the end of Mary's speech, both in the play and in the film, she stands, pauses, and as O'Neill stunningly describes her gesture in the stage directions, "She passes her hand over her forehead as if brushing cobwebs from her brain." The ceiling-angled long shot changes abruptly to an extreme close-up of Mary as she says the final lines of the play:

> That was in the winter of senior year. Then in the Spring something happened to me. Yes, I remember. I fell in love with James Tyrone and was so happy for a time.[21]

O'Neill's strong and ironic ending lines are notable in many of his plays, but this one stands above all others in its poignant irony. Lumet takes great advantage of the lines by cutting from long shot to tight close-up. We enter Mary's mind, her feelings, her lost world, by the jarring contrast in physical perspective from the previous shot to this one. As she holds her hands against her face, a small detail is prominent in the film that would be lost on the stage; we see clearly her wedding ring on her left hand and the irony of the final lines is clearer. Following Mary's final words, we see a close-up in turn of each of the Tyrone men. First, we see James Tyrone; his face reflects strange numbness which conceals great pain. Next, we see Jamie; his expression is somewhat less emotional than that of his father, yet reflects deep unhappiness and frustration. Next, we see Edmund; his head is tilted pathetically to one side, eyes almost closed from sorrow, reflecting enormous emotional pain. Following the four final close-ups, the camera returns to the long shot from above. We again see the lights passing slowly across the windows and hear the melancholy sound of the foghorn. The mood of these final moments is completed by the strangely mournful piano music, which is quiet, slightly discordant, and atonal.

The music for single piano composed for the film by André Previn has been skillfully and evocatively used at various points throughout the film. It is most noticeably heard at the beginning with the titles and again during the final scene, mentioned above, after Mary has vainly attempted to play the piano. Elsewhere in the film the music has been used only between moments of dramatic and emotional tension, as if to punctuate the action. Lumet has wisely chosen not to use musical soundtracking to underline the emotions of a particular scene, which would detract from the realism of the film. The music, besides being discordant and atonal, which is appropriate to the moods of the action, has a slow and faltering quality, which suggests Mary's hopeless desire to play the piano again. The score subtly supports, while it in no way distracts from, the performances, which are of paramount importance in the film.

Indeed, much of the artistic success of the film version of *Long Day's Journey into Night* is attributable to the superb individual performances and ensemble work of its cast, who were honored with a joint best-acting award at the Cannes Film Festival. Katharine Hepburn's performance as Mary remains one of the high points of her distinguished career. She was at the time physically perfect for the role, somewhat gaunt, with a fragile and ethereal beauty, and she captured all of the nervous agitation of the character. Vocally, Hepburn projected the quavering timidity of Mary as well as her strength and even cruelty in moments of psychic and emotional dominance. Ralph Richardson's Tyrone is equally fine. He is every inch the robust, arrogantly proud, self-made immigrant—once a great actor, now a miserly landowner. Richardson's speech captures the trained, self-conscious, theatrical quality of the character mixed with the Irish brogue that betrays his origins. And it is curious to note that Richardson, in the film, even looks very much like James O'Neill from the several photographs of him that exist. Jason Robards and Dean Stockwell both deliver superb performances as the Tyrone sons. Robards's Jamie is aptly bitter and malicious, yet he also reflects the character's sensitivity and enormous affection for the other Tyrones. Dean Stockwell as Edmund delivers one of the finest performances of his career. Stockwell's playing is eminently sensitive, brooding, melancholy, and pained without ever degenerating into sentimentality.

Noted for his outstanding work with actors, Lumet has stressed the close relationships between himself and the cast, saying: "The closeness in the work with the actors is the heart of the picture."[22] He goes on to say that much of his success in directing the actors in the film was dependent upon finding the right way of dealing with each of the individual styles of the performers. With Richardson he used a kind of "musical shorthand"—"a little less timpani here, a little more bassoon," which, he says, was immediately translated into acting. With Dean Stockwell he worked in a more "internal-method" fashion, analyzing each moment in the character. With Jason Robards purely technical elements of the role were primarily discussed. And with Katharine Hepburn he says he resorted to technical matters only when her enormous energy and acting instinct became depleted.

Not only has Lumet managed to evoke splendid individual performances from the cast, but also, and perhaps more importantly, he has managed to fuse the four performances into genuine ensemble playing. The tremendous power of each of the roles, as well as the commanding presence of each of the performers, could have resulted in individual tours de force, but this is not the case. The individual acting styles blend, support, and complement each other. Each actor, just as each character, has his moment of glory, of triumph. The characters continually rise and fall in terms of psychic strength and emotional dominance, lashing out at others during moments of intense emotional energy and yielding resignedly during moments of weakness and counterattack. The performances and the directorial point of view maintain this important equilibrium.

Lumet's skillful work with the actors in the film is but one of the reasons for the artistic success of the adaptation of *Long Day's Journey into Night*. That this film constitutes a splendid—if not the definitive—performance of one of the greatest of American plays will assure its lasting importance. While it is reverentially faithful to a long and complex stage work, it nonetheless reflects a rethinking and reworking from stage dynamics to those of the screen. Lumet has said that the film medium allowed him "a superb method of focusing the play through the use of the camera."[23] He has used such things as composition, lighting, camera angle and movement within the deliberately confined physical space of the film to create a dynamic cinematic space that is charged with emotional meaning. The film's superb cast and Lumet's use of cinematic resources focus and intensify the battles, internal struggles, as well as the poignant appeals for sympathy and understanding of the characters that O'Neill called the "four haunted Tyrones."

NOTES

1. Louis Sheaffer, *O'Neill: Son and Artist* (Boston: Little, Brown and Company, 1973), p. 635.
2. Moira Walsh, *America* 107 (November 24, 1962): 1158.
3. Jay Jacobs, *Reporter* 27 (September 27, 1962): 42.
4. Ibid.
5. Stanley Kauffmann, *New Republic* 147 (September 24, 1962): 147.
6. Ibid.
7. Robert L. Hatch, *Nation* 195 (November 1962): 227.
8. Ibid., p. 228.
9. Dale Luciano, "Interview with Sidney Lumet," *Film Quarterly* 25 (Fall 1971). See pages 20–29 for Lumet's views on filming *Long Day's Journey*.
10. Byron Bentley, *Theatre Arts* 46 (October 1962): 16.
11. Eugene O'Neill, *Long Day's Journey into Night* (act 4) (New Haven, Conn.: Yale University Press, 1956), p. 151.
12. Ibid. (act 1), p. 46.
13. Hatch, p. 227.
14. Kauffmann, p. 147.
15. Graham Petrie, *Film Quarterly* 21, no. 2 (Winter 1967–68): 12.
16. *Long Day's Journey*, pp. 149–53. Lumet has added to this scene the theatrical metaphor of the wig, which further underlines the theatrical (or unreal) metaphor that O'Neill used throughout this scene—that of a card game. Edmund and Tyrone are falteringly playing cards, and the line "Who's play is it?" is frequently repeated as each one desperately tries to communicate with the other.
17. *Long Day's Journey* (act 4), p. 125.
18. Ibid., p. 151.
19. Ibid. (act 1), p. 46.
20. Especially in act 4, but throughout the film, Lumet uses medium and relatively close-up shots of Mary as she speaks of her hair being out of place, which reflects her nervous awareness of the fact that all are staring at her.
21. *Long Day's Journey* (act 4), p. 176.
22. Luciano, p. 21.
23. Ibid., p. 20.

9
The Iceman Cometh

(1973)

O'Neill's monumental late play, *The Iceman Cometh*, is currently the last of his works to have been put on film. It stands as a worthy monument to the extraordinary careers of O'Neill himself, as well as Fredric March and Robert Ryan, who both gave their last performances in this film. Produced by Ely Landau as the premier release of the American Film Theatre—a subscription series of modern plays adapted to film that exited for two seasons between 1973 and 1975—the film was considered by most an auspicious start to Landau's bold but commercially risky plan. The aim of the American Film Theatre was, as stated by the organization's vice-president, "to bring to audiences everywhere great works of the theatre, performed by consummate artists, under the guidance of major directors, on film."[1] A similar idea was envisioned by Dudley Nichols in his film version of *Mourning Becomes Electra* in his hope that it might become a "road show with Theatre Guild backing . . . might even become a cultural must."[2] The AFT films did, in a sense, become "cultural musts" and the subscription-ticket sales and block booking of the films created a successful first season. The original plan was to show these films only during the seasons of subscription sales and then destroy them. But as prophetically suspected by Jay Cocks in his *Time* review of *Iceman*, "Success has a way of changing such plans."[3] and all of the films produced for ATF are now being commercially distributed by Paramount. It is indeed fortunate that the film version of O'Neill's *Iceman* still exists.

Much of the success of *The Iceman Cometh* (as is true of other AFT films) is owing to the superb cast assembled for the film adaptation, a cast that would be virtually impossible to gather for any regular stage run. Nonetheless, Landau was insistent from the inception of the project that these films were not to be merely photographed stage plays, but cinematized versions of the stage works. John Frankenheimer's adaptation of *The Iceman Cometh*, while it is faithful to the text of O'Neill's outsized play, manages also to invest the work with a cinematic life of its own. This film, like *Long Day's Journey into Night*, is not opened up for film treatment. Both of these works thematically necessitate confined space, which would be destroyed by any traditional attempts at opening up. Both are long works and intensely verbal, and both have led to critical controversies over the nature of stage-to-screen adaptations, and to critical pronouncements on what can be viably translated from one medium to the other. While fewer critics were so obsessed or upset with the confined space of *Iceman* (as had been the case with *Long Day's Journey*), nonetheless much of the adverse criticism of Frankenheimer's film reflects what Susan Sontag, in her fine essay on film and theater, cited as a "basic disapproval of films that betray their origins in plays."[4] A survey of some of the critical responses to the film will clarify this attitude.

Stanley Kauffmann advised his readers that this was "not going to be a film at all," but then goes on to say that "questions about the medium fade beside the general quality of the acting."[5] Nora Sayre asserted that "the play doesn't flourish on film" and later went on to say that "the play is an inescapably great experience, and that fact isn't muffled by the film."[6] Vincent Canby complained that the film had been so "Balkanized" that one loses cognizance of the spatial relationships between characters, yet he goes on to say later that "even this kind of cinematic fragmentation cannot destroy its impact."[7] Each of these critical attitudes suggests Sontag's point, and each of the three reviewers seems to try to separate the experience of the play from the medium of the experience—the film itself. Much that has been written of the Landau-produced *Long Day's Journey into Night* evidenced similar preoccupations.

Several other critics found the play enhanced by its adaptation to the film medium. Pauline Kael made two key points about the advantages and disadvantages of putting such a work on film. She said that what is lost of the actual "presence" of the actors is gained from the quality of the cast, and that what might be lost of the ensemble work of a live performance is gained in "closeup view that allows us to see and grasp each detail."[8] This balance is important to the dynamics of the film, as will be discussed later. Paul Zimmerman called the adaptation "a great movie of a great play, rich in the kind of profound multi-level performances that movies rarely have the time to develop, intimate yet majestic in a way that is special to film."[9] Jay Cocks, writing in *Time* magazine called *Iceman* a "film of extraordinary beauty and power," and he goes on to say that "it is not only a worthy production of a great play, but also possesses moments . . . of its own greatness."[10]

As can be seen from these several attitudes toward the film version of *Iceman*, whether positive or negative, no critic questioned the greatness of the play itself. This was not always the case—*Iceman* is a particularly demanding and difficult stage work and one that was not immediately received with the kind of adulation it now generally enjoys. Because many of the problems of stage production transfer to its film adaptation, a brief look at the nature of the play and its production history will serve as a useful introduction to an analysis of the film itself.

When *Iceman* was first produced in 1946 by the Theatre Guild, O'Neill himself carefully supervised the production, and it was to be the last of his works that he would see on Broadway in his lifetime. The main problem for the director and cast was the unusual length of the work, but O'Neill was more than usually adamant in refusing any cuts except the few which he made during rehearsals. (O'Neill would later secretly send Carlotta to check the text of the play with productions to ensure that no cuts had been made.[11]) The play was also repetitious. When it was pointed out to O'Neill that a character repeated himself eighteen times, he responded "if it is said eighteen times it is meant to be."[12] O'Neill insisted that *"Iceman* was something that I wanted life to reveal about itself, fully, deeply, roundly,"[13] and the length and repetitiousness were part of the fabric of the work. Actors complained about the difficulty of the roles and the enormous amount of concentration necessary over so long a period of time. They are all on stage throughout most of the production, only occasionally putting their heads down on the tables as if dozing off. Several actors complained about the roles invading their private lives, such was the power of the characterizations.[14] The production suffered, according to most accounts, from inadequate performances, especially James Barton's Hickey. Barton virtually fell apart, breaking into tears twice during Hickey's long monologue at the end of the play. It was not until the superb Circle in the Square production, directed by José Quintero in 1956 and starring Jason Robards, Jr., that the play was fully realized on stage, and the length and repetitiousness of the work were seen as necessary rather than problematic. Critical opinion of the play changed radically with the second production. A highly acclaimed television version of *Iceman* was made in 1960, also starring Jason Robards, Jr., as Hickey and directed by Sidney Lumet. By the time that Frankenheimer came to adapt *Iceman* to film, it had already become firmly established as an American classic, and the AFT backing allowed it to be faithfully rendered on film. The effectiveness of the film lies in its superb cast as well as the ways in which Frankenheimer has accepted the difficulties of the work and managed to find cinematic ways of dealing with them.

Frankenheimer wrote about his experience filming *The Iceman Cometh* in *Action* magazine in 1974, calling it "the finest experience of my professional life."[15] He outlined the three central problems in adapting it to film: first, the extraordinary length of the original; second, the fact that the entire action takes place in one room; and third, the fact that "the impact of the play comes from the cumulative effect of the ensemble playing."[16] He, along with film critic Thomas Quinn Curtis, edited and reworked the text, cutting out about an hour and a quarter of dialogue. Frankenheimer also mentioned that in the first draft of the shooting script they "fell victim to the old trap of 'opening-it-up' " (beginning the film on the street, going out with certain characters, and showing Parritt throw himself off the fire escape). But during the actual shooting he replaced about half of the lines that had been cut and abandoned the scheme of opening it up. He found that lines cut earlier made later lines unplayable, the repetitions were seen as necessary to the cumulative effect of themes and characterizations within the work. As for doing away with the exterior shots, he stated:

> In spite of the fact that *Iceman* claims to be a very realistic play, it is not at all—rather, to quote Stanley Kauffmann, it is a 'symbolic play.' Thus it had to be kept within the romantic or idealized setting of the four walls.[17]

Whether the play is "realistic" or "symbolic"—it certainly seems to be both of these things—it is clearly a play about entrapment, which is thematic reason enough to keep the characters within the confines of the bar. The third problem that Frankenheimer found was the most difficult to solve. To maintain the impact of the ensemble playing of the several actors, Frankenheimer stated that he "planned the entire film as a montage of shots, utilizing maximum depth of focus."[18]

A closer look at the two last, and related, problems will more clearly suggest the aptness of Frankenheimer's approach to the play. The decision not to open it up seems a wise one since this play (like *Long Day's Journey into Night*) requires a claustrophobic sense within both the physical walls of the setting and the psychic walls of the characters' own self-defeated egos. Each of the "inmates" (as they are often called) has a "pipe dream" about escaping the confines of the bar. The philosophical character Larry Slade aptly says of Hope's establishment:

> It's the No Chance Saloon. It's Bedrock Bar. The End of the Line Cafe. The Bottom of the Sea Rathskeller! Don't you notice the beautiful calm in the atmosphere? That's because it's the last harbor. No one here has to worry about where they're going next, because there is no farther they can go.[19]

Even when the once dissolute but now reformed Hickey—the iceman of hope, salvation, and death—comes to the bar to shake all of its inhabitants out of their fear of the outside world, they can make only futile and aborted attempts at escape. It is neither necessary nor desirable for the camera to follow them out of doors during these brief interludes of escape, which will ultimately be irrelevant to their immuration.

Two scenes in the play that Frankenheimer originally considered opening up for film treatment are good examples of the wisdom of not doing so. One is the scene in which Harry Hope, through Hickey's encouragement, finally gets up the courage to go out of the bar, which he hasn't done in twenty years. Hope is mortally afraid and thinks of several excuses to keep from doing so—finally in rage at Hickey's taunting, he "pushes the door open and strides blindly into the street." Inside the bar the others watch him through the window and comment on his frightened behavior. Shortly, Harry rushes back into the bar with the story of an automobile that nearly ran him over. Hickey again taunts Harry, telling him to give up "that ghost-automobile." Harry's next line, one of the most poignant in the play (and made even more so by the brilliant acting of Fredric March), is: "Yes, what's the use now? All a lie! No automobile. But, bejees, something ran over me! Must have been myself, I guess."[20] Our imaginative recreation of the fearful panic that Harry felt outside the security of the bar is greater than any actual visualization could present, and the pathetic poignance of this self-discovery is enhanced by not having opened up the film at this point. Nonetheless, Frankenheimer has used other cinematic means of intensifying Hope's fear of the outside. Throughout this scene, as indeed throughout the series of temporary leave-takings that come from the third act of the play, Frankenheimer generally has the camera shooting toward the door. Most of the shots in this section of the film are composed with the door prominent in the background and a glaring light coming through its window. The light coming from outside, in contrast to the dimness inside, intensifies the dichotomy between the comfortable illusory world within and the fearful real world without. At one point in the scene just before Harry goes out, there is a close-up shot of his face, and the light from the window reflects in his spectacles, obscuring his eyes. He, as well as the other inhabitants of the saloon, like Plato's cavedwellers, prefers the security of his dim world of illusions.

The second major scene that Frankenheimer considered opening up was the suicide of the young Parritt, who has betrayed his anarchist mother. Close to the end of the film Parritt, in guilty despair, throws himself off the fire escape of the saloon. Frankenheimer decided during the shooting not to show this event. This seems to be a wise decision since one very important point about Parritt's death is how completely unimportant and unaffecting it is to all the other inmates of Hope's saloon, except Larry, who is the only one who knows the meaning of the muffled sound outside. The rest think it might have been a mattress that some "bum" had used to sleep on the fire escape, and they go on with indulgent self-absorption. Parritt's suicide is the only "action" in this film that is devoid of traditional kinds of action, and to visualize it would break the mood and tone of the whole. But Parritt's suicide has been visually foreshadowed throughout the film, most clearly during the scenes that come from the third and fourth acts of the play. Parritt is often seen with the window prominent in the background of the shot; likewise, we often see Larry framed by the window as he suggests to Parritt that the only way of ridding himself of the guilt he feels is by ending his own life. During Hickey's final monologue, which is the immediate catalyst to Parritt's suicide, the shadow of the fire escape is clearly cast on the window and is seen in several shots. Here again, without resorting to opening up, Frankenheimer has intensified the action through a purely cinematic kind of composition.

The other major problem, besides that of the necessarily confined space of the film, that Frankenheimer cited as an obstacle in adapting *Iceman* was that of maintaining the impact of the ensemble playing of the large cast of characters. To achieve this, he wanted maximum depth of focus used throughout the film. Technically he relied on the film's excellent cinematographer, Ralph Woolsey, who talked about this aspect of the film's production in an American Film Institute interview. He said that the depth of focus was "critical to the audience's never losing a sense of the geography of the film."[21] He mentions further that the exposure level of the film stock was altered in order to allow maximum depth of field in all shots. Woolsey pointed out also that most of the film was shot with varying degrees of wide-angle lenses which augmented the overall compositional area available in each shot.[22] Such cinematic tactics certainly have worthy precedents, such as Gregg Toland's similar use of wide-angle deep-focus photography in his work on Ford's adaptation of O'Neill's *Long Voyage Home* as well as Wyler's adaptation of *The Little Foxes*. In both of these films, as in *Iceman*, the photographic style uncramps and visually dynamizes confined space, helps to maintain the sense of ensemble playing, and allows for an interesting dramatic play between objects or people in the foreground and the background of a shot.

The deep-focus shots allow the important overall atmosphere of the bar to be maintained at all times. Often there will be a character speaking in the foreground of the shot while the listening (or sleeping) characters are seen in the background. Many of the shots in the film are done from a low angle, also with deep focus, allowing the ceiling of the bar to be seen. Having the ceiling visible adds to the sense of claustrophobic confinement within the establishment. Bottles of whiskey are often prominent in the foreground of shots and they visually comment on the state of intoxication of the characters. The whiskey bottles take on greater importance and visual prominence during the series of leave-takings from act 3 of the play. As several of the characters fearfully and haltingly attempt to leave, the camera is often positioned at table level, with whiskey bottles prominent in the foreground of the shot. In the background of the shot is the door with glaring light coming through its window. The bottles become synonymous with the besotted security inside the bar and the light synonymous with the harsh reality outside. Another important example of effective depth-focus shooting occurs during the banquet for Harry Hope's birthday. Several of the tables in the bar have been pushed together to make a long banquet table that crosses the screen on a diagonal line. The diagonal composition, as so often used in film or even in Tintoretto's famous *Last Supper*, which this arrangement resembles, gives kind of disquieting tension to the scene. The table is shot in depth focus and the audience can choose its own focal point during the scene. The arrangement here is also reminiscent of the banquet scene in *Citizen Kane*, where extreme depth focus was used to much the same end. The sequence at the banquet table ends with a slow zoom-in to Hickey, who has been at the head of the table; as he announces that his beloved wife, Evelyn, is dead, and we get closer to the truth of Hickey's reformation, the zoom-in brings us both physically and psychically closer to the character.

Camera movement, in general, is an important way in which the film maintains the continuity and impact of ensemble playing. Frankenheimer and cinematographer Woolsey plotted the shots of the film utilizing as much fluid camera movement as possible, to avoid cutting, which would break the dramatic momentum. Woolsey used a device that he calls "table-scrapers"—a kind of dolly upon which the camera is positioned at exactly table level—to effect easily movement from one group of characters to another, or to alter slightly the camera positioning in relation to a group of character sitting at a single table.[23] Since so much of the film takes places at the tables of Hope's saloon, this device proved quite successful in maintaining the continuity of the work with a minimum of cutting. Throughout the film the camera movement is slow and unobtrusive. During Hickey's long monologue at the end of the film, the fluidity of camera movement is most impressive. Hickey's speech has important ramifications for all the other characters. It is important that we see the reactions of the listeners to his story. The camera follows Hickey as he moves from one group of listeners to another in a fluid and unobtrusive way, maintaining the continuity of ensemble playing at this climatic moment in the film. Quick cutting is used for emotional impact only when Hickey first says the words "And so I killed Evelyn."[24] There are brief shots of the astonished faces of each of the listeners, and the jarring contrast between the smoothness of the shooting of the rest of the speech and this series of quick cuts is effective in the pacing of the whole sequence.

As the camera movement in the film is simple and unobtrusive, so is the prevailing visual style of this adaptation. This notwithstanding, Frankenheimer has managed to enhance the viewer's experience of the work through a variety of purely cinematic devices, such as composition, meaningful blocking of characters within the shots, careful attention to details, and atmosphere. Most of the characters in the film are usually seen in group shots; they are grouped according to their thematic interrelatedness. Only the characters of Parritt, Larry Slade, and Hickey are frequently given single shots. Isolating these characters in the frame underlines their varying degrees of isolation from the rest of the group. Parritt, the newest denizen of Hope's establishment, is shunned by the others. Larry Slade, who "lives life from the grandstand," deliberately separates himself from the others and his sense of alienation is stressed by the many shots of him alone in sullen pensiveness. Hickey, as the flippant messiah and salesman of truth, sets himself apart from and above the others—and, indeed, he is often filmed from a low angle to magnify his size. A portrait of Harry's dead wife, Bessie, figures prominently in the composition of many shots in the film, most importantly in a shot in which Hickey stands directly beneath the portait as he confesses to secretly hating his wife, Evelyn, which links Hickey's "pipe dream" of killing his wife out of love, to Harry's false idealization of Bessie, whom he secretly despised. Just as compositional details take on great significance in a film which is so spatially confined, so does the general ambience of the work become paramount.

Frankenheimer's film, assisted by the superb art direction of Jack Martin Smith and fine costumes by Dorothy Jeakins, evokes precisely the atmosphere of the lower depths that O'Neill's moribund work requires. The grimness of Hope's "cheap ginmill" is captured in the texture of the walls, the surfaces of the tables, the sawdust and debris on the floor, dust on bottles and other objects, and the harsh glare of ceiling lamps. To contribute further to the atmosphere of the bar the film's color was, as Woolsey put it, "desaturated," that is, most of the color was bled out of the film to give it a monochromatic look that would intensify the overall sordidness of the milieu.[25] There is a slightly exaggerated graininess to the film, resulting from altering the exposure level of the film stock to allow maximum depth of field, and this also contributes to the effectively somber look of the film.

While there is much that is visually impressive in Frankenheimer's apt and adroit direction of *Iceman*, it is unquestionable that much of the triumph of this film adaptation is owing to its superb cast. It is difficult to imagine a more perfect Harry Hope than Frederic March. The veteran actor March was

THE ICEMAN COMETH (1973) American Express Films and Ely Landau Org. Directed by John Frankenheimer. With Fredric March. (Harry Hope—"who tries to hide his defenselessness under a testy, truculent manner.")

seventy-six when the film was made and had been on both stage and screen for over fifty years. He is the very embodiment of the character O'Neill described as "a bag of bones . . . a soft-hearted slob who tries to hide his defenselessness behind a testy truculent manner."[26] Harry Hope is an assemblage of contradictions—he is doddering and willfully powerful; he is good-natured and cantankerous; he is weak and self-defeated, yet possessed of some pride and dignity as the landlord of the lower depths. Fredric March's performance skillfully captures all of Hope's subtleties and inconsistencies. O'Neill, in a small detail in the stage directions, mentions that Harry's cheap store-bought teeth click as he talks,[27] and March even captures this quality in the quavering rhythms of Harry's speech. Hope's character must combine both comedy and pathos, and March maintains the balance beautifully throughout the film. In Harry's key moments in the film—his vainly disguised childish excitement at the birthday festivities, his comic despair at discovering the liquor no longer has a "kick" after Hickey's arrival, his pathetic and long-overdue attempt to leave the bar, and his jubilant sense of relief in discovering that Hickey was "insane," enabling the bar's inhabitants to return to their set ways of life—March's acting, as focused upon and magnified by the camera, creates unforgettable screen moments. The role of Harry Hope was to be the last of March's film performances, and it is a superb conclusion to a distinguished career.

Robert Ryan, in the important and demanding role of Larry Slade, gave a performance that deservedly received unanimous critical praise. Ryan, who played the death-obsessed "Grandstand Foolosopher" Larry, died shortly after completion of the film. Ryan never got to see the film in which he played the role that, according to Frankenheimer's report, "he had waited all of his artistic life to play." Larry Slade is an intense and complex character whom O'Neill described as having "a mystic's blue eyes with a gleam of sharp sardonic humor."[28] He is a jaded, self-loathing former anarchist who can no longer believe in politics, or, indeed, anything at all; who, like Edmund in *Long Day's Journey into Night*, is fond of quoting the lines from a Heine poem:

> Lo, sleep is good; better is death, in sooth,
> The best of all were never to be born.[29]

He sees himself as "condemned to be one of those who has to see all sides of a question," and realizes that "when you're damned like that, the questions multiply for you until in the end it's all question and no answer." Robert Ryan's performance captures the profound world-weariness and pained endurance of Larry's character. Paul Zimmerman said that it was "Robert Ryan, his face a wreck of smashed dreams, who provides the tragic dimension that makes this *Iceman* a moving, unforgettable experience."[30] And Pauline Kael praised Ryan, saying that "he is so subtle he seems to have penetrated to the mystery of O'Neill's gaunt grandeur."[31] Such praise is indeed warranted.

The role of Larry is full of psychological tensions—a tension between commitment to ideas and intellectual nihilism; a tension between social interrelatedness and alienation; and a tension between the absolutes of life and death, of being and nothingness. Ryan plays Larry with such penetrating honesty and integrity that the profound tensions within the character become palpable. This is especially evident in his scenes with the young Parritt, whose mother had been Larry's lover, and who might even be Larry's own son. Parritt demands Larry's involvement, wanting him to control his destiny—to become his executioner, in expiation of the sin of betraying his mother. Larry does finally become involved, "ordering" Parritt's suicide. The death of Parritt becomes a substitute for Larry's own desire to kill himself. Ryan's portrayal of the profound self-disgust that Larry feels at his own cowardice is remarkably skillful and poignant. Larry's last lines, spoken to himself as no one else is listening, are "Be God. I'm the only real convert to death Hickey made here. From the bottom of my coward's heart I mean that now."[32] Ryan is shot in close-up during this speech; the close-up intensifies the "sardonic grin" that O'Neill wanted Larry to express at this point of bitterly sincere self-realization.

Jeff Bridges in the role of Parritt also gives a fine performance. He projects the youthful vigor, naiveté, nervousness, childishness, and obsessive sense of guilt that combine to make up Parritt's character. Don Parritt is the new comer to Hope's saloon; he is the youngest and physically the least dissipated of the group, yet he is the most desperate and driven of the saloon's inhabitants. He is haunted and hounded by the guilt he feels at having informed on his mother's anarchist activities, an action that he tries to attribute to political motives, but one that clearly reveals his Oedipal jealousy of her several love affairs. Parritt's guilt is obvious almost from the moment he enters the saloon; it is a predictable and schematic characterization. Yet Bridges's performance gives it vitality and depth through his shadings of O'Neill's deliberately iterant lines.

Before examining the pivotal and highly controversial performance of Lee Marvin as Hickey, some note should be taken of several of the fine performances in smaller roles in the film, since the ensemble work is so important to this particular adaptation. Bradford Dillman's performance as Willie Oban, the Harvard Law School alumnus who once had a successful legal practice and who now is hopelessly lost to drink, nervously twitching with the DT's, was singled out by most critics as superlative, or as Pauline Kael put it, "a small but flawless performance."[33] Dillman is both funny and pathetic in his subtle portrayal of Willie, a role that is so full of nervous mannerisms that it almost invites caricature. Dillman's controlled underplaying of the role makes it cinematically apt and effective. Tom Pedi, as the tough but sentimental bartender Rocky, acts with a veteran's assurance, having performed the same role in the 1946 stage production and the 1960 television adaptation. John McLiam, as Jimmy Tomorrow, combines the naive optimism and pitiful self-delusion that Jimmy displays. Moses Gunn gives an intensely powerful performance as Joe Mott, a black man who was once the mogul of a successful gambling saloon and who now has fallen to the position of doorman. Martyn Green and George Voskovec are convincingly mottled and childishly cantankerous as the British infantry captain and general of a Boer command, who endlessly relieve the Boer War. Sorrell Booke, as Hugo, the former editor of anarchist publications, skillfully captures the tone and mannerisms of a man who lives in a semidelirious mental state, one who can only express himself in momentary bursts of disconnected idea and images. The rest of O'Neill's motley assortment of pimps, whores, and broken-down, self-deluded dreamers give striking performances, in roles which are small but vitally important to the tone and ambience of the film.

Lee Marvin's performance in the catalytic role of Hickey was the most controversial aspect of Frankenheimer's adaptation. Most critics of the film found Marvin's portrayal of Hickey the greatest shortcoming of the adaptation. Nora Sayre said that Marvin was "deliberately charmless, and too rationally earthbound for a part that needs the touch of a magician," and that Marvin lacked the "quality of maniac spellcaster"[34] necessary to the role. Vincent Canby similarly complained of Marvin's lacking any "hint of mania" and the "demonic"[35] quality that must be present in Hickey. Jay Cocks saw Marvin as having "the hype and patter" of the character but lacking the necessary "bravura," and continued by saying that Marvin's Hickey "does not stand apart from the others but becomes just another victim."[36] Pauline Kael found Marvin "all wrong for the part" and his performance to be all on one level, lacking any sense of the "interior life of the character."[37] Marvin was inevitably compared to Jason Robards, Jr., who had played Hickey in both the 1956 stage production and the 1960 television version of the play. Robards, as did many critics, considered the role to be his alone and he was shattered by Frankenheimer's choice of Marvin to play Hickey.[38]

Frankenheimer considered Marvin essential to his interpretation of the play, which he feels hinges on the question of Hickey's sanity in the murder of his wife and subsequent zealous obsession with truth and sense of mission to spread the gospel of life without illusions. Talking about his interpretation of the play and choice of Marvin to play Hickey, Frankenheimer said:

> *Iceman* is not a work about having to live with illusion but rather one that explores the necessity and the horrible pain of living without it. . . .To make this concept of *Iceman* work, it must be perfectly clear to an audience that Hickey is sane . . . sane when he killed his wife and sane when he comes to the bar. . . . With this concept in mind I was determined to get Lee Marvin for Hickey. Lee had the strength, the presence, the humor that the role demanded and, most of all, he shared my point of view about the character.[39]

THE ICEMAN COMETH (1973) American Express Films and Ely Landau Org. Directed by John Frankenheimer. With Lee Marvin, Hildy Brooks, Nancy Juno Dawson, and Evan Evans (Lee Marvin dominates and manipulates at Harry Hope's birthday party.)

Frankenheimer is certainly right in insisting on the sanity (within the psychological and ethical context of the play) of Hickey. When he says he was insane when he killed his wife, it is merely another illusion, or "pipe dream," which both eases the guilt he feels and prevents him from having emotionally and intellectually to recognize that he did it because he hated Evelyn—hated her love for him, the guilt which it created (a guilt with which he could no longer live), and the inadequacy of his repayment of her love. The illusion of insanity also frees the inhabitants of Hope's saloon from the tortuous self-examination that Hickey had led them into. In an interview in 1946 O'Neill said that the philosophy of the play was simply that "there is always one dream left, one final dream, no matter how low you have fallen, down there at the bottom of the bottle."[40] Hickey's "insanity" is that last dream for himself and all the others. When Hickey leaves with the two policemen, the air is cleared and the liquor starts to get its "kick" again.

Much of the negative criticism of Marvin's portrayal of Hickey stresses the lack of maniacal and demonic qualities in the character. But Hickey is neither

THE ICEMAN COMETH (1973) American Express Films and Ely Landau Org. Directed by John Frankenheimer. With Fredric March and Lee Marvin. (Hickey, as the bringer of happiness, is welcomed by Harry Hope to his saloon.)

monster nor maniac. Marvin was criticized as being one-dimensional, but Hickey throughout the play does exist on just one level—that of obsession with a single idea. Lee Marvin's performance as Hickey seems much more skillful than most of the original critics of the film found it to be. One problem with accepting him in the role was the fact that he was cast against type—having been associated with tough-guy roles in action films—and another difficulty seems to have been the comparison of his portrayal to that of Jason Robards, Jr. Marvin's physical presence and commanding voice contrast effectively with the state of dereliction in Hope's saloon. He captures much of the haughty air of Hickey's sense of superiority to the others without ever becoming condescending. Marvin's voice seems naturally suited to what O'Neill described as Hickey's "salesman's mannerism of speech, an easy flow of glib, persuasive convincingness."[41] There is a certain monotony in Marvin's delivery, but this is suitable to the character who, rather insensitively, harps on a single issue throughout the film. Hickey does not really grow or change until the final monologue, when he discovers his real feeling toward his dead wife, and even this recognition is deliberately masked. The schematic repetitiousness of Hickey's role is signaled by the fact that the first three acts of the play ironically end with Hickey saying the word "happy": "All I want is to see you happy" (act 1), "Why all that Evelyn wanted out of life was to make me happy" (act 2), and "It's time you began to feel happy" (act 3). Happiness is what Hickey had sought for himself in killing his wife, and what he wants to bring to those he considers to be his former compatriots in the misery of self-delusion.

Hickey is oblivious to the real needs and wants of the denizens of Hope's saloon, and Marvin's playing of the role captures the heedless well-meaningness of Hickey's self-appointed mission. In trying to convince the others to accept the truth about life, he is really trying to convince himself—he is both apart from them and equally victimized by the conflict between two different levels of reality—the psychological reality of what one believes, and often contradictory reality of the way one lives and acts. Hickey's long, final monologue is as much aimed at self-conversion as it is aimed at converting the others, and it is very much a rationalization for culpable past actions. Marvin's delivery of the monologue is essentially dispassionate, yet the flatness of delivery paradoxically underscores the passion beneath the surface. It is noteworthy that O'Neill, in writing Hickey's final speech, did not overburden it with stage directions suggesting the exact emotional quality of lines and sections of the speech. O'Neill often uses a plethora of emotional directives, but here they are surprisingly absent, which suggests the aptness of Marvin's interpretation of the speech. Hickey must, at this point, become a spellcaster, and the levelness of Marvin's delivery helps to cast the spell. Only a few emotional outbursts (signaled by stage directions) break what O'Neill called the "strange running narrative manner"[42] of the speech. These sudden shifts in tone (and change in editing rhythm, as discussed earlier), primarily involving the truth about his feelings toward his wife, are played with a controlled intensity. The dominant mood of Hickey's monologue and the word most often repeated in the stage directions is "obliviously," and this is what Marvin's performance skillfully manifests.

One reviewer of the film who faulted Lee Marvin's Hickey made the interesting point that Marvin's weakness in the role "does not so much throw the production out of balance as readjust the emphasis. . . . The weight of the production falls on Robert Ryan."[43] This may well be not so much a reemphasis of the play's focus as a reclamation of the balance that the work should have, without the overshadowing force of a too dominant Hickey.

The character of Larry Slade is, in many ways, the most interesting character in the play and subsequent film adaptation. He is the character who seems to understand the most, to suffer most, and finally to change most. It is true, as noted by many O'Neill critics and biographers, that Larry is discernibly the authorial spokesman in the work, and as such he is most clearly aware of the paradoxes of existence, of belief, and of the multileveled and nefarious nature of reality. Analogizing the work to Plato's allegory of the cave, Hickey brings the "light of the reality beyond" to Hope's cave; its inhabitants like the comfort of the darkness; only Larry can see the impossibility of reconciling this duality. He remains "condemned" to the dualistic point of view—"looking with pity at the two sides of everything," as he says, until the day he dies.

Frankenheimer ends the film with a lingering close-up of Robert Ryan's face. In the background there is a cacophony of random noises and songs, as the others celebrate the revivifying effects of intoxication. They sing snatches of old songs, shout lines of poetry, pound on tables, and laugh with abandon, which is all possible again now that the nagging soul-searching that Hickey introduced into their world is removed. Only Larry is silent and morose, staring blankly into space, oblivious to the noise around him. The selective vision of the camera, isolating Larry in close-up, can clearly focus this final moment of *The Iceman Cometh*, making it rich with meaning and poignancy. There is pain and desolation in Ryan's expression, mixed with a sense of tranquillity and a pitying acceptance of his own sorry lot in life as well as that of those around him.

Shortly after completing *Iceman* O'Neill said:

> There are moments in it that suddenly strip the secret soul of a man stark naked, not in cruelty or moral superiority, but with an understanding compassion which sees him as a victim of the ironies of life and of himself. These moments to me are the depth of tragedy, with nothing more that can possibly be said.

The final close-up of Robert Ryan as Larry becomes one such moment in this skillful film adaptation. The effectiveness of Frankenheimer's version of *Iceman* is precisely in an accumulation of such moments throughout the film. This film, like Lumet's version of *Long Day's Journey into Night*, demonstrates that cinematic resources can be employed within confined physical space to focus and intensify the thematic and experiential core of the original work.

NOTES

1. Vincent Canby, *New York Times*, January 24, 1974, p. 7.
2. *Time* 104, no. 24 (November 24, 1947): 104.
3. Jay Cocks, *Time* 102 (November 12, 1973): 122.
4. Susan Sontag, "Film and Theatre," reprinted in *Film Theory and Criticism* (New York: Oxford University Press, 1974), p. 250.
5. Stanley Kauffman, *New Republic* 169: 24.
6. Nora Sayre, *New York Times*, October 30, 1973, p. 36.
7. Vincent Canby, *New York Times*, November 11, 1973, section 2, p. 1.
8. Pauline Kael, *New Yorker* (November 5, 1973): 149.
9. Paul D. Zimmerman, *Newsweek* 82 (November 12, 1973): 119.
10. Cocks, p. 122.
11. Louis Sheaffer, *O'Neill: Son and Artist* (Boston: Little, Brown and Company, 1973), p. 574.
12. Ibid., p. 572.

13. Ibid.
14. Ibid., p. 575.
15. John Frankenheimer, "Filming *The Iceman Cometh*," *Action* 9, no. 1 (January–February 1974): 37.
16. Ibid., p. 37.
17. Ibid.
18. Ibid.
19. Eugene O'Neill, *The Iceman Cometh* (New York: Random House, 1940), p. 25.
20. Ibid., p. 200.
21. Ralph Woolsey, *American Cinematographer* (February 1974), p. 156.
22. Ibid.
23. Ibid., p. 157.
24. O'Neill, *The Iceman Cometh*, p. 241.
25. Woolsey, p. 157.
26. O'Neill, *The Iceman Cometh*, p. 7.
27. Ibid., p. 8.
28. Ibid., p. 4.
29. Ibid., p. 32.
30. Zimmerman, p. 120.
31. Kael, p. 150.
32. O'Neill, *The Iceman Cometh*, p. 258.
33. Kael, p. 155.
34. Sayre, p. 127.
35. Canby, p. 130.
36. Cocks, p. 122.
37. Kael, p. 151.
38. Barbara Gelb, *New York Times Magazine*, October 11, 1976, p. 124.
39. Frankenheimer, pp. 35, 36.
40. Scheaffer, p. 579.
41. O'Neill, *The Iceman Cometh*, p. 76.
42. Ibid., p. 228.
43. Zimmerman, p. 120.

Conclusion

The translation of any work from one medium into another unavoidably seems to require that both artistically valid changes as well as damaging compromises be made. The fifty-year history of O'Neill's work on the screen suggests that changes made in structure or emphasis in the process of adaptation are often useful, but that compromises seldom, if ever, benefit the adaptation. Compromises, while sometimes necessary, more often tend to be merely expedient, or else are based on ephemeral considerations. Several of the O'Neill adaptations suffer from concessions to expediency, to formulas, or to public morals and from fear of the censor's shears. Often these varieties of compromise overlap in a single adaptation.

For example, *Summer Holiday* suffers from the expediency of using a screenplay that MGM had on hand from an earlier film version of O'Neill's play. The conventionalizing tendency of the earlier screenplay became magnified in the second screen version, and the central character became broadened into caricature. Another financial expediency was the casting, because of assumed box-office appeal, of Mickey Rooney, who was wrong for the role. Similarly, in *Strange Interlude* the casting of Norma Shearer and Clark Gable in the principal roles, ill-suited to them, was box office-minded. In neither case did the casting make the films commercially successful, and both were flawed artistically by having inappropriate stars. And *Strange Interlude* is the most damagingly flawed of the O'Neill adaptations by concessions to censorship. This play, which commingles passion and philosophy, is stripped of both, and the power of censorship is reflected in the cutting of all words to do with passion as well as all references to God. All of the other adaptations of O'Neill managed to escape such bowdlerization, if not a certain toning down or prettifying of characters and actions in conventional ways, as in the 1930 version of *Anna Christie*, and both film versions of *Ah, Wilderness!*

Hollywood has consistently exhibited a bent for the formulaic, and one of the most enduring formulas is that of the "love story." Several of the O'Neill adaptations have had their dramatic and thematic proportions altered by an insistence on romance whether or not it is relevant to—or even used consistently throughout—the film. This tendency is clearly evidenced all the way from the 1930s to the 1950s, from *Anna Christie* to *Desire under the Elms*. The two versions of *Ah, Wilderness!* turn O'Neill's bittersweet comedy of family life into what is essentially a teenage love story, and the play must be restructured to accommodate the romance. In *Strange Interlude* a patently unromantic marriage based on self-sacrifice becomes a typically romantic affair. In *Desire under the Elms* a generally sordid and latently incestuous relationship is gratuitously and inconsistently treated in a visually conventional romantic way. The film version of *The Emperor Jones* introduces two female characters to allow romantic affairs and rivalries extraneous to the theme and the major actions of the work. And in the sound version of *Anna Christie* one inconsistent scene is added to enhance the romantic formula.

The preparation and, to a great extent, evaluation of stage to screen adaptation had been persistently influenced by another formula—the convention of opening up, or breaking out of the confines of limited stage or studio space. Compromises in this direction have lessened the effectiveness of several of the O'Neill adaptations, simply because they have been merely formulaic and not part of a larger reworking of the play for film. Quite frequently such alterations are connected to the reapportioning of the romantic elements in the transition from stage to screen. For example, the exterior scenes in *Desire under the Elms* and *Strange Interlude* are part of the inconsistent romantic qualities of the works. Both films have exterior scenes irrelevant to the themes and atmosphere of the whole film, and are presented in an unconvincing way. The tendency toward conventional opening up is seen also in *Mourning Becomes Electra*, which has generally opted to follow the theatrical and thematic form of the original. In all of these cases, if for somewhat different reasons, the exterior scenes merely underline the hybrid film/theater nature of the cinematic versions.

Other, more effective films, such as *The Long Voyage Home*, *Long Day's Journey into Night* and *The Iceman Cometh*, substantially avoid the merely formulaic, employing the device of opening up only as it is relevant to both the thematic core of the original work and its recreation on film. Ford's *The Long Voyage Home*, the most fully realized in atmosphere of the O'Neill adaptations, uses exterior scenes beautifully and consistently throughout, but only as part of a unified reworking of the original for film. The exterior sequences, apart from their technical competence and convincing realism, spring naturally from the work as the mere formulaically included scenes in other of the O'Neill adaptations do not. A masterful director such as Ford can also accept the essentially confined physical space of the original and use this to cinematic advantage. It is important to note in this regard that technical developments in the late 1930s made it possible to shoot confined physical space with greater visual interest, because of the increased depth of field possible and increased camera mobility. Ford and his technically innovative cameraman, Gregg Toland, use these possibilities to make the interior sequences as dynamic as the outdoor scenes. This point is relevant also to *Long Day's Journey* and *Iceman*, both of which essentially retain the confined physical space of the original, but rework compositional space into viable cinematic form. Neither film makes formulaic concessions to opening up, which would be thematically counterproductive, but neither film can be called simply a filmed stage play because of the significant and significating intervention of the camera between the work and the audience's experience of it. Ford, Lumet, and Frankenheimer have made cinematic form follow thematic function, and all three were both skillful and highly sympathetic to the O'Neill work in their direction of these adaptations.

John Ford was decidedly the best director to bring O'Neill to the screen. Very often the adapted works of O'Neill were entrusted to far less capable directors, notably Robert Z. Leonard, whose direction of *Strange Interlude* lacks force and significance; Dudley Murphy, who takes little advantage of the expressionist visual potential of *The Emperor Jones;* Delbert Mann, whose work on *Desire under the Elms* is often clumsy and inappropriate; and Dudley Nichols, who, while highly capable as a screenwriter and sympathetic to O'Neill's work, lacked imagination in his direction of *Mourning Becomes Electra*.

Other, more accomplished directors brought O'Neill to the screen with varying degrees of effectiveness, depending to a great extent on the stylistic suitability of the director to the adapted work. The style of the remarkable producer-director-editor Thomas Ince was well suited to the silent version of *Anna Christie*. Clarence Brown, the conventionally skillful MGM director of many star vehicles for Greta Garbo and Joan Crawford in the 1930s, was not stylistically suited to the tone and atmosphere of *Anna Christie*. Brown's style, inclined to rather lush and romantic visual effects, seems much more appropriate to the nostalgic *Ah, Wilderness!* Rouben Mamoulian, an often extraordinary and innovative director, directs the musical numbers in *Summer Holiday* with far more skill than the dramatic scenes, and the work becomes uneven. And Sidney Lumet and John Frankenheimer, the highly capable recent directors of O'Neill on film, have done some of their finest screen work in the adapting *Long Day's Journey* and *The Iceman Cometh* to the screen.

While directorial sureness is of foremost importance, much of the ultimate effect of a film necessarily relies on its performances. The indomitable and magnifying eye of the camera demands physical aptness as well as craft on the part of the performer. The intensified visual dynamics of film also demand uniformity of acting styles. The O'Neill adaptations have been variously enhanced by superb performances and diminished by ones that are either inadequate or inappropriate. The individual performances of, say, Greta Garbo or Paul Robeson have substantially contributed to the effectiveness of the O'Neill films in which they star. On the other hand, the inappropriateness

Conclusion 165

of Mickey Rooney in *Summer Holiday* or Burl Ives in *Desire under the Elms* or Norma Shearer in *Strange Interlude* has had deleterious effects on both O'Neill's characterizations and the film adaptations. Perhaps even more crucial on film is the compatibility of the acting styles of an entire cast of a work. The film versions of *The Emperor Jones, Mourning Becomes Electra,* and, most noticeably, *Desire under the Elms* are flawed by the incongruous acting styles of the players. Both of the O'Neill adaptations directed by Clarence Brown are notable in their ensemble playing; a single dominant mood emerges from the acting in *Ah, Wilderness!*, and, to a lesser extent, in the sound version of *Anna Christie*, owing to the screen power of Garbo. *The Long Voyage Home* is greatly enhanced by the fine assortment of character actors whose performances are skillfully fused. The most remarkable ensemble playing, however, occurs in the last two O'Neill's works brought to the screen—*Long Day's Journey* and *Iceman Cometh*. The meaning and emotional effect of both works stem from an intense interaction among the characters, and the individual performances and exceptional ensemble playing account for much of the artistic success of both adaptations. It should be noted in this connection that both Lumet and Frankenheimer had far greater autonomy in casting than did the directors working under the corporate structure of the studio system in the adaptations of O'Neill in the decades prior to the 1960s.

In all of O'Neill's major work the characters of the plays are profoundly affected by the atmosphere and environment in which they exist. The film medium has distinct advantages in the creation of atmosphere and expressive settings, and the most effective of the O'Neill works on the screen recreate O'Neill's dramatic milieu in striking cinematic form. This is often the result of the sympathetic and long-term alliance of director and cinematographer, as with John Ford and Gregg Toland in *The Long Voyage Home*. The collaboration resulted in the most compelling film translation of O'Neill's mystique of the sea. The sympathetic alliance of Clarence Brown and William Daniels, successful in many films of the late 1920s and 1930s, accounts for much of the vivid recreation of atmosphere in *Ah, Wilderness!* The combination of Sidney Lumet and his frequent cinematographer, Boris Kaufman, resulted in a superb film realization of the claustrophobic ambience essential to O'Neill's *Long Day's Journey into Night*. And most recently, the stifling atmosphere of O'Neill's lower depths was vividly given filmic form in the collaboration of John Frankenheimer and cinematographer Ralph Woolsey.

As suggested in the introduction to this study, a primary function of adapting a stage work to the screen is to revivify or recreate the essential atmosphere, mood, characters, and themes of the original work within the aesthetic dynamics of film. While all of the O'Neill films treat the original with some fidelity, some are faithful in outline rather than in essence, such as

Strange Interlude or *Desire under the Elms*. Several other, while having striking moments and some superb performances, are flawed as film recreations of the original play because of the accentuation of elements only tenuously connected to essential considerations of characters and themes of the original, as discussed from various angles in the specific analyses of *Anna Christie* (1930), *The Emperor Jones*, *Ah, Wilderness!*, and *Summer Holiday*. While admirably retaining the essentials of theme, character, and mood, *Mourning Becomes Electra* would also be less than fully realized according to this idea of adaptation because it does not sufficiently recreate and revivify these elements into cinematic form. A variety of other considerations, of course, having to do with production and direction values, acting, screenplay, and cinematography also play important roles in any evaluation of these adaptations, as discussed above.

The most effective adaptations of O'Neill yet on film are, discernibly, Ford's *The Long Voyage Home* and Lumet's *Long Day's Journey into Night*. While the two films work in very different ways, both recreate and restore the essential core of the adapted works in striking cinematic form. Ford's *The Long Voyage Home*, in a wealth of atmospheric details, superb ensemble performance, and exceptional cinematography, captures in a kind of cinematic poetry all of the richness and diversity of O'Neil's imagery associated with the sea. Similarly, the fusing of superb visual details, ensemble playing, and cinematography in Lumet's *Long Day's Journey into Night* finds a visual language in shots and rhythms which revivifies O'Neill's language on the screen, and focuses the emotional core of the work. It is indeed remarkable that such disparate original works and stylistically different films should result in the most artistically successful screen translations of O'Neill's work.

Contrasts abound. The original short plays which make up *The Long Voyage Home* are slight compared to the *Long Day's Journey*—O'Neill's masterpiece. Ford's film relies to a great extent on the atmosphere of nature and natural forces—Lumet's film is almost totally confined within the walls of a house. Ford's film takes verbal and structural liberties with the original—Lumet's film follows the original script religiously. Contrasts could be extended into the realm of characterization, thematic differences, length of the works, verbal dynamics, and so forth, but the essential point is that superior adaptations can be made from widely ranging dramatic sources. What the two films do share is a probing and revitalizing treatment of the original material, which is actualized by skillful directorial control, uniformaly excellent and suitable performers, and a visual style which finds precisely appropriate means of translating the dramatic, thematic, and emotional core of a stage work into masterful cinematic form.

Ideally, the process of stage-to-screen adaptation should be reciprocal—the film translation should not only shine with a light of its own, but should also help to illuminate the original work. Ford's *The Long Voyage Home* and

Conclusion

Lumet's *Long Day's Journey into Night* certainly enhance our understanding of these works of O'Neill. Much the same can be said of Frankenheimer's trenchant version of *The Iceman Cometh*, and Nichols's intelligently compressed *Mourning Becomes Electra*. But the merger of O'Neill and Hollywood may perhaps be longest remembered for Lumet's *Long Day's Journey* and its illumination of the painful past that so influenced the career of Eugene O'Neill.

Filmography

Anna Christie

Released: 1923
Producer: Thomas H. Ince
Director: John Griffith Wray
Adaptation: Bradley King
Photography: Henry Sharp

Cast
Anna Christie: Blanche Sweet
Mat Burke: William Russell
Chris Christopherson: George F. Marion
Marthy: Eugenie Besserer

Anna Christie

Released: March 1930
Producer: Irving B. Thalberg
Director: Clarence Brown
Adaptation: Frances Marion and Clarence Brown
Screenplay: Frances Marion
Cinematographer: William Daniels
Film Editor: Hugh Wynn

Cast
Anna Christie: Greta Garbo
Chris Christopherson: George Marion
Mat Burke: Charles Bickford
Marthy Owens: Marie Dressler
Bartender: James T. Mack

Strange Interlude

Released: September 1932
Producer: Irving B. Thalberg

Filmography

Director: Robert Z. Leonard
Screenplay: Bess Meredith, C. Gardner Sulivan, Robert Z. Leonard
Adaptation: Robert Z. Leonard
Cinematographer: Lee Garmes
Film Editor: Margaret Booth

Cast
Nina Leeds: Norma Shearer
Ned Darrell: Clark Gable
Sam Evans: Alexander Kirkland
Charlie Marsden: Ralph Morgan
Gordon: Robert Young
Mrs. Evans: May Robson
Madeline: Maureen O'Sullivan
Professor Leeds: Henry B. Walthall
Gordon as a boy: Tad Alexander

Distributed by Metro-Goldwyn-Mayer

The Emperor Jones

Released: November 1933
Producers: John Krimsky and Gifford Cochran
Director: Dudley Murphy
Photography: Ernest Haller
Adaptation and Screenplay: DuBose Heyward
Musical Director: J. Weldon Johnson

Cast
Brutus Jones: Paul Robeson
Smithers: Dudley Digges
Jeff: Frank Wilson
Ondine: Fredi Washington
Dolly: Ruby Elzy
Lem: George Stamper
Marcella: Jackie Maybie
Treasurer: Blueboy O'Connor
Carrington: Brandon Evans

Distributed by United Artists
Running time: 72 minutes

Ah, Wilderness!

Released: December 1935
Producer: Hunt Stromberg

Director: Clarence Brown
Screenplay: Albert Hackett and Frances Goodrich
Cinematographer: William Daniels
Musical Score: Herbert Stothart

Cast
Nat Miller: Lionel Barrymore
Richard Miller: Eric Linden
Essie Miller: Spring Byington
Sid: Wallace Beery
Lily: Aline MacMahon
Tommy Miller: Mickey Rooney
Muriel: Cecilia Parker
Mr. McComber: Charles Grapewin
Arthur Miller: Frank Albertson
Wint Selby: Edward Nugent
Belle: Helen Flint

Distributed by Metro-Goldwyn-Mayer
Running time: 100 minutes

The Long Voyage Home

Released: October 8, 1940
Director John Ford
Producer: Walter Wanger
Cinematographer: Gregg Toland
Scenarist: Dudley Nichols
Music: Richard Hagerman
Art Director: James Basevi
Special Effects: Ray Binger and R. T. Layton

Cast
Ole Olson: John Wayne
Aloysious Driscoll: Thomas Mitchell
Smitty (Thomas Fenwick): Ian Hunter
Cocky: Barry Fitzgerald
Captain: Wilfred Lawson
Freda: Mildred Natwick
Axel Swanson: John Qualen
Yank: Ward Bond
Donkeyman: Arthur Shields
Joe: Billy Bevan

Distributed by United Artists
Running time: 105 minutes

Filmography

Mourning Becomes Electra

Released: November 1947
Director: Dudley Nichols
Producer: Dudley Nichols
Adaptation and Screenplay: Dudley Nichols
Musical Director: C. Bakaleinikoff
Music: Richard Hageman
Film Editors: Roland Gross and Chandler House
Cinematographer: George Barnes

Cast
Ezra Mannon: Raymond Massey
Christine Mannon: Katina Paxinou
Lavinia Mannon: Rosalind Russell
Orin Mannon: Michael Redgrave
Adam Brant: Leo Genn
Peter Niles: Kirk Douglas
Sarah Niles: Nancy Coleman
Seth Beckwith: Henry Hull

In association with the Theatre Guild and RKO Radio Pictures, Inc.
Running time: 175 minutes

Summer Holiday

Released: June 1948
Producer: Arthur Freed
Director: Rouben Mamoulian
Screenplay: Albert Hackett and Frances Goodrich
Music: Harry Warrens
Lyrics: Ralph Blane
Director of Photography: Charles Schoenbaum
Art Direction: Cedric Gibbons

Cast
Richard Miller: Mickey Rooney
Muriel: Gloria De Haven
Nat Miller: Walter Houston
Uncle Sid: Frank Morgan
Tommy: Butch Jenkins
Belle: Marilyn Maxwell
Cousin Lily: Agnes Moorehead
Mrs. Miller: Selena Royle
Arthur Miller: Michael Kirby
Mildred: Shirley Johns
Mr. Peabody: Howard Freeman

Mr. McComber: John Alexander
Mrs. McComber: Ruth Brady

Photographed in Technicolor, released by Metro-Goldwyn-Mayer
Running time: 92 minutes

Desire under the Elms

Released: March 1958
Producer: Don Hartman
Director: Delbert Mann
Cinematographer: Daniel Fapp
Original Music: Elmer Bernstein
Conductor: Richard Hageman
Screenplay: Irwin Shaw

Cast
Anna Cabot: Sophia Loren
Eben Cabot: Tony Perkins
Ephraim Cabot: Burl Ives
Simeon Cabot: Frank Overton
Peter Cabot: Pernell Roberts
Lucinda: Rebecca Welles
Florence: Jean Willes
Eben's Mother: Anne Seymour
Fiddler: Roy Fant

Distributed by Paramount Studios
Running time: 114 minutes

Long Day's Journey into Night

Released: October 1962
Producer: Ely Landau
Director: Sidney Lumet
Cinematographer: Boris Kaufman
Art Director: Richard Sylbert
Musical Score: André Previn

Cast
Mary Tyrone: Katharine Hepburn
James Tyrone: Ralph Richardson
Jamie Tyrone: Jason Robards, Jr.
Edmund Tyrone: Dean Stockwell
Kathleen: Jeanne Barr

Distributed by Embassy Pictures Corporation
Running time: 170 minutes (uncut version), 136 minutes (cut version)

The Iceman Cometh

Released: October 1973
Producer: Ely Landau
Director: John Frankenheimer
Text Editor: Thomas Quinn Curtiss
Cinematographer: Ralph Woolsey
Film Editor: Harold Kress
Production Design: Jack Martin Smith

Cast
Hickey: Lee Marvin
Harry Hope: Fredric March
Larry Slade: Robert Ryan
Don Parritt: Jeff Bridges
Willie Oban: Bradford Dillman
Hugo Kalmar: Sorrell Booke
Margie: Hildy Brooks
Pearl: Nancy Juno Dawson
Cora: Evan Evans
The Captain: Martyn Green
Joe Mott: Moses Gunn
Pat McGloin: Clifton James
Jimmy Tomorrow: John McLiam
Chuck Morello: Stephen Pearlman
Rocky Pioggi: Tom Pedi
The General: George Voskovec
Moran: Bart Burns
Lieb: Don McGovern

Bibliography

Anderson, Lindsay. "The Method of John Ford," as reprinted in Lewis Jacobs's *The Emergence of Film Art*. New York: Hopkinson and Blake, 1974.

Bakshy, Alexander. Review of *Strange Interlude*. *Nation* 135 (September 28, 1932): 292.

Baxter, John. *The Cinema of John Ford*. New York: A. S. Barnes and Co., 1971.

Bazin, André. *What Is Cinema?* Berkeley: University of California Press, 1967.

Benét, William Rose. Review of *Mourning Becomes Electra*. *Saturday Review* 30 (November 29, 1947): 41.

Bentley, Byron. Review of *Long Day's Journey into Night*. *Theatre Arts* 46 (October 1962): 16.

Bentley, Eric. *The Playwright as Thinker*. New York: Harcourt, 1946.

Bogdanovich, Peter. *John Ford*. Berkeley: University of California Press, 1968.

Brown, John Mason. Review of *Mourning Becomes Electra*. *Saturday Review* 30 (December 13, 1947): 22.

Canby, Vincent. Review of *The Iceman Cometh*. *New York Times*, January 24, 1974, p. 7.

Cargill, Oscar, N. Bryllion Fagin, and William J. Fisher, eds. *O'Neill and His Plays*. New York: New York University Press, 1961.

Cavender, Kenneth. "Interview with Harold Pinter and Clive Donner." *Behind the Scenes: Theatre and Film Interviews*, edited by Joseph McCrindle. New York: Holt, Rinehart and Winston, 1970.

Clair, René. "The Art of Sound." Reprinted in *Film: A Montage of Theories*. New York: Dutton, 1966.

Cocks, Jay. Review of *The Iceman Cometh*. *Time* 102 (November 12, 1973): 122.

Costello, Donald P. *The Serpent's Eye: Shaw and the Cinema*. Notre Dame, Ind.: Notre Dame Press, 1965.

Crowther, Bosley. Review of *Mourning Becomes Electra*. *New York Times*, November 14, 1947, p. 38.

―――. Review of *Desire under the Elms*. *New York Times*, March 13, 1958, p. 24.

―――. Review of *Long Day's Journey into Night*. *New York Times*, October 10, 1962, p. 57.

―――. Review of *The Long Voyage Home*. *New York Times*, October 9, 1940, p. 30.

Dale, Luciano. "Interview with Sidney Lumet." *Film Quarterly* 25 (Fall 1971): 20–29.

Eisenstein, Sergei. *Film Form: Essays in Film Theory*. Edited and translated by Jay Leyda. New York: Harcourt, Brace and World, 1949.

Bibliography

Engel, Edwin. *The Haunted Heroes of Eugene O'Neill.* Cambridge, Mass.: Harvard University Press, 1953.

Frankenheimer, John. "Filming *The Iceman Cometh.*" *Action* 9 (January–February 1974): 37.

Gassner, John, and Dudley Nichols. *Twenty Best Film Plays.* New York: Crown Publishers, 1943.

Gelb, Barbara. "Possessed by the Tormented Spirit of Eugene O'Neill." *New York Times Magazine,* October 1, 1976, p. 124.

Gelb, Barbara and Arthur. *O'Neill.* New York: Harper's, 1960.

Hall, Mordaunt. Review of *Anna Christie. New York Times,* December 10, 1923, section 5, p. 22.

———. Review of *The Emperor Jones. New York Times,* September 20, 1933, section 2, p. 26.

Hartung, Phillip. Review of *Mourning Becomes Electra. Commonweal* 47 (November 28, 947): 175.

———. Review of *Long Day's Journey into Night. Commonweal* 74 (October 19, 1962).

———. Review of *Desire under the Elms. Commonweal* 67 (March 22, 1958): 95.

Hatch, Robert L. Review of *Mourning Becomes Electra. New Republic* 117 (December 8, 1947): 41.

———. Review of *Long Day's Journey into Night. Nation* 195 (November 1962): 227.

———. Review of *Desire under the Elms. New York Herald Tribune,* November 7, 1927.

———. Review of *Desire under the Elms. Nation* 186 (April 5, 1958): 304.

Hurt, James. *Focus on Film and Theatre.* Englewood Cliffs, N.J.: Prentice-Hall, 1974.

Isaacs, Hermine Rich. Review of *Mourning Becomes Electra. Theatre Arts* 32 (November 1957): 31.

———. Review of *The Long Voyage Home. Theatre Arts* 24 (December 1940): 867.

Jacob, Jay. Review of *Long Day's Journey into Night. Reporter* 27 (September 27, 1962): 42.

Jacobs, Lewis. *The Rise of the American Film.* New York: Harcourt, Brace, 1939.

Kael, Pauline. *I Lost It at the Movies.* Boston: Little, Brown and Company, 1964. Bantam Books.

———. Review of *The Iceman Cometh. New Yorker* 49 (November 5, 1973): 149.

Kauffmann, Stanley. "Notes on Theater and Film." *Performance* 1, no. 4 (September/October 1972). Reprinted in *Focus on Film and Theatre,* edited by James Hurt. Englewood Cliffs, N.J.: Prentice-Hall, 1974.

———. Review of *Desire under the Elms. New Republic* 38 (April 7, 1958): 81.

———. Review of *The Iceman Cometh. New Republic* 169 (November 30, 1973): 24.

———. Review of *Long Day's Journey into Night. New Republic* 47 (September 24, 1962): 147.

Kennedy, Margaret. "The Mechanized Muse," in *Film: An Anthology,* edited by Daniel Talbot. Berkeley: University of California Press, 1967.

Knight, Arthur. Review of *Long Day's Journey into Night. Saturday Review* 45 (October 6, 1962): 30.

———. Review of *Desire under the Elms. Saturday Review* 41 (March 15, 1958): 95.

Kracauer, Siegfried. "The Theatrical Story." *Theory of Film: The Redemption of Physical Reality.* New York: Oxford University Press, 1960.

Lawson, John Howard. *Film: The Creative Process*. New York: Hill and Wang, 1964.

Life. Review of *The Long Voyage Home*. Anonymous. *Life* 9 (November 11,1940): 83–84.

McCarten, John. Review of *Desire under the Elms*. *New Yorker* 34 (March 22, 1958): 95.

McCrindle, Joseph. *Behind the Scenes: Theatre and Film Interviews*. "Interview with Harold Pinter and Clive Donner" by Kenneth Cavenner. New York: Holt, Rinehart and Winston, 1971.

Macgowan, Kenneth. Review of *Desire under the Elms*. *Theatre Arts* 42 (April 1958): 81.

———. *Behind the Screen*. New York: Dell, 1965.

Mapp, Edward. *Blacks in American Films: Today and Yesterday*. Metuchen, N.J.: Scarecrow Press, Inc., 1972.

Marion, Frances. *Off with Their Heads*. New York: Macmillan Company, 1972.

Marx, Samuel. *Mayer and Thalberg: The Make-Believe Saints*. New York: Random House, 1975.

Mitchell, George. "The Films of Thomas Ince." *Films in Review* (October 1960): 481.

Mitry, Jean. "Interview with John Ford." *Cahiers du Cinema* 45 (March 1955). Translated by Andrew Sarris, reprinted in *Interview with Film Directors*. New York: Avon, 1967.

Murray, Edward. *The Cinematic Imagination*. New York: Ungar, 1972.

Newsweek. Review of *Desire under the Elms*. Anonymous. *Newsweek* 51 (March 17, 1958): 106.

Newsweek. Review of *Mourning Becomes Electra*. Anonymous. *Newsweek* 30 (November 24, 1947): 92.

Nichols, Dudley. *The Writer and the Film*. New York: Crown Publishers, 1943.

Nicoll, Allardyce. *Film and Theatre*. New York: Crowell, 1936.

Noble, Peter. *The Negro in Films*. New York: Arno Press and The New York Times, 1970.

O'Neill, Eugene. *Anna Christie*. New York: Boni and Liveright, 1922.

———. *Desire under the Elms*. In *Nine Plays*. New York: Random House, 1954.

———. *The Iceman Cometh*. New York: Random House, 1940.

———. *Long Day's Journey into Night*. New Haven, Conn.: Yale University Press, 1956.

———. *The Long Voyage Home*. In *Seven Plays of the Sea*. New York: Random House, 1946.

———. *Mourning Becomes Electra* In *Nine Plays*. New York: Random House, 1954.

———. *Strange Interlude*. In *Nine Plays*. New York: Random House, 1954.

Panofsky, Erwin. "Style and Medium in the Moving Pictures." *Critique* no. 3. Reprinted in Daniel Talbot, ed., *Film: An Anthology*. Berkeley: University of California Press, 1970.

Peet, Creighton. Review of *Anna Christie*. *Outlook* 29 (February 26, 1930): 350–56.

Sarris, Andrew. *Interviews with Film Directors*. New York: Avon, 1967.

———. *The American Cinema*. New York: E. P. Dutton and Co., 1968.

Sayre, Nora. Review of *The Iceman Cometh*. *New York Times*, October 30, 1973, p. 36.

Scott, James F. *The Medium and the Maker*. New York: Holt, Rinehart and Winston, 1975.

Shaw, Bernard, and Archibald Henderson. "Drama, the Theatre and the Films." *Table-Talk of G.B.S.* New York: Harper's, 1925.

Sheaffer, Louis. *O'Neill: Son and Artist*. Boston: Little, Brown and Company, 1973.

———. *O'Neill: Son and Playwright*. Boston: Little, Brown and Co., 1968.

Sheridan, Bart. Review of *Long Day's Journey into Night*. *McCalls* 90 (November 1962): 228.

Bibliography

Simon, John. *Private Screenings*. Berkeley: Berkeley Medallion Edition, Berkeley Publishing Co., 1971.

Skinner, Richard Dana. Review of *The Emperor Jones*. *Commonweal* 18 (October 6, 1933): 532.

———. Review of *Strange Interlude*. *Commonweal* 16 (October 15, 1932): 539.

Sontag, Susan. *Styles of Radical Will*. New York: Farrar, Straus and Giroux, 1960. "Theatre and Film," 99–122.

Talbot, Daniel. *Film: An Anthology*. Berkeley: University of California Press, 1967.

Time. Review of *Desire under the Elms*. *Time* 71 (March 17, 1958): 106.

Time. Review of *Mourning Becomes Electra*. Anonymous. *Time* 104, no. 24 (December 8, 1947): 37.

Time. Review of *The Long Voyage Home*. Anonymous. *Time* 36 (October 28, 1940): 82.

Time. Review of *The Emperor Jones*. Anonymous. *Time* 22 (September 25, 1933): 31.

Troy, William. Review of *The Emperor Jones*. *Nation* 317 (October 11, 1933): 419.

Walsh, Moira. Review of *Long Day's Journey into Night*. *America* 107 (November 24, 1962): 1158.

Watts, Richard, Jr. Review in *New York Herald Tribune* as quoted in *The Literary Digest* 114 (September 24, 1932): 18.

Woolsey, Ralph. "On Filming *The Iceman Cometh*." *American Cinematographer* (February 1974), p. 156.

Work, John W. *American Negro Songs*. New York: Crown Publishers, 1940.

Young, Stark. Review of *Strange Interlude*. *New Republic* 72 (September 14, 1932): 124.

Zierold, Norman. *Garbo*. New York: Stein and Day, 1969.

Zimmerman, Paul D. Review of *The Iceman Cometh*. *Newsweek* 82 (November 12, 1973): 119.

Index

Ah, Wilderness!, 12, 66–77, 78, 79, 87, 104, 162, 164, 166
Albertson, Frank, 67
All God's Chillun Got Wings (O'Neill), 51
American Film Institute, 151
American Film Theatre, 13, 114, 146
Anderson, Lindsay, 101
Anheuser-Busch Gardens, 83
Animal Crackers (Heerman), 47
Anna Christie (1923), 11, 21–27, 94, 101, 164, 166
Anna Christie (1930), 12, 27–37, 38, 60, 73, 94, 101, 122, 162, 163, 164, 165, 166
Anna Karenina (Brown), 29, 73
Applause (Mamoulian), 77

Bakshy, Alexander, 40, 45
Barretts of Wimpole Street (Thalberg production), 38
Barrymore, Lionel, 67, 71, 74, 84
Barton, James, 148
Baxter, John, 98, 100, 102
Bazin, André, 16
Becky Sharp (Mamoulian), 77
Beery, Wallace, 67, 71, 74, 84
Behind the Screen (Macgowan), 25
Benchley, Robert, 39
Benét, William Rose, 105
Bentley, Byron, 135, 136
Bentley, Eric, 14
Benton, Thomas, 83, 90
Bergman, Ingmar, 132
Bernstein, Elmer, 129
Beyond the Horizon (O'Neill), 101–2
Biddle, George, 90
Blacks in American Film: Today and Yesterday (Mapp), 60
Blane, Ralph, 86
Bogdanovich, Peter, 100
Booke, Sorrell, 156
Bound East for Cardiff (O'Neill), 89, 93

Bridges, Jeff, 155
Brooks, Hildy, 157
Brown, Clarence, 29, 32, 33, 36, 66, 67, 72, 73, 74, 77, 164, 165
Brownlow, Kevin, 74
Byington, Spring, 67, 71, 74, 84

Cabinet of Dr. Caligari, The (Wiene), 11, 14, 61
Camille (Cukor), 15, 38
Canby, Vincent, 147
Cannes Film Festival, 144
Caretaker, The (Pinter), 16
Carousel (play, dir. Mamoulian), 77
Cat on a Hot Tin Roof (Williams), 116
Censorship, 31, 39, 42, 43, 44, 45, 93, 103, 104, 114, 115, 119
Cerf, Bennett, 131
Chapin, James, 90
Cinematic Imagination, The (Murray), 49, 51
Citizen Kane, 90, 93, 151
City Streets (Mamoulian), 48
Circle in the Square, 148
Clair, René, 111
Cocks, Jay, 146
Cohan, George M., 74
Coleman, Nancy, 104
Color, use of: in *Iceman Cometh*, 153; in *Summer Holiday*, 82, 83
Confession of a Co-ed (Murphy), 51
Constant Woman, The, 12
Craig, Gordan, 61
Crawford, Joan, 164
Crewe, Regina, 48
Crowd, The (Vidor), 14
Crowther, Bosley, 79, 91, 105, 122, 125
Curtis, Thomas Quinn, 148

Dancing Lady (Leonard), 38
Daniels, William, 36, 165

De Haven, Gloria, 84, 85, 87
Desire under the Elms, 11, 12, 49, 55, 116–30, 163, 165, 166
Digges, Dudley, 52
Dillman, Bradford, 155
Dinner at Eight (Cukor), 15
Douglas, Kirk, 104, 105, 108
Dream Play, The (Strindberg), 61
Dressler, Marie, 25, 30, 32
Dreyer, Carl, 132
Dr. Jekyll and Mr. Hyde (Mamoulian), 77

East of Eden (Kazan), 137
8½ (Fellini), 48
Emperor Jones, The, 11, 51–65, 163, 165, 166
Eustis, Morton, 68
Evans, Evan, 157
Expressionism, 14, 51, 52, 59, 61, 142, 164

Fapp, Daniel, 129
Ferguson, Otis, 68, 74
Fiene, Ernest, 90
Film and Theatre (Nicoll), 13
"Film and Theater" (Sontag), 14, 16, 147
Films of John Ford, The (Baxter), 98, 100, 102
Film: The Medium and the Maker (Scott), 100
Film Quarterly (Lumet interview), 136, 139
Fitzgerald, Barry, 90, 94
Flesh and the Devil (Brown), 29
Focus on Film and Theatre (Hurt), 14
Ford, John, 89, 90, 94, 99, 163, 165, 166
Fordin, Hugh, 78, 85, 87
Frankenheimer, John, 146, 147, 148, 149, 150, 151, 152, 153, 156, 160, 164, 165
Freed, Arthur, 86
Freeman, Howard, 83
Freud, Sigmund, 44

Gable, Clark, 38, 41, 42, 162
Garbo, Greta, 12, 21, 25, 27, 28, 29, 30, 31, 33, 35, 36, 104, 105, 164, 165
Gelb, Arthur and Barbara, 118
Ghost Sonata, The (Strindberg), 61
Gibbons, Cedric, 82, 83
Gilpin, Charles S., 51, 62
Gish, Dorothy, 23
Gish, Lillian, 23
Glückliche Hand, Die (opera, dir. Mamoulian)
Goodrich, Frances, 66, 69, 79, 82
Great Ziegfeld, The (Leonard), 38
Green, Martyn, 156

Greenwich Village Theatre, 119
Gunn, Moses, 156

Hackett, Albert, 66, 69, 79, 82
Hairy Ape, The, 11, 12, 118
Hall, Mordaunt, 32, 40, 48
Haller, Ernest, 58
Hamlet (Olivier), 48
Hartman, Don, 116, 119
Hartung, Phillip, 105, 123
Hatch, Robert, 79, 105, 122, 132, 138
Hayes, Helen, 47
Hedda Gabler (Ibsen), 70, 108
Heine, Heinrich, 154
Helburn, Theresa, 103
Hepburn, Katharine, 103, 104, 134, 135, 136, 141, 144
Heyward, DuBose, 51, 52, 61
Homer, Winslow, 84
Hunter, Ian, 90
Hurt, James, 14
Huston, Walter, 84

Iceman Cometh, The, 11, 13, 101, 145–61, 163, 164, 167
Ince, Thomas, 21–27, 164
Informer, The (Ford), 98
In the Zone (O'Neill), 89, 93, 96, 98
Isaacs, Hermine Rich, 105
Ives, Burl, 116, 117, 122, 123, 165

Jacobs, Jay, 132
Jacobs, Lewis, 26, 27
Jeakins, Dorothy, 153
John Ford (Bogdanovich), 100
Johnson, J. Weldon, 63
Judith of Bethulia (Griffith), 23
Juno, Nancy, 157

Kael, Pauline, 14, 147, 154, 155
Kauffmann, Stanley, 53, 119, 122, 124, 125, 132, 138, 147, 149
Kaufman, Boris, 136, 140, 141, 165
Kennedy, Margaret, 57
Kirkland, Alexander, 42
Knight, Arthur, 122, 123, 125, 128
Kracauer, Siegfried, 14
Krutch, Joseph Wood, 39

Landau, Ely, 12, 131, 146, 147, 153, 157
Langner, Lawrence, 68
Leonard, Robert Z., 38, 41, 48, 164

Index

Lifeboat (Hitchcock), 101
Linden, Eric, 67, 70, 71, 76
Littell, Robert, 39, 40
Little Foxes, The (Wyler), 15, 16, 100, 151
Lonedale Operator, The (Griffith), 23
Long Day's Journey into Night, 12, 40, 69, 77, 91, 94, 100, 101, 122, 131–45, 147, 149, 154, 160, 163, 164, 165, 166, 167
Long Voyage Home, The, 12, 23, 89–102, 121, 122, 151, 163, 165, 166
Loren, Sophia, 116, 117, 121, 122, 123, 124, 125, 126, 127
Lower Depths, The (Kurosawa), 16
Lumet, Sidney, 131, 133–45, 148, 164, 165, 166, 167

Macbeth (Shakespeare), 15
McCarten, John, 123
Macgowan, Kenneth, 119, 125
McLiam, John, 155, 156
MacMahon, Aline, 74
Mamoulian, Rouben, 48, 66, 73, 77, 78, 82, 84, 85, 86, 87, 164
Mann, Delbert, 116, 117, 119, 121, 123, 125, 127, 128, 164
Mapp, Edward, 60
March, Fredric, 146, 150, 153, 154, 158
Marco Millions (O'Neill), 77
Marie Walewska [Conquest] (Brown), 29, 73
Marion, Frances, 32, 34
Marion, George, 25, 26
Marty (Mann), 116
Marvin, Lee, 155, 156, 157, 158
Marx, Groucho, 47
Massey, Raymond, 105, 106, 114
Maxwell, Marilyn, 85
Mayer and Thalberg: The Make-Believe Saints (Samuel Marx), 28, 38
Mayer, Louis B., 83, 103
Meet Me in St. Louis (Minnelli), 86, 87
Meredith, Bess, 38
Metropolis (Lang), 14
Milne, Tom, 79, 82
Mitchell, George, 21
Mitchell, Thomas, 90, 94
Moon of the Caribbees, The (O'Neill), 89, 92
Moorehead, Agnes, 74, 84
Morgan, Ralph, 42
Motion Picture Production Code, 44, 56, 93, 104
Mourning Becomes Electra, 12, 49, 55, 101, 102, 103–15, 122, 146, 163, 164, 165, 166, 167
Movie Man, The (O'Neill), 11

Murphy, Dudley, 51, 52, 54, 55, 58, 59, 61, 62, 164
Murray, Edward, 49, 51, 61
Music, use of: in Anna Christie, 31; in Ah, Wilderness!, 71, 74, 75, 77; in Emperor Jones, 63; in Long Day's Journey into Night, 143; The Long Voyage Home, 92, 99; in Mourning Becomes Electra, 107; in Summer Holiday, 83, 86, 87
Mutiny on the Bounty (Thalberg), 38

Nathan, George Jean, 39
Natwick, Mildred, 90, 98
Negro in Films, The (Noble), 60, 63, 64
Nichols, Dudley, 15, 89, 90, 96–99, 103–6 108, 110, 111, 114, 164, 167
Nicoll, Allardyce, 13, 14, 55
Nobel Prize, 13
Noble, Peter, 60, 63, 64

O'Neill, Carlotta Monterey, 131, 148
O'Neill, Eugene, attitude to film adaptations 11, 27, 28, 39, 49, 51, 62, 63, 78, 89, 103, 119, 131
O'Neill, James (father of Eugene), 114
O'Neill: Son and Artist (Sheaffer), 38, 39, 47, 69, 118
Oresteia (Aeschylus), 103
Overton, Frank, 127, 128
Ozu, Yasujiro, 132

Panofsky, Erwin, 16, 137
Parade's Gone By, The (Brownlow), 74
Parker, Cecilia, 72, 73, 76
Paxinou, Katina, 104, 105, 113
Pedi, Tom, 155
Perkins, Anthony, 116, 117, 118, 121, 122, 124, 125, 127
Petrie, Graham, 138, 139
Phillip, Robert, 90
Pickford, Mary, 23
Plato, 150, 159
Plunkett, Walter, 85
Porgy (play), 77
Porgy and Bess (play), 77
Previn, André, 143
Provincetown Players, 89
Pulitzer Prize, 12, 13, 39

Qualen, John, 90
Queen Christina (Mamoulian), 77
Quintanilla, Louis, 90
Quintero, José, 49, 148

Radio City Music Hall, 66

Rebel without a Cause (Ray), 137
Reckless (Fleming), 12
Redgrave, Michael, 105, 114
"Regarding Mr. O'Neill as a Writer for the Cinema" (Watts), 118
Richardson, Sir Ralph, 135, 139, 140, 144
Rise of the American Film (Jacobs), 26, 27
Robards, Jason, Jr., 135, 139, 144, 148, 156, 158
Roberts, Pernell, 127, 128
Robeson, Paul, 51, 52, 59, 61–64, 164
Romeo and Juliet (Thalberg production), 38
Rooney, Mickey, 69, 74, 79, 80, 81, 85, 87, 162, 165
Royle, Selena, 84
Russell, Rosalind, 104, 105, 106, 108, 114
Russell, William, 25
Ryan, Robert, 146, 154, 155, 159

Saint Joan (Shaw), 28
Sayre, Nora, 147, 156
Schreiber, George, 90
Scott, James, 100
Sennwald, Andre, 68, 74
Shakespeare, William, 15
Shaw, George Bernard, 11
Shaw, Irwin, 119
Sheaffer, Louis, 38, 39, 47, 69, 118
Shearer, Norma, 38, 41, 162, 165
Simon, John, 123, 138
Sisk, Robert, 49
Skinner, Richard Dana, 35, 40, 42, 59
Smith, Jack Martin, 153
Sontag, Susan, 14, 16, 147
Soyer, Ralph, 90
Sport Parade, The (Murphy), 51
Stagecoach (Ford), 90
Stockwell, Dean, 134, 135, 139, 144
Stothart, Herbert, 74
Strange Interlude, 12, 38–50, 103, 114, 162, 163, 165, 166
Streetcar Named Desire, A (Kazan), 15, 16, 137, 138
Strindberg, August, 61

Sullivan, C. Gardner, 38
Summer Holiday, 12, 66, 73, 74, 77–87, 162, 164, 165
Sweet, Blanche, 21, 23, 24, 25

Thalberg, Irving, 28, 38, 41
Theatre Advancing, The (Craig), 61
Theatre Guild, 66, 68, 102, 104, 114, 146, 148
Theory of Film: The Redemption of Reality (Kracauer), 14
Third Man, The (Reed), 137
Throne of Blood (Kurosawa), 15
Toland, Gregg, 90, 93, 94, 97, 100, 151, 164, 165
Twentieth Century (Hawks), 15
Two Women (De Sica), 124

VistaVision, 129
Voskovec, George, 156

Walsh, Moira, 132
Wanger, Walter, 90
Warren, Harry, 86, 87
Watts, Richard, Jr., 11, 41, 42, 118
Way Down East (Griffith), 15
Wayne, John, 90, 98
Welles, Rebecca, 127
Who's Afraid of Virginia Woolf? (Mike Nichols), 15
Wilia, Jean, 127
Willard, A. M., 84
Williams, Tennessee, 11, 118
Wood, Grant, 83, 90
Woolsey, Ralph, 151, 152, 153, 165
World of Entertainment: Hollywood's Greatest Musicals (Fordin), 78, 85, 87
Wray, John Griffith, 21–27
"Writer and the Screen, The" (Nichols), 111
Wyler, William, 100, 151

Young, Stark, 40

Ziegfeld Girls, (Leonard), 38
Zimmerman, Paul, 147, 154